T0245610

TWIST

AN AMERICAN GIRL

A Memoir

Adele Bertei

ZE BOOKS

Published by ZE Books of Houston, TX
in partnership with Unnamed Press of Los Angeles, CA

www.zebooks.com

Cover Design by With Projects Inc.
Typeset by Jaya Nicely

ISBN: 978-1-736309-33-9

eISBN: 978-1-736309-34-6

Library of Congress Control Number: 2022947826

Distributed by Publishers Group West

This book is a work of nonfiction.

First ZE Books Printing: March 2023

Printed in North America by McNaughton & Gunn

First Edition

2 4 6 8 9 7 5 3 1

for Maria

CONTENTS

AUTHOR'S NOTE

This memoir is narrated by Maddie Twist. Maddie Twist is a Trojan horse. Like Ulysses, I needed protection while taking the journey back through the war zones of my youth. Some names have been changed to protect the innocent *and* the guilty. I have no appetite for revenge. Or maybe this book is a story of compassionate revenge.

Twist: An American Girl is a diaristic love letter to my mother, Kitty, and to the motherless girls I've known—Lizzy Mercier, Ivonne Casas, Edwige Belmore, and others—who did not live long enough to tell their own tales. Motherless daughters don't always make it down here on Earth. Some choose the exit rather than face the loneliness or turn into their own forsaken mothers. For others, the only escape is into fantasy.

I watched my mother bring wonders and horrors to life while trying to escape a world she refused to belong to, a world that continues to be cruel to women. Her wild imagination is my inheritance, compensation for her neglecting six of the seven Greek demonstrations of love. *Storge* was thoroughly abandoned. *Eros*, she knew well. We lost each other when I was young. We find each other in dreams, in the face of love, and in the pages of this book.

The memoir takes place in Cleveland, Ohio, from 1965 through 1973—a cultural climate extremely foreign to where we live today. And yet, many injustices remain in place. Especially those that punish women for being born women. It's 2022 as I write, and the Supreme Court has reversed a federal law from 1973 granting women the right to control their own bodies.

I was born to working-class white European parents (Italian, French, and Irish). The Italians were virulent racists. My Irish mother suffered from paranoid schizophrenia and was physically abused by my father, and who really knows what came first? The chicken or the egg? In the early 1960s, televised news presented the vivid horrors of racism: peaceful black protestors beaten by white racists, fighting off attack dogs, sprayed with fire hoses. Kitty identified with their pain. My father punished her for this and other perceived crimes.

He punished his children by proxy, withholding child support. The weave of poverty and Kitty's mental illness spread through our lives like a poisonous gas until the state intervened. Kitty was sent to a mental institution; my brothers and I, to foster homes and various state-controlled placements. In each new situation, I tried my best to adapt and survive.

Twist: An American Girl is true to the cultural time and how it felt to be me between 1965 and 1973: white, working class, poor, queer, abandoned, and hungry for belonging. I have remained faithful to the way people talked and how they acted. When I describe people and events, I'm expressing my teenage thoughts through the lens of memory. History cannot be whitewashed and put through a rinse cycle of lies and omissions to avoid triggering another's feelings, group sensitivities, or collective guilt.

I will not be that child condemned to silence and shame, trapped in the basement of Ursula Le Guin's story "The Ones Who Walk Away from Omelas." I walk alongside those who break from the path of systemic oppression that evil pursues on its journey into human hearts. Society is not color blind; evil is. *Twist: An American Girl* tells of how I learned this truth and how faith in the goodness of people—and having the courage to keep looking for and finding that goodness—is the antidote to suffering and the heart-song of communion.

Shame makes the heart a fist of bees.
—Maddie Twist

There's light enough for what I've got to do.
—Charles Dickens, *Oliver Twist*

TWIST

AN AMERICAN GIRL

PART I

1

PETER PAN'S BASTARDLY BEGINNINGS

Call me Maddie Twist. My mom shies away from anything ordinary, so she named me Madeleine Marie Baptiste.

"Your father wanted to call you Maria Maddalena after your Nonni. All the women on your father's side for generations were named after Mary Magdalene, the most famous prostitute of all time."

Kitty smiles, teeth twinkling through the cigarette smoke. Kitty: my crazy mother.

"Your name sounds melodious," she says. "You can pretend you're French and your father isn't a dago bum."

"Yeah, but Maria Maddalena is a cool name. It sounds like music, like it's going somewhere. Madeleine Marie hits a dead end."

I love all things French—especially Paris and Leslie Caron—but irritating my mother can be fun.

"Life is hell for women as it is, Maddie—let alone when you're named after a prostitute. Just look at Nonni. She's rusted and miserable!"

Kitty flounces around the room smoking a Kent, singing "Maria" from *The Sound of Music* in her panties. She shimmies, trilling out, *Flibbertigibbet!* Taking a little bunny step each time she flips a word up into the next octave. Some mother she is—always warning me about this world being no place for a woman or a girl. Kitty calls men's things their "third legs," says that's where they carry their brains.

Last night I dreamed the whale Moby Dick swallowed up every woman and girl on the face of the earth, including me. All of us, pulverized into mush. My eyeballs were intact, so when the whale turned on its side I crawled into the its head to peek through his blowhole. With all the women gone from the earth, the men's heads and third legs exploded into nothingness—headless, third-leg-less bodies running amok and in circles like cartoon road runners.

I know the words to "Maria," but I don't join in. The warm beer smell coming off Kitty's body makes me turn away. She was named after Saint Catherine, but she is a dancing sacrilege.

"Can you please put your clothes on? The neighbors!"

She ignores me. To her, clothing is not necessary inside the house. I yell at her, "Terpsichore, I said put some clothes on!"

"It's too hot! A girl's gotta breathe!"

She loves the Greeks, but did she even notice I called her Terpsichore? If I lit myself on fire, would she blink?

"Don't stare at my bits, Maddie!" she chirps, vanishing around a corner, wiggling into her bedroom just as our neighbor the Italian fireman strolls past the picture window, head bobbing like a chicken's. I yank the curtains closed and open the front door.

"Hey, Mr. Carpucci! Don't you have any fires to put out today?"

Head down, he walks quickly past our house.

It's Monday morning and I'll be late for the first day of school because Kitty didn't wake me up.

I grab my book of poetry. Where's the green jacket? Gone missing from the closet. Well, well, here comes Kitty. In she struts, holding my jacket open like a gentleman for a proper lady. I play along and slide my arms in.

"Have a good time at school, Frenchie!"

Poof. She disappears.

Frenchie is fine by me. Ever since I saw *An American in Paris*, I've dreamed of dancing like the beautiful Leslie Caron across the rooftops of Paris, with the Saint Thérèse of Lisieux prayer to the Queen of Heaven on my lips: *"to obtain for me by her powerful intercession, the grace I yearn for so ardently."* My mother never prays, but I do. At night, alone in my room, I kneel like a good soldier, praying to find a way, a compass, a pathway through to a new world. I pray to Saint Thérèse, whom the aviators wear on their wings. To Saint Brendan, protector of sailors. And to the prostitute who watched Jesus roll away the stone.

Kitty calls herself a bastard because she never knew her father. Beloved Grandma Jo got pregnant with Kitty when she played piano in bars during the Depression. Grandma wrote the name Frank Harris on Kitty's birth certificate as the father, but no one had ever heard of him. Grandma was also a bastard, daughter of an Irishwoman in Nova Scotia living with the Micmacs *without* a man. I'm the third bastard on my mother's side, born when she wasn't married. My father was in Korea at the time. His mother, Nonni Maria Maddalena, curses Kitty in Italian. Gives her the evil eye, the malocchio, and says, "La bambina è una bastarda!"—then looks at me with pity and hands me a Torrone candy.

My mother's half brother, Jack, gave her the nickname Kitty. He thinks she looks like Kitty Twist, Jane Fonda's character in *Walk on the Wild Side*. The name suits my mom perfectly, the way she bounces around like a kitten, appearing out of nowhere and scrambling away just as fast. The Italian guys on my father's side grabbed hold of that nickname like mongrels with a steak bone. They stuck Ballou on the end, a name from another Jane Fonda film. They love to shout when they see her, laying on the *-lou* like it's a bomb going off. Kitty Bal-LOU!

They call my father Big Al because he's short but acts tough like he's Al Capone. If I call him Big Al, he swears at me in Italian. And I love Italian. "Dio cane, a fanabla, vaffanculo!"

Kitty calls him a son of a bitch because she doesn't like his mother (the bitch) or him either these days. They were divorced a few months ago. Big Al still hangs around, saying his boys need him. Never mind me. My brothers need that gambling wife-beater Big Al like they need a hole in their heads. Little brother Louie is six, and he's kind of crazy—"hyperactive," the doctor called him. He rocks on the couch and bangs his head, sometimes for hours. Next comes Chance. He's only three and hardly speaks, a little mouse with pale blond hair. He watches the shenanigans in this nuthouse through sad, curious blue eyes.

Big Al is supposed to pay Kitty alimony, but he refuses, so we keep running out of food. She doesn't care so much because she pops pills that make her fly around the house like a wild-eyed tornado. Jack calls them her "speedy-to-go pills." When she asks Big Al for money, he's always crying broke. He blames not having a steady job on the shines, the spooks, the moolignons, who he says are stealing all the good jobs. And that's not the worst he calls black people, even though his own skin turns deep dark in the summer when he works outside at the brickyard. Kitty says his buddies call *him* a moolignon, which means "eggplant" in Italian.

The Italian family hates black people, but they hate most people who aren't like them. Big Al and his buddies have names for everyone: Micks, Spics, Polacks, fairies, sluts, and tramps. Some vocabulary. Kitty hates it when he talks this way, especially when he says the n-word. A dirty grin spreads across his face when he says it, like he's sucking on a piece of candy he stole from a child. Kitty thinks we shouldn't call them "colored"; we should call them "black," because of black power and black being beautiful. She likes to torment Big Al, going on about handsome Jim Brown the football hero, and sometimes he'll just haul off and smack her. She yelps, but just takes it and walks away.

Our neighborhood is called Maple Heights. Black people don't live here. I see them on TV getting beaten up by cops or chased by dogs and angry white guys with sharp mean faces. Kitty and I watched the news when Martin Luther King Jr. and crowds of people marched in Alabama for equal rights. Kitty says they shot Malcolm X because his message wasn't peaceful like Dr. King's. The men who run the country don't want black people to be equal. Jack says most white people are scared that if black people get equal rights, they'll just take revenge on white people for making them slaves.

"Wouldn't you want revenge if some guy kept Grandma and your mother as slaves and beat them till they bled?"

"But that's what Big Al does to Mom, smacks her around. Makes her do things she doesn't want to."

When Jack visits and asks where Big Al is, Kitty rolls her eyes—"Oh, he's off somewhere polishing his Bates six-footers!"—and they laugh like hell. Jack says the Bates are shoes designed with lifts in-

side to make short men taller. They laugh about Al, but even Jack
admits he's handsome and a sharp dresser. Al used to take Kitty out
on the weekends to Captain Frank's for dinner looking like a movie
star in his crisp white shirts, wingtips so shiny you could see your
own reflection. Al irons his pants into creases sharp enough to slice
a finger.

Big Al's brother Caesar is a criminal. He's spent most of his life
in and out of prisons. Kitty says when Caesar was twenty-eight, he
robbed the Union Loan and Discount Company of $439 and never
looked back. I heard Jack talking to Kitty about the Cleveland mob-
sters, how they set off at least thirty-five car bombs in a ten-year
stretch. He called the car bombs "lethal popcorn," said shooting is
not enough for the Mob. They prefer blowing their enemies to bits.

Once every five years or so, Uncle Caesar gets sprung and shows
up at Nonni's dinner table looking handsome, never failing to
hand me a crisp twenty-dollar bill with his baby-bottom-smooth
hands. The moment Caesar turns his back, Big Al curses those
pretty hands.

"Good-for-nothing bastard never worked a goddamned day in
his life!"

Caesar's back in prison now, a place called Allenwood in Penn-
sylvania. Al loves to mouth off about gangster glory like he's one of
them. I hear names like Danny "the Irishman" Greene, "Big Ange"
Lonardo, "Little Frank" Brancato, and Jimmy "the Ice." I asked
what "the Ice" meant, and Al grinned, saying Jimmy murdered
people with an ice pick. He complains about Mob guys almost as
much as black guys. He'll start in on a tirade about how "this testa
di cazzo controls the city's jukeboxes!" and "that frochio finocchio
took over the garbage-hauling contracts! Minchia!"

Big Al wanted a seat at the wise guy table, but he never had a
quarter of the smarts of a Jimmy Cagney–style gangster. He started
off working the vending machine route—a big racket for the Mob,
which washes money through the "limitless supply of untraceable
coin" from jukeboxes and vending machines. He graduated to running bets from the local bars out to the racetrack. Maybe that's why
the index and middle fingers of his left hand stop clean at the second

knuckle. He says a Korean sniper shot them off. Must have been some sniper, to make that neat of a slice. Jack thinks the stubs were punishment for Big Al getting caught with his mitt in the Mob's cookie jar.

It's the first day of sixth grade and I'm walking up the steps to my elementary school holding a book of poems—Percy Bysshe Shelley. The book makes the kids gossip about what a weirdo I am, reading poetry and all, but it protects me, like a shield against the nitwits. *My name is Ozymandias, king of kings: / Look on my works, ye Mighty, and despair!* There's a gang of kids behind me laughing loud, so I turn and they're all red-faced, howling and pointing at me. Stringbean Coco, the tallest and meanest girl in the school, waltzes up and gets in my face.

"Whore!" She spits out the word with an ugly hyena laugh.

"Fuck you, Olive Oyl!" I yell.

She picks up a clump of dirt and throws it right into my eyes.

The nurse in the school infirmary hangs up my jacket and freezes in place.

"Who did this to you?"

She holds up the back of the jacket. Written in messy red nail polish on the green wool is the word WHORE.

"Uh . . . I don't know. That's weird."

The nurse is kind, gentle, but she's giving me the "sad" look of pity, the look I hate more than anything. Even when my eye hurts like this, I never cry—even when the bees get all worked up, buzzing and stinging and turning my heart inside out, making my face burn red hot beneath the pitiful look.

"It'll be okay. Let's see that eye. Should I call your mother to pick you up?"

"Please don't. I'm fine."

Back in class, I sniff the air through an open window. It smells good from the coming storm, the electric rain deepening the other smells: the squeaky-clean classroom, the chalk and erasers, the brand-new school supplies, and the books, which mean everything to me. Like music, books are boats to sail away on to strange and wondrous shores.

There are Cindys, Debbies, and Cathys to the left of me, Tommys, Stevies, and Pats to the right. Some Irish last names, some Polish and Italian, and others that sound boring: a Lewis and a Long, a Waddell and a Wynn. And I'm here in the middle. Bucky Beaver, they call me. Because of my buck teeth.

Last year, Big Al won a bet on a horse named Balboa Moon and took me to an orthodontist for braces. The sweaty man had to pull two teeth on the sides to make room for my front teeth to move backward. It was painful! And with braces on, I had to learn to talk without sounding like Sylvester from *Looney Tunes*. I tried, but everything came out sounding like *thuffering thuccotash*. I didn't speak much for a whole summer, but I sang to myself whenever I was alone and could *thuffer* in peace. Dionne Warwick's spooky songs are the best to sing along to. The lyrics, like in the song "Walk on By," make me wonder if love is a miserable state to find yourself in and about things I don't understand but want to.

I like the blue sound of Gerry and the Pacemakers' "Ferry Cross the Mersey." And soul singers: Barbara Mason singing in that begging sweet voice, *Yes, I'm ready*. And the Kinks' "All Day and All of the Night." CKLW is always playing in our house, mostly soul music. The last time I danced with Kitty, we went nuts to "Papa's Got a Brand New Bag." She's such a good dancer! Before marrying Big Al, she taught dance at the Arthur Murray Dance Studios. Lately she doesn't dance so much. She's either flying around like a banshee talking to herself or giggling on the phone in her bedroom. Or reading *In Cold Blood* or other books about murder, or books about sex and pills, like *The Valley of the Dolls*. Kitty takes a lot of pills. Sometimes she's drunk and dopey, mooning around to "Since I Fell for You," by Lenny Welch. I like Bob Dylan, a real poet like Percy Shelley. Too bad he can't sing to save his life. Jack calls him a philosopher. Jack has a record collection of great singers—Elvis, Roy Orbison, Gene Pitney, and the Righteous Brothers—so for him to play that 45 record "Subterranean Homesick Blues" by a guy who sings through his nose means a lot. Kitty can't stand Dylan. Whenever "Like a Rolling Stone" comes on the radio, she groans and spins the dial.

Today it's hard to concentrate in class. I stare out the window at heavy gray clouds ready to burst, streaked through with purple and dark golden light. The loudspeaker over the teacher's desk crackles with a tinny voice announcing my name, *and* I leave the snickering class and run the empty hall to the office. The principal's assistant says my mother called; there's been an emergency.

The streets are as quiet as sleep, lined by maple trees with leaves on fire. I watch a few fall gently to the ground, a sharp breeze spinning delicate oranges and reds into a circle. I join in and twirl. We twirl like ballerinas, graceful and strong. I'm Jimmy Cagney dancing with Leslie Caron in my autumn-colored daydream. I dance along the sidewalk, down streets with rows of matching GI bungalows: small houses built for soldiers coming home from the war. Korea, I guess, where Big Al fought. He says he nearly didn't get the veteran's loan for the house because the banks are "full of crooks, all of 'em." Each lawn is a perfect square and the brightest of greens in summer, edges sharp as a GI's buzz cut. Our yard is all patchy dry green-and-brown crabgrass. The scraggly stalks crawl up past my bare calves in the summer and itch like the devil. The grass feels worse when it's cut, too sharp to walk on barefoot. Soft grass is beautiful, especially when it's freshly mown and smells like it looks, bright green. I secretly wish I could lie on our neighbor's lawn with the sun on my face smelling all that fresh green. The kind of green you want to roll around in. Color of emeralds, like Kitty's eyes.

"Hey, Al, when you gonna cut that grass, buddy?" Ray Ciccolini, the cop next door, always asks, standing on his front steps and hitching up his pants over his belly. Big white smile pasted on his mug to torment my dad. Ray's lawn is perfect, like he trims it every day with nail clippers.

"When hell freezes over, Ray!" Al replies, flipping him the Italian bird as the crabgrass rustles in the breeze, our very own flag of independence.

I was eight when Al won a bet on another horse and spent his winnings on aluminum siding for the house. He said it was good protection for when the commies dropped the bomb on us, because the aluminum would soak up the radiation. He loved showing that siding off to his buddies, so proud about how it would keep us all alive. I didn't buy the stories about commies or radiation for a minute because, as ashamed as I am to admit it, Big Al is an ignoramus. The only thing he knows how to read is a racing form.

We had a hailstorm in 1964, and boy, what a grand storm it was, hail big and hard as baseballs. Kitty thought the world was ending. When President Kennedy was shot dead, it sent her into hysterical fits about the apocalypse and sent me into days of tears. We loved him so much. This hailstorm had her wailing out another banshee tangent that the world was coming to an end.

It happened on a weekend afternoon. My little brother Louie was rocking, banging his head while the couch hit the wall, *boom boom boom.* I was busy memorizing "The Raven," by Edgar Allan Poe, because I loved the ghostly beauty of the words and wanted to impress Jack. He's gone now. Drafted. Fighting strangers somewhere in Vietnam.

The sky turned dark and bruise blue, so I went out into the front yard to watch as a blue-black cloud flew straight up the street at me, and right out of that cloud came hail balls firing at the ground so fierce they could have split a skull. I rushed inside as the cloud aimed for our house. When it hit, the noise on the siding was like a hundred cannonballs! Like that poem by Alfred Tennyson. I stood up on the coffee table, reciting,
Came through the jaws of Death,
Back from the mouth of hell,

All that was left of them,
Left of six hundred.

while Kitty screamed her throat raw.

As quickly as the hail balls came, the cloud of thunder vanished, followed by an eerie silence. Kitty warned me not to go out when the noise stopped. I couldn't help myself; I ran out to scoop up a bunch of ice balls for her and Louie to gawk over. You should have seen the aluminum siding. Dented all over. Like an army of giant woodpeckers had gone to town.

When he came home after the storm, Big Al nearly had a heart attack, stomping around, swearing about how he would sue the company that sold him the crappy siding.

"Fa male, Dio cane! Weatherproofing my ass!"

He cursed for a half hour, then said he was going to the store for more beer and didn't return until late, thank sweet Jesus.

A few weeks later after another beatdown, Kitty threw him out for good.

I've been summoned home. *Again.*

It's quiet inside. I call for Mom. She answers from the bathroom:

"I'll be right out, honey!"

"What's the emergency?"

"Hold on a minute!"

After Kitty threw Big Al out, she named her bedroom La Cave after a nightclub downtown. La Cave is decorated with blond furniture she calls "modern" and I call "boring." Hideous new lamps have drawings of amoebas on the shades. We hardly eat, but she has money for this ugly stuff? Kitty would like our house to look like something straight out of *Life* magazine, modern and dull. Once upon a time, a painting in a golden frame hung over her bed, of two girls in long sweeping dresses playing a piano and a harp. I loved that picture, would stare at it longing to go back in time, to be in the room listening to the elegant girls playing their instruments. A banner has replaced the musical ladies above her bed; it spells out CARCINOMA IN-SITU in messy black letters. When she came home from the hospital, she hung the banner as her way to "commemorate her missing womb."

The only beautiful thing left in the house was Electric Jesus, a picture of Jesus in a golden frame on Kitty's bedroom dresser, but he's gone now. His Sacred Heart lit up and glowed with fire, his right hand moved to make the sign of the cross, and a music box inside played "Ave Maria." Nonni gave her the Jesus as a present, I guess with the hope he might save Kitty from being a bad mother.

One time I was in her room copying a picture from the Bible of Jesus nailed to the cross, humming a hymn Grandma would sing, and a miracle happened: Electric Jesus's heart lit up! "Ave Maria" played, and Jesus made the sign of the cross, then froze. I ran over to the picture feeling as blessed as Saint Bernadette from the movie, and lo and behold, Electric Jesus was NOT plugged in! My heart nearly exploded! I screamed for Kitty.

"Mom! Mom! A miracle happened, come quick!"

When she saw me in such a state ranting about the Jesus sitting dark and lifeless on her dresser, she laughed and threw me out of her bedroom.

She's been locked in the bathroom for an hour, so I seize the opportunity to invade her room and rustle around in her purse, through little bottles of Chanel No. 5 and Arpège, tubes of bright red lipstick smelling as much as the perfume, musty and sweet. I'm the Artful Dodger, peeling out a few bills from her wallet, picking a pocket or two.

"What are you doing in my purse?"

She stands behind me reflected in the mirror, her face painted and teeth floating like white Chiclets in the center of the brown makeup. She's decked out in a cream-colored turtleneck, hoop earrings, and big fake eyelashes, crowned by a huge curly black wig. A giant cloud of a thing. Her eyes bug out wilder than ever, and she's talking way too fast and fizzy.

"Come on! Maddie, let's go up to Southgate, I want to get some groceries—don't I look beautiful?—let's go shopping!"

"You made me come home from school to go shopping? Looking like that?"

A weird tickle crawls up my spine. I know she's on the pills. Waving her hands around her face like she's trying to cool down, she sings her own melody: "Black is beau-tee-full!"

"You look crazy! Where did you get the money for that stuff?"

The room smells like beer, cigarettes, and her sweat. My stomach hurts. She has a sketch pad and has been drawing, an Egyptian queen wearing a high headdress filled with hieroglyphics. Patting her wig, she sits regally on the unmade bed and points to the glyphs—"This is the crow announcing bad omens, this is the eye of Horus the Great . . ."—her eyes gleaming with green fire.

I am mesmerized. And scared out of my wits. She tucks a stray wisp of blond hair under black elastic. Now she's jumpy, up again, all wound up and heading toward me with hands flapping, eyes darting like frightened baby birds searching for a safe place to land. I let my eyes be strong, be her target so she doesn't see me sliding the dollar bills into my pocket.

"Cleopatra was a black queen, and I'm her reincarnation."

"What?! You're Cleopatra?"

"I bet you didn't know Cleopatra was black."

I cross my arms tight. "If that's true, why didn't Diahann Carroll play Cleopatra in the movie? Elizabeth Taylor isn't black! And if Big Al sees you, he will beat you into a lump of hamburger! Please, wipe off the makeup and take that wig off. Please?"

A curtain comes down over her face as she shoves me out the door.

Roy Orbison sings "In Dreams" from the radio. If only Kitty would sing, would walk and talk with me. Dance with me again like she used to when I was little. She's really sick, isn't she, Jack? I think of you in your MP uniform, ducking behind tanks in Vietnam where bombs fall and children run the streets screaming for their mothers. What do I do when the bees in my heart start stinging? When there's nowhere to hide? All of Kitty's colors churn in my belly. I want to open that bedroom door, step right through her curtain, and tell her yes, she is Cleopatra with eyes the color of emeralds. I want to whip the horses and drive her off in a chariot like Ben-Hur, but the makeup stains on the rim of her turtleneck make it all seem too late, I don't know what for.

Our house is full of so much hurting. There are fights, and strange whispers behind closed doors, and bruises. Kitty hardly leaves her bedroom, and the walls are all empty now, just blank white spaces. We used to have a shadow box with little bird sculptures and a clock in the shape of a golden star, but Kitty likes to throw things down the basement steps. I came home from school one day to find Electric Jesus shattered in the basement pile. She says hearing the crash soothes her nerves.

When I get home from school today, Louie is banging and rocking the couch as usual, so I put the Beatles on the hi-fi to calm him down. He likes the Beatles. Big Al won't pay for his medication, so he keeps banging, and Kitty lives in a dream world where we don't exist.

I steal a cigarette from Kitty's pack and head out to the overgrown backyard jungle to lean on the junker, a pink-and-black 1955 Chevy. Tall grasses and weeds have taken over, weaving nets of tangled green through the rusted shell and broken windows. I light up. Inhale. Blow out a perfect smoke circle, my concentration like an arrow aimed straight through the traveling O, imagining myself with hair slicked back behind pointy ears. I'm Peter Pan, dancing across the rooftops of Paris with Miss Leslie Caron. Lifting off, we glide on air.

Tinker Bell has flown into the Chevy. I see her light through the rear window, and it's fading but blinking in Morse code, a code only known to the fireflies and we two. *Danger!* spells Tink. I stomp the cigarette out and clap hard—*Don't die, Tink!*—and her glow starts to swell, then whooshes and sweeps across me, a lighthouse beam through the weed nest. I wonder if she has a little bell down there. Does it ring when her wings flutter? I want to know, to find out if faerie girls are just like me. I want to hear Tink's bell, I'll make it ring! I clap, chanting, *"Please, Tink, don't die!"* while behind me: the dirty dishes, the boys whining for food where there is none, the naked Cleopatra. Yellow submarine of a rock 'n' roll record spinning into life everlasting, have mercy on us, Lord Jesus Christ.

2

JACKPOT EYES

Ann-Margret runs toward us in the dark theater wearing a bright yellow dress. Red hair on fire, she sings "Bye Bye Birdie" against a deep blue sky. I want to jump out of my skin and into the movie screen!

Aunt Joanie and I celebrate her birthday at the movies, and afterward, we have cake. I dance around Grandma's living room singing "Honestly Sincere," thrusting my hips like Conrad Birdie. I speed up the action with double thrusts. Aunt Joanie blushes while Grandma laughs and taps her foot.

The phone rings. *Please, please, don't be Mom!* Grandma Jo answers with her Irish lilt. "Hello? Oh, hi, darlin' . . . Yes, Joanie will bring her back tonight." She cups the phone and says to me, "Give me one to hang, Maddie."

I pull a Pall Mall from the pack. Grandma's lips pucker as she takes a puff off the unlit cigarette, leaving a bright red lipstick print on the white paper. She's stopped smoking since her heart attack, but when she doesn't drag on dry tobacco and pretend, she's unhappy and constipated.

"Why are you complaining? You could have married that nice Joel Grey. He was so talented"—and the cigarette slips from Grandma's fingers. "Kitty! Will you stop crying? It's going to be all right. Hello? Hell—I can't believe she hung up on me!"

Grandma puts the phone down. A little teary-eyed, she walks over to her piano as Joanie whispers, "Kitty's having trouble with your dad. She told me she didn't marry Joel because he was nellie, not because he's a Jew." Joanie giggles whenever she says the word *nellie*.

"The Jews are the chosen people," I say to no one in particular as she spins me in a circle to Peggy Lee singing "Chi-Baba, Chi-Baba."

"You two are silly, the pair of you." Grandma's mood instantly changes, and she can't help but play along to the record. The lady was made for music.

I have a thing about the Jews ever since I saw the movie *The Diary of Anne Frank* and read about concentration camps in *Collier's Encyclopedia*. I couldn't believe it, this proof of human evil: how the Devil can take over entire countries. What scared me most was the scene where Anne dreams she sees her best friend, Simone, in the camp rocking back and forth, looking lost in those striped pajamas they had to wear—and Anne wakes up screaming. I dreamed I was in the same camp planning our escape but woke up before we jumped the barbed wire.

Grandma shimmies on the piano bench in time to the rhythm of her left hand on the keys.

"Your mother was one helluva dancer, Maddie. Before your father came along, Kitty was a chorus girl in musical revues, always hobnobbing with the stars at the Theatrical where she met that Joel fellow. He was something special, all right. She could have married a bona fide showbiz man, but no, she wanted the tough guy. Now look at the state she's in."

The story goes that, full of muscles and attitude, Big Al showed up one night on Short Vincent Avenue looking for action in a GI uniform, showing those Mack the Knife teeth. Kitty is a sucker for tough guys. She hooked herself a live one with Big Al. He took her to see *On the Waterfront* for their first date. Jack says I was born nine months later, back in the days when Big Al coulda been a contender. Well, he's certainly no contender, driving her crazy with his gambling and beatings and being broke all the time. Dreaming about winning some imaginary jackpot.

I wish Kitty would have married Joel. So what if he's nellie? *Nellie* is not in the dictionary, but I guess it means "girlish." Big deal. You can call all the men who happen to be entertainers girlish, especially dancers. Fred Astaire, my hero, and Gene Kelly, who wears ballet slippers in *An American in Paris*. Men dance. And men can be pretty too, especially when their feet move like raindrops pounding pavement. Suppose Kitty had married Joel instead of Al. She'd still be dancing, maybe in musicals alongside him, and I coulda been a contender myself.

"Listen, Maddie, and watch my left hand."

Grandma is playing a boogie-woogie, pounding so hard you'd think the piano would crack through the floorboards. With her right hand she plays light, rhythmic notes that dance up into the air like a flock of happy blackbirds flying in formation. She sings her favorite Boswell Sisters song: *Crazy people, crazy people / Crazy people like me go crazy over people like you!*

"I wanna play!"

She sits me on her left side and guides my fingers, picking out four notes. "Find the rhythm, honey; I know you can do it. You do it with the cards all the time. It's just like that."

Sometimes on nights I stay over, Grandma Jo and I smack the kitchen table in beats with the plastic playing cards, which is more fun than rummy. I play a rhythm opposite hers with my stack, and we get a great thing going. The beats change and shift and go on forever. She tells me I have natural rhythm, and I blush. Nobody can beat out a rhythm like Grandma Jo.

"Grandma, did you have any black relatives back in your family?"

She grabs me way too tight and whispers, "Don't you ever say that to anyone about me, you hear? Ever!"

She starts pounding the keys again like nothing happened, singing with that vibrato Jack calls "as deep and as dark as the old Cuyahoga."

I love hearing her sing. Aunt Joanie has a beautiful voice too, but softer and sweeter. Sometimes when Joanie joins in singing with her best friend, Ella, the harmonies grow wide and thick and beautiful enough to blow the roof right off with the joy of it. Ella's big like Mama Cass and just as good of a singer. I pray that my voice will be that amazing one day. But I'm probably too skinny. Maybe humans are like bells. The bigger the size, the deeper and more beautiful the notes—notes that change like Grandma's face when she sings, with its strange shade of color, mixed up into the way she plays piano by ear. The mystery of this and that.

After Kitty was born, and with no man to take care of them, Grandma made a living during the Great Depression playing piano and singing in the speakeasies near Kingsbury Run. Kitty would sit on the floor hanging on to the piano leg, bass notes vibrating through her tiny body. Jack thinks Kitty's childhood made her crazy, because she never knew her father and they didn't have a pot to piss in. He says that Grandma was so poor, they lived in people's attics, where a rat once ripped Kitty's teddy bear right out from beneath her tiny arms. If I ask Kitty about those days, she gets wild-eyed, says Grandma didn't treat her very well and it's nobody's business. Grandma won't talk about it either, preferring to "accentuate the positive."

"Didn't you ever wonder why your mother's such a good dancer?" Grandma asks. "You betcha, this is why. She grew up holding on to the piano leg with me playing stride!"

I begged Big Al for a piano every year before my birthday so I could learn to play like Grandma Jo. The last time I begged, he made a big deal out of how my wish nearly came true.

"I had yer goddamned piano in the truck, and I'm coming up Warner Road hill and the back gate flew open. It fell out. Smashed to pieces," he told me. "So, I got you one, but it's laying all over that hill right now."

Imagining black and white keys flying in a thundering crash of bum notes from a bum father, I jump down to the carpet and wrap my arms around the piano leg. Grandma's low, rhythmic music hums through my bones.

I don't tell Grandma about home, where Kitty's punches in the poor house erase the music and turn me blank. That being poor makes me shudder more than punches. Poorness is a tumble down a well with nobody throwing you a rope.

Kitty was happy for a while, once upon a time. We were buddies: dancing buddies, talking buddies, movie buddies. We listened to music on the hi-fi and the radio, singing along while she whipped the meringue for pie or pulled fabric through the sewing machine. She'd go on and on about how much she loved to dance before Big Al came along. She took me to see *West Side Story* when I was little. I used to cry and wail constantly, but at the movies and the drive-in, I never made a peep, was hypnotized for hours. There's not much I remember about life in the days between her having Louie and then Chance. But the movies and music! The dance at the gym! The Sharks and the Jets! I remember so well.

Kitty bought the soundtrack album, and we danced and sang every word. She was Maria. I wanted to be Tony, but she preferred when I danced and acted like Bernardo, the bad boy, so I tried my best to look tough and mean. And wow, could she sew! Skirt suits in the style of Jackie Kennedy for herself and school dresses for me—that is, before she went crazy and ripped up all my clothes. I don't like wearing skirts or dresses anyway. I want to be a boy. Maybe I was born in the wrong skin. I know the truth: boys are the ones who get to be free and go on adventures. Girls have to be slaves to boys. Who in their right mind would stand for it? What if I could change? Be a boy and be free, like in my imagination? A boy with wings. A faerie boy.

At twilight in the summer, Kitty, Louie, and I used to sit on the front steps listening to the transistor radio—"Not Fade Away" by the Rolling Stones, yeah!—dancing while fireflies swooped around us. Big Al calls them "lucciole." The boys on this block catch and stomp them on the sidewalk. The poor bugs end up as streaks on cement, glowing in the dark for idiots.

I'd catch a bunch in a mason jar, with holes poked in the top so they could breathe. Kitty would say, "Switch off all the lights, Maddie, quick!" and we'd gather around the kitchen table, the jar blinking like a magic lantern.

Back then, she didn't run into her room and lock the door all the time. Big Al didn't gamble away his paychecks. He'd come home from the brickyard, tired and happy, singing along to his Mario Lanza records in his fake opera voice: *'O sole mio, sta nfronte a te!* Kitty cooked nice meals for us, like pork chops and green beans, with strawberry shortcake and whipped cream for dessert. They were proud of my grades. I wasn't left alone to take care of the boys, begging relatives and scrounging for food like a wolf in the wild.

Now Kitty drinks all the time and Big Al gambles. She says he is gambling away the money for the house and soon we'll be living in a tent in Grandma's backyard. The neighbors act like we're from Mars but I bet creatures on Mars aren't this crazy. When Kitty had Chance, the nutsiness accelerated like a train picking speed and running right over us all. Poor Chance. It wasn't his fault that everything is falling apart. She didn't give him the name of a French king like Louie or a whore from the Bible, but it sure wasn't ordinary, that name. It hung over him like a curse. Big Al could have used a lucky break, but Chance wasn't it. When Kitty handed Big Al the birth certificate, he went nuts.

"Minchia! He's not a horse!"

Now Chance is three, a blond elf with hungry blue eyes that follow me everywhere. He's looking for something from me that I don't know how to give.

It's a sunny Saturday afternoon, but the curtains are closed tight. So are all the windows and doors. The house reeks of cigarettes. She'll smack me if I try to open a window or even a curtain. She's allergic to sunlight these days, sitting in her chair with a beer, chain-smoking.

"Can you help me clean the house?" I ask her. She stares off into space.

"These fights will never amount to anything as great as the battles of the Spartans."

Huh? And then:

"Do not. Touch. Those. Curtains! You're the one always closing them. I thought you'd be happy."

"You have clothes on today, for a change."

"Katherine Anapolous. That's my name. And the dark is my home." She waves a cloud of smoke away from her face, talking to ghosts. Not to me, that's for sure.

"Are you a Greek vampire now? Should I build you a coffin to sleep in?"

The answer: silence and smoke. I fall on the floor, fake choking on the poisonous air. She ignores me. I stand up and begin to recite Poe: *It was many and many a year ago / In a kingdom by the sea . . .*

It doesn't impress her one bit. She's somewhere else, eyes flashing green with excitement. I want her to play with me. I get close to her and whisper dramatically (Kitty loves drama): *'Twas brillig, and the slithy toves . . .*

Finally, she stares at the daughter who just dropped down from outer space onto the carpet. Shaking her head, she laughs. Finally! Maybe now she'll play. But no. Off she dashes, locking herself into her bedroom. I turn from hopeful Martian poet into Casper, the Friendless Ghost Girl.

My transparent hands pick up her book of Greek mythology, my see-through head gets lost with Orpheus. He is a better friend to me than Katherine Anapolous. He sings and plays music so enchanting that the oak trees pull up their roots to follow him. I follow too— until my brothers start wailing for food, until I scrape the peanut butter jar clean and give them what's left, hands and head becoming solid again.

Jack reminds me of James Dean. He's got the haircut, the moves, the jeans, the tight white T-shirt. I open the door of his beloved Austin-Healey Spider, careful not to smudge the chrome handle, while he runs his hands through his hair and gives me his *I look handsome, don't I?* pose. We race through the streets from Dunham onto Corkhill Road, radio pumping "Wooly Bully." Flying along in Jack's spit-shined coupe with the top down and the music blasting. Total freedom. Jack pulls in tight to the curb and there's the Rocket 88, parked in its usual spot across the street from our house. Big Al's arm hangs over the open window, a Lucky Strike dangling between his finger stubs. Since Kitty divorced him, we see him more than we did when they were married. Kitty says he's spying on her.

"Hey, Al, how ya doin' in there?"

"Your car looks like a maraschino cherry. Cars are supposed to look like tanks, not fruit, fer Christ's sake."

"How about you making sure your kids can eat, huh Al?"

"Mama's baby, Papa's maybe, Jack."

What the hell is that supposed to mean?

"Watch this fruit fly, Al!" Jack peels out and away.

Big Al grumbles. "*Faccia di culoh* with his fancy car."

I stomp over to the Rocket, murder in my heart.

"You chased him away! He was gonna come in!"

Big Al presses the button on his car window, rolling it up real slow. I plant my face inches from the glass.

"Very funny. Come on, give me some money. We need groceries."

"I'm broke, Maddie."

He starts the engine, revving it like he's about to pull off, and I run to the front of the car and slap my hands on the hood. He beeps his horn. I'm not going anywhere. Let him run me over. So he gives in and reaches into his pocket. Peels off a bill from the wad. The liar. I return to the driver's side as he rolls down the window, hands me a dollar, then tugs it back, the jerk.

"Don't give it to your mother. She'll drink it," he says. "You wanna come to the track with me?"

"No way! A dollar? That won't buy peanuts! Pay up or I'll tell Ray Ciccolini you're hitting Mom and you're starving us all to death."

His smile flips. "You got a smart mouth, you know that?"

Clenching his teeth, he moves for the door handle like he's going to come after me while I kick the door of his car and run for my life toward the house. I hit the steps and watch while he tosses a lit Lucky Strike out the window, rolling off in his mint-green chariot.

Big Al took me horseback riding once. The riding instructor had us going at a slow pace, but when we cleared the forest and my horse saw the humongous stretch of green grass between the forest's edge and the stable, well, that horse took off like a bullet! Racing through the air with my butt rising above the saddle, gripping the reins, I felt like Liz Taylor riding the Pie to victory in *National Velvet*. The horse I rode was so beautiful and strong, and I was scared, but what a magical feeling, the power and the terror! Big Al watched that horse lift off with me, light as a feather on its back, and that was it. He started strutting around the track telling everybody I was going to be a jockey.

"She's the perfect size and weight and can fly on those horses. Jackpot! We'll be rich!"

The idea of wearing those satin outfits in dazzling colors sure was tempting, along with the magic of riding and flying. Then he brought me to Thistledown Race Track to meet some goombah about a job on weekends as a stable girl, and that did it, no more jockey dreams for me. The boss was a guy with a surly mug who looked me over like he was eyeballing a piece of prime rib. When I thought about me—once feather, now steak—and this guy doing the grilling, I got queasy. As we were leaving, we passed a legless jockey in a wheel-chair yakking it up in a circle of healthy two-legged jockey buddies. That poor jockey decided for me. Not a chance, Big Al. Your jackpot just disappeared.

The TV news is on with a story about Cynthia Gabrinski, a neigh-borhood girl whom I kind of knew in second grade. Cynthia's parents came home one Saturday afternoon and called her name. When she didn't answer, they went upstairs to her attic bedroom, a gabled room like mine in a house exactly like ours, two streets away. They found her on the bed with blood streaming down her face. A stranger had broken into the house and shot blanks into Cynthia's eyes. She'll live, but her condition is unstable. She'll be permanently blind.

I change the channel so the boys can watch *The Jetsons*. Louie's not interested, he keeps banging. I pretend to be Henry VIII, traips-ing around with a colander on my head shouting, "Off with their heads!" while Louie nearly rocks the couch through the wall. That's it. I'm locking him up in Ye Olde Tower of London (the living room coat closet). Chance stares like he's watching the best cartoon he's ever laid eyes on.

Louie howls from the closet. Then suddenly, he's dead quiet. I imagine he's suffocating in there, so I open the door and out he scuttles, head tucked like a bug, over to the couch. How rotten it was to close him up in there. I'm about to go off to my room to say a prayer of contrition—*Oh, my God, I am heartily sorry for having offended Thee*—when Kitty decides to come out of hiding. She nearly trips over Chance sitting there on the rug, all sorrowful eyes, playing with a stuffed bunny.

Kitty's slurring, waving a piece of paper. She flops down naked on the couch next to me, and the pain in my stomach starts up again, sharp and bitter. It's a note from the school nurse. I went to her the other day because of my stomachache, and she had a doctor come in to see me.

"An ulcer. At your age."

"There's nothing in the kitchen, just beer and Cap'n Crunch. Go back to your room and leave me alone."

She slaps me hard across the face. Runs to her bedroom. Slams the door.

The next day after school, I make the rounds, house to house, with a Maxwell House coffee can. Taped to the can is a sign I made of construction paper: THE CYNTHIA GABRINSKI FUND.

"Would you like to make a donation to help with Cynthia's medical expenses?"

It's mostly mothers who answer the doors, their eyes going all soft as they say what I'm doing is very sweet, so kind. They practically trip over themselves, running for their pocketbooks. One lady gives me a ten-dollar bill!

I buy lunch meat with cash instead of the food stamps Kitty gives me that are so embarrassing. Wonder bread, potato chips, and pop. And Tang, the favorite drink of astronauts. Watching the light of the sky turn magical and lonely, I wonder if a girl will ever be allowed to travel to space. I slow my step, peeking into people's windows, searching for families gathered around their kitchen tables. I imagine Cynthia, her eyes bandaged at the dinner table as she slowly reaches around with her hands, her mother helping, gently placing her fingers around Cynthia's fork and guiding the food to her mouth. Stroking her hair. The father is about to cry but holds back his tears so he doesn't upset her.

I hope Cynthia's not in pain. That she'll forgive me. But how can we forgive someone if we don't even know they've wronged us? I want to tell her what Grandma told me a long time ago when we watched that movie about Helen Keller: that the blind can see with their hearts.

Fireflies weave patterns around me, signaling a mysterious future in their glowing Morse code. I answer, blinking my eyes, dot-dot-dash.

Weave me a majestic suit of armor, lucciole. Make me your Captain of the Lightning Bugs, so I can fly.

My father sees the world through jackpot eyes. But not me. You can't just wait around for luck to find you, especially when you're invisible. I'm beginning to see the light.

3

BLOOD! RUBIES! FIRE!

Kitty drinks beer on the couch while we watch *The Ed Sullivan Show*, a rerun with Maria Callas. Kitty says when I was only a toddler, I watched Maria Callas sing and tried to stand up, squealing and reaching my fat baby arms toward the TV.

Big Al has been hanging around outside in his car. Tonight, he decides to stroll right in, and she doesn't bat an eyelash. Why does she let him inside? He throws a few measly dollar bills on the coffee table. Kitty glances at the money, eyes bouncing back to the TV. I hear the pop and fizzle from the kitchen, the beer cap clatter on the counter. He returns and sits on the couch, staring dull-faced at the TV. Kitty ignores him.

When Maria Callas hits a high note, her face twists into something both beautiful and ugly as if she's in pain, like Jesus on the cross suffering for God. I close my eyes and listen. Maria's notes turn into a stream of rubies cutting through sunlight straight into my heart. She finishes the song and I'm frozen, holding on to the wonder of her voice. Big Al breaks the spell, spitting words at Kitty.

"Where the hell did you go last night?"

"None of your business, you deadbeat! We're divorced. You don't live here anymore, remember? Get out!"

She screams, throws an ashtray full of butts at his head. He ducks. The glass shatters as it hits the wall. I run to my bedroom. Louie is crying, but nothing can stop him when he starts. I wrap a pillowcase around my head to muffle the sounds. Puck stares back at me in the mirror, a faerie boy of a midsummer's night smiling in silence and peace. I open the Bible and *Lives of the Saints*, carefully placing them next to each other, seams straight on the avocado-green carpet. Perfect. I think about the nature of fire—how it destroys *and* gives warmth. Life.

There is no other book filled with more horrors and wonders than *Lives of the Saints*. Its pages are filled with mysteries, with stories of ashes and lilies, of bells and battles. My favorite saints are Michael the Archangel (slayer of Lucifer), Saint Joan of Arc, Saint Bernadette, whom our Mother Mary appeared to in France, and Saint Thérèse de Lisieux, with her shower of roses. Whenever I pass a rose bed, I imagine Saint Thérèse is there assuring my protection. It's Saints Michael and Joan who counsel me to fight, to be a warrior. Saint Bernadette teaches me to be true to my visions. In return for my devotion, the saints hang around as my private army, always ready to teach something wondrous—usually something about bearing up to suffering, but such is the Way of the Cross.

Oh, how I wish Kitty and Grandma Jo could be strong like Saint Joan. I want to be a warrior like Saint Joan but am not sure how the Devil gets into people and how to get him out to fight, or why anyone would choose to be burned at the stake. What makes Big Al so mean? Makes my mother crazy? Makes mean white men beat or hang people because of the color of their skin, or gas people to death in concentration camps? What makes men drop bombs on babies in Hiroshima, in Vietnam? The Catholics talk about the Devil, but it's men who invented bombs and guns. Didn't God make man in His own image? Does this mean God is really the Devil, and maybe Adam was the real bad guy, not Eve? Why are women bad and men always the heroes, no matter how horribly cruel men are?

This is a man's world, sings James Brown. I hardly ever cry, but the first time I heard that song, the tears came because James Brown doesn't sing the truth—he sings about all the great things man makes, but not the horrible things that cause death and destruction. I cried because there are hardly any women heroes in the Bible and only one Jo in an ocean of Little Women. I cried because deep down, I know why Kitty is crazy. Being born a girl means I may never have the life I dream of. Girls can't be heroes. Or be in love with other girls like I am, secretly, in my dreams. I want to be a boy. I want to be a hero.

.

The next night, Big Al bursts through the door and starts right in on Kitty.

"*Puttana!* I oughta kill you right now. You're sick!"

I will punch his lights out if he goes near her. We've hardly eaten in two days because he won't pay her alimony, and I'm too ashamed to keep calling relatives for food.

"What the hell are those magazines I found under the bed? You wanna get tied up, huh? Is this what you want?"

He punches her hard in the stomach. I shout, "The Lord is with thee! Stop! Please! Stop!" but he hits her again, this time in the face, and she crumples to the floor. He grins like a cartoon devil while I fly at him and wrap my legs around his waist, trying to gouge his eyes out, but he throws me off and lifts Kitty up like he's about to help her, that crazy grin on him the whole time. Taking her head in his hands gently with the biggest smile yet, he smashes her face into a sharp corner where two walls meet. A hollow crack. Her scream ripping through me.

"No! Leave her alone!"

Kitty's body crumples and blood streams from her mouth. I hear Maria Callas's highest note, a blood ruby cutting her heart in two. Kitty wails, "Police! Help!" and Big Al throws his arm back like he's going to give her another smash in the face. I try to pull him away, but she's in his grip now as he lifts her off the ground, her legs kicking like a toy dolly. He hisses through clenched teeth, up close to her bloody face.

"Bobby Delardi? You'd do that, you whore? Screw my boss?"

She wails. A strange animal sound.

I remember Kitty running around the house with this goofy face, saying, "Ooooh, Bobby Delardi!" The phone ringing, and her dashing back out into the kitchen, giggling. "Ooooh, he hung up on me, that devil!"

The boys are crying in their bedroom. Poor little guys. A sense of calm comes over me, and in my mind I'm dressed in armor like Joan of Arc. I walk next door to tell the cop Ray Ciccolini that my dad is beating up my mother. He hitches up his pants and runs right over there while I sit down on his front steps, invisible again, wishing that Kitty and Al would vanish instead, once and for all. Both of my parents, rotten. Rotten to the core.

The police show up. Nosy neighbors are out on their front steps watching as they shove Al into the back of their squad car. Aunt Joanie arrives to take Kitty to the hospital, and Kitty doesn't make a peep in the car, not even a goodbye to us when Joanie drops the boys and me at Nonni's house. Joanie tells me, "Be brave, Maddie. Push on."

Aunt Joanie bought us groceries, so I made Louie and Chance sandwiches, gave them baths, and put them to bed. We're back home now with Kitty. Who knows where Big Al is? She sits very still in a bathrobe drinking a highball, watching the Mamas and the Papas sing "Monday Monday." I curl up on the carpet to watch and listen.

"Mama Cass is so fat." Kitty sighs and takes a drink.

I can't believe her—the Mamas and the Papas is the best singing group on Earth, and all she can think about is fatness? "Mom, who cares? Listen to the harmonies!"

Kitty laughs a little, ice cubes tinkling. I can tell she is hurting in her very soul, her face and mouth swollen like that. It's a mess of purple and yellow and red smears. I wish I could ask her about Bobby Delardi and the magazines with pictures of ladies tied up, but I can't get the words out. I try to feel sad for her, for my brothers, but something is wrong with me. Instead, I think of my heart as a crippled hunchback hanging on a rope, swinging away from this hell-house to the sound of a beautiful bell. Tolling out my time left here. Counting down the days, hours, and minutes. Ticktock.

I'm in bed reading William Blake's poem "Tyger" from Kitty's poetry anthology. The poet wants to know: Who is it that made such a beast, and why? And if it's God, did He mold the Tyger out of pure fire? Which makes sense, because of its gold and orange stripes and ferocious nature. *And what shoulder, & what art / Could twist the sinews of thy heart?* The poets often talk about all of us being part beast, part angel. Poe talks about it too. Wasn't poor Annabel Lee killed by devious angels?

I can't seem to concentrate on anything but the poems I love, the music I sing. My excitement about starting sixth grade has vanished since my grades have turned to crap and it's embarrassing, as are these buck teeth that all the kids make fun of. I wish I didn't have to go to school tomorrow.

Pulling the covers into a tent over my head, I sing "Alfie," which makes me feel heavy around the heart. Partly because it's such a sad melody, but also because I wish I were a boy named Alfie and Dionne was singing to me. Grandma Jo says I'll never be a good singer without vibrato. Vibrato sounds spooky sometimes, but mystery in a voice is good. If you take an index finger, press it to your Adam's apple, and wiggle it up and down, it kind of works but sounds fake. I know that one day I won't have to fake, because an angel will fly into my voice, and the songs will follow her back out. I wonder if the angel will be devious. I hope she's kind.

Hours later I hear Kitty mumbling from the living room while Big Al moans about being sorry. He's back, but she won't let him in her bedroom. The springs squeak on the couch as he settles in.

"Fire! Jesus, Al, wake up, fire!"

Kitty bursts through my bedroom door, waves of thick smoke follow her in and flames flicker behind her and she's wild and screaming, dragging me out into the hallway. I stare at the blaze leaping from the linen closet.

"Chance!"

Chance is standing in front of the burning linen closet in the hallway, fire lighting up his face. I scoop him up and race for the front door, past Big Al, still asleep on the couch . . . but I see him cocking an eyelid open, just a slit. Peeking. Kitty screams at him, "Al, get up, for Christ's sake, wake up!"

She grabs Louie's hand as I pass her with Chance, while Big Al mutters from the couch, "What the hell, what's going on?" like he's half asleep and doesn't understand what's happening even though the house is filling with smoke. Somebody called the fire department, thank Jesus. The siren screams of the fire engines get closer, drowning out Kitty's yelling. Finally, Big Al rushes outside, a mad bull shouting, "Who started the goddamned fire?" looking at Louie, then Chance, then Kitty, then me. Everything is happening so fast. Now he's picking up Chance, waving a pack of matches around his head, and yelling, "Chance! I told you not to play with matches!"

Chance, the mouse who never cries, rips out a terrified wail while he tries to pry himself free from Big Al's hands. Kitty won't stop screeching like she's being burned alive, and here come the neighbors out on their front lawns to see what the commotion is about. They gawk. No wonder! Kitty is not only hysterical; she's buck naked. She won't let Al cover her up.

I cross the street and sit on the curb while the crazy scene on the lawn turns into a pinwheel of color, fire trucks washing the house in red lights.

Unchained from her fiery stake in the sky, Saint Joan of Arc marches toward me from the hurting house. She looks me straight in the eye, her own eyes burning like little fires. She hands me a sword, its handle engraved with birds and red crosses. So beautiful.

"It's time to prepare," says Joan. "Be brave, Maddie. *Push on.*"

The best birthday I can remember is my seventh, when Big Al brought home the *Collier's Encyclopedia*. I opened the boxes to discover the greatest of treasures, running my hands along the black, red, and gold bindings and screeching with joy while Big Al hugged Kitty, proud of himself for giving me such a wonderful gift. I opened the first volume, A–APO (Apollyon), and inhaled the smell of the crisp pages, a strange new smell, imagining, *This is what the most wondrous libraries in the world must smell like.* Kitty taught me to read early on, and I went to the *Collier's* at least once a day to investigate something I'd heard about in school or on the radio or TV. The rest of my birthdays, I can hardly remember. Kids in the neighborhood have parties. We never celebrate birthdays.

This birthday is my eleventh, and its different because I'm staying at Grandma Jo's for the weekend and Grandma made me a cake. Jack's home on leave for the first time. Grandma wrote him a song called "Each Star I See," the only song she's ever written. It's very pretty but sad, like Grandma is since Jack went off to war.

Each star I see in its glittering light
beckons to me, you appear through the night . . .
so dream with me, my darling, and pray our dreams come true,
and the next star I see may be you.

Jack nearly cried when he heard her play the song. He brought her two beautiful dolls from Vietnam. His coolest show-and-tell is a Vietnamese switchblade. I wonder if he's ever used it. The blade shoots straight out the top of the pearl handle, not like the ordinary ones that flip open from the side. And the handle has a dragon on it. It's a beauty.

An idea pops into my head, planted there by my current crush, Hayley Mills. Hayley plays Gillie in a movie called *Tiger Bay*. She's a tomboy like me, wants to hang out with the local boys, but she's a girl, so of course they won't allow it. One day while she's sneaking around being nosy, she accidentally witnesses a handsome Polish sailor shoot his girlfriend. The girlfriend's a real creep and has been using the sailor for the money he sends her while he's off at sea. And the girlfriend has another boyfriend, the two-timing schemer. The sailor comes home all excited to see his girl, and she pulls a gun on him! They wrestle with it, he shoots her—but I think he doesn't really mean to because he's trying to protect himself. Gillie watches the sailor hide the gun in what he thinks is a secret place. The sailor takes off, and Gillie steals the gun, maybe because she wants to help the sailor, maybe because she thinks it's cool to be bad. Probably a little of both.

I steal Jack's knife to have something precious of his to keep close. And also because girls prefer bad boys, and I want to be a bad girl-boy who gets the girlfriend. I also steal from my step-grandfather Karl because he deserves it. Karl keeps a sock stuffed with tip money in a dresser drawer, moron that he is. I take about twenty five-dollar bills off the roll and hide the knife and cash in a hole under a floorboard upstairs in Grandma's attic. Before finishing the job, I slick my hair back with Vaseline, playing the kind of dangerous boy Hayley Mills could fall for.

Karl is a crabby parking lot attendant who is just awful to Grandma. Kitty despises him. She shudders whenever he comes near, like she's just seen a ghost. I think he did something mean to her when she was little.

The only time I hear him speak is when Grandma plays the piano. And then it's a yell.

He has a vocabulary of about ten words and most of them are insults. His real last name is Weiss (Grandma told me), a German name that he changed to Chong, and he won't tell anyone why he changed it. Now, it's easy to put two and two together here, and I'm betting an escaped Nazi might want to hide his true identity. Why would anyone hunting Nazis ever suspect a man with a Chinese name? Karl is meaner than a gutter rat. Whenever he catches me looking at him, he makes a hideous bug-eyed face and flips his dentures out. It's disgusting.

Grandma, Joanie, and I will be singing at the piano having a fantastic time, and here comes Karl Chong: "You're all going to hell!" His huge, clumsy feet thud into the living room and there he'll stand, lord of the manor, sneering at us. Vacuuming up every ounce of joy from the room.

"Stop. STOP that colored music, you hear? I pay the bills! I need peace!"

There goes Grandma's sparkle. Her hands freeze.

"I can play something slow, if you don't mind, Karl."

Her body slumps as she begins singing a slow hymn. But no matter the change of joyous to woeful, her music whooshes out love. She can't help it, can't hold back the hurting from the notes and I am learning that love hurts. Chong never utters a kind word to Grandma in my presence. In turn, my thoughts concerning his health are far from kind.

When Chong is home, we leave the piano and head out to the rose garden in Grandma's backyard.

"He can't understand, can't hear the music like we do. Saint Thèrése understands. She knows he's a poor, poor man."

She places a hand ever so gently on my shoulder. How can she be so kind in the face of Chong's cruelty?

Jack discovers the knife is missing. He's furious. I confess and give it back, telling him I'm sorry, that I only wanted something special of his to hold on to. He understands but is not about to give up his pearl-handled switchblade. He offers me some Vietnamese money, and I act like it's a fantastic gift even though it's pretty, but useless.

Karl is another story. Even though I return his lousy money he hits the roof, forbidding Grandma from letting me visit ever again. Karl pays all the bills, so whatever Karl says goes. I'm out on my can. Back to the nuthouse. I say goodbye to Grandma, and she looks sadder than a broken doll. Joanie told me Karl is replacing her piano with a Hammond organ because he can't stand seeing her happy. Grandma can't play her stride rhythms on an organ! You *press* organ keys; you can't *beat* them!

Grandma hugs me tight. "Take care, Maddie," she says, like it's the last time she'll lay eyes on me.

I swear if I ever see Karl again, I will punch those dentures down his Nazi gullet.

Jack drives me home. He pulls his Spider over a block away from Grandma's house and parks.

"Let's go for a walk, Maddie. It's a nice night."

This feels weird, him pulling over, wanting to walk. I bring along my transistor radio, a gift from Aunt Joanie. It's after suppertime. Twilight, my favorite time of day, when the sky turns magical. We stroll past teenagers hanging out on porches, families playing ball and stuff with their little kids on the lawns. Leaves are turning gold, orange, and red all over the oak and buckeye trees, and the air smells fresh and clean like it does when the sun is just about to go down for the night.

"Things are pretty nutty right now, huh?" he says.

"You can say that again."

I don't look people in the eye if I can help it, especially when something sad is about to happen.

"Maddie, it wasn't Chance who set the closet on fire. He's four years old."

"But Big Al said he did it."

"Come over here. I want to show you something."

He takes me across the street to where his neighbors the Mallions are playing hopscotch with their kids on the sidewalk. The littlest one stands on the sidelines, watching and squealing in delight. These kids have really gone to town with the colored chalk. The dusty blue light makes the colors stand out sharp and super bright.

"Hey, Bob! How old is Ruthie?"

Jack's neighbor Bob wipes his hands on his pants and smiles. "Ruthie? Tell Jack how old you are!"

Little Ruthie grins at us. She holds up three fingers. She's real cute, a living doll.

"Three and a half," says Bob proudly.

One of Ruthie's front teeth is missing. The gap makes her grin even cuter.

"Mind if I conduct a little experiment?"

"Ah . . . sure. Go ahead, Jack."

Bob doesn't look too thrilled about saying yes. Jack pulls out a pack of matches and hands them to Ruthie. Bob's eyebrows lift.

"Hey, wait a minute there! You're giving her matches?"

"Don't worry, Bob, I told you it's an innocent experiment. I've got my eyes on her."

"Yeah, well, so do I, buddy." Bob crosses his arms tight. He doesn't like these shenanigans one bit.

"Can you light a match for me, Ruthie?"

The little girl turns the matchbook around in her fingers, then tries to put it in her mouth for a taste. Jack snatches the matches out of her tiny hand, and here comes Bob, marching toward us in a huff.

"Ruthie, that's dirty, don't touch it!"

Ruthie starts to cry as Bob swoops her up and away from Jack.

"I'm sorry, Bob. I just wanted to see if she could do it."

"Smart-ass. That's the last thing I need, is my kid playing with matches."

"No harm done, honest. I'll see you around, Bob."

Bob glares. Ruthie waves at us over her dad's shoulder as Bob walks away.

"You see? Unless Al taught Chance how to light a match, he couldn't have started the fire."

"Maybe he did teach him how to light a match."

"Why would he do that? Chance is four years old."

I'm trying to think it through, but I'm so tired. Maybe I'm just too tired right now.

"Your brother didn't start that fire, Maddie. Your dad set the fire because he wanted the insurance money."

"What do you mean, insurance money? We all could have been killed."

Jack searches the sky, like the answer is floating on a cloud up above his head. He crouches down and holds my arms, gentle-like, which makes me nervous.

"I don't want to scare you, but more trouble is on the way. Your dad would never really try to hurt you kids, but he's a bum. He beats your mother, and she can't take much more. She's sick, Maddie. Do you understand what I mean? Can't you tell?"

My voice is lost somewhere deep in my throat and won't come out. I turn away to watch Ruthie, now just a speck bobbing on her dad's shoulder. Jack follows my eyes.

"I'm going back to 'Nam tomorrow. Your own war is right here, kid, so we both need to be brave soldiers. Promise me that whatever happens, you'll stick to the books. You keep crawling right inside them. The books are your foxholes, you hear me? And music, you love music, right?"

I nod. Don't want to cry. He'll think I'm weak.

"Hell, you better start practicing taking good care of yourself. You're too skinny. Let's go back to Corkhill. I'll cook you a hamburger, okay?"

I don't want Jack to leave. What if I lose him forever?

He hoists me up as high as he can and carries me over his shoulder just when the song "Whiter Shade of Pale" comes on the transistor. That song sounds too spooky, but Jack starts tickling me. I can't help but laugh till the tears come down. He carries me to the car, waltzing around like Charlie Chaplin with a rag doll as the chalky sidewalk colors fade to night.

4

THE WAY OF THE CROSS

Winter changes the buckeye trees into knobby skeletons, their twisted arms crying out with nothing to protect them. Jack is gone, and I can't visit Grandma anymore. Karl won't have it. Big Al is nowhere to be found when you need money or food. When we don't need him, he's there—sitting in his spy-mobile, snooping on Kitty's comings and goings. She filed a report with the police yesterday, and we haven't seen him since. Good riddance.

Junior high school has begun, but it's a disaster. I can't concentrate, and this new teenage way of being and dressing is so confusing. Kids I knew in sixth grade are acting like high school seniors and movie stars. The girls dress like Twiggy and Gidget in new clothes that smell like department store perfume, and they're always looking to see if any boys are watching them as they parade by with their new breasts. I'm practically in rags, wearing Kitty's blouse with the lacy sleeves rolled up. The girls all snigger at me and the boys ignore me completely. Like it was in elementary school, here I am, the cheese standing alone.

Our English teacher tells us we can study one of three languages. Although I want to learn French, I choose Latin, because poets use Latin words and Jack says it's the root of all romance languages. But I can't study. Life at home is crazier every day.

After the fire, we moved into a much bigger house on a street called Evelyn in a suburb called Seven Hills, which Big Al likes because it's the name of a film starring Mario Lanza. Sure enough, he bought the house with the insurance money like Jack said he would, but he's not allowed to live here with us. Although I can see the houses on either side of ours, if I throw a stone as hard and as far as I can, it won't hit either, making it the perfect match for Kitty's fits. We don't want the neighbors knowing what goes on in our nuthouse.

I play hooky a lot and spend my time watching TV. Or sometimes, after feeding the boys and walking Louie to school, I bundle up beneath the great willow tree fanning out its fountain of pale green in our new backyard. Leaning against its strong trunk feels good, solid. I read Edgar Allan Poe and *Alice's Adventures in Wonderland*, imagining what it would be like to have a friend to talk with. A girl like me who has a lot to say and no one else to say it to. I want to stay like this, thinking about my invisible girlfriend, watching the light dance while the breeze sings music through the leaves of the willow—leaves like long pale green fingers to whistle through.

Winter's coming on quickly. Winter here is what I dream the deepest, darkest days of Alaska must be like, with snow so deep and air so cold you can't step out of the house for fear your nose will crack right off your face. Winter is worse than awful because no one wants to drive through a snowstorm to bring us food, and who can blame them? Sometimes Kitty will give me money, and I'll put on her fur coat and trudge to the grocery store on Pleasant Valley Road. People stare and whisper. I'm used to the weird looks. On my way home, I sing the song "Impossible" from Cinderella, sing it loud and strong. Singing keeps me warm, and songs, even the corny ones, are the only things that seem to make me happy these days. I sing to some-one in my head—my invisible girlfriend, the one I tell absolutely no one about because they'd call me a queer nutcase. It seems like nothing can be worse in this life than being queer. And looks like queer is what I am when I sing and when I listen to music, dreaming about meeting her one day—the lonely girl meant for me. Only for me.

Sometimes Big Al picks Louie up for a weekend, but he always leaves Chance and me behind. He doesn't bring food or money, and he doesn't care that we live on peanut butter and crackers. Kitty is out most nights. I think she's dating Dr. Etchy, the creepy psychiatrist who diagnosed her as a paranoid schizophrenic. She doesn't come home until late and is usually drunk, ornery, and looking for trouble.

January is two degrees above zero cold, and the gas company almost turned off the heat, but Joanie came through and paid the bill. Kitty seems much worse in the new house. Her eyes roll back into her head like Saint Sebastian's. She's naked most days, heater blasting, screaming about Dr. Freud and the sadists, sounding like she's speaking backward in a language I can't understand. I try to steer clear. She nearly killed me by smashing a whiskey bottle over my head the other day, but I flew out of the way just in time.

Today she tried to rip my hair out in the kitchen. I had enough. I grabbed back. Took her wrists and threw her down with all my strength, down to the kitchen floor. She just lay there with the strangest begging look in her eyes, like she was excited that I threw her down. Like she wanted me to do something else to her, twisting her naked body around like a snake. I stepped around her and got out of there. A feeling like a poison ball churned in my stomach. I tried and tried but couldn't throw it up.

It's a freezing cold night. Kitty isn't home yet. I reheat the spaghetti Nonni sent over, thinking about my First Communion, when I was nine years old. How eerie it is to eat Jesus's body and drink his blood, knowing it's just bread and juice. The Catholics are nuts, but I love the paintings, the statues, and the sculptures! The art is fantastic, all bloody and beautiful. And I like the safety of prayerful places, churches where incense burns and people pray for hours and hours and the air grows holy. It's as if all those prayers turn every molecule of air into a song of holiness. Sometimes I can get Louie and Chance to pray before eating, and they like it. It feels like they're always waiting for someone to tell them what to do, and it makes them feel calm when it's something nice, like praying. They can't remember the words no matter how hard I try to teach them, but they fold their hands obediently, playing along, Louie grinning and Chance looking up toward heaven while I recite the Prayer of St. Francis, *Lord, make me an instrument of your peace: where there is hatred, let me sow love.* This feels nice, praying and eating around a table like a real family. So normal and sweet.

Kitty comes home. Unwraps her fur coat, flops into a chair, and stares me down, bleary-eyed and wearing her mean face.

"Who called me?"

"Nobody."

I wipe sauce from Chance's chin.

"You're lying. I know you are."

"The phone didn't ring once, I swear."

"Why are you lying, Maddie? Do you think I'm stupid?"

She punches me right off my chair. I stare into her bloodshot eyes. The Saint Francis prayer—*"Lord, where there is despair, let there be hope; where there is darkness, light..."*—comes out from under my breath. She hits me again, this time in the mouth. A front tooth smashes against my lip and I can feel blood drip down my chin. I refuse to cry.

"Where there is hatred, please. Let me sow love . . ."

"You're praying? Do you think the Lord can save you from me?"

"Mom, nobody called. I'm not lying. Please stop."

Louie stutters, his eyes flying back and forth. "Mommy, sh-she— it's true, n-nobody called you!"

She slams her fist into my stomach. I double over. She drags me by the hair to the front door and throws me outside in the snow. Slams the door and locks it.

It's just the cold, the snow, and me. The clear night sky filled with stars. I run around the house trying the basement windows, but everything is locked. I have on a sweater and pants and socks, but no coat, no shoes. As much as it kills me to beg, I bang on the door, screaming, "PLEASE!" Praying my voice will hit her in the heart. Praying she'll have pity.

Louie and Chance are at the living room window mouthing my name. Louie cries. Chance stares like he sees a ghost. Steam from their breath fogs the glass. If she hurts those boys, I will kill her, I will sin and sin again. I hear Jack in my head: *She can't help it, she's crazy. It's a sickness*—words I chant to myself to try to make it all right, but her craziness doesn't warm things up out here and there's no-where to hide, nowhere to run. Nothing can save me, not the prayer of Saint Francis or the stars so clear and clean in the cold night sky. The stars. Icy blue pinpoints of light a zillion miles away. I pray to conjure them closer, imagining my body and head surrounded and glowing with their fires. It's so quiet. The only thing I hear is the sound of my teeth chattering inside my skull. Numb skull crowned in stars.

A light goes on in our basement window and the clothes dryer starts up. I make it over to the vent, muscles tight from the icy cold, feet and hands numb as I curl up next to the vent for warmth, praying the warm air lasts, praying Kitty has taken a diet pill and decided to do all the laundry in the house tonight. Or maybe she has mercy left for me after all. Or maybe I'll die out here. *It is in dying that we are born to eternal life. Amen.*

I've lost track of time. I bang on the door, but she won't come near. It's painful to knock with these numb hands. I ball them into fists, ram them under my sweater, and rush over to the vent. The dryer clicks off. My face begins to burn, skin searing icy edges over my cheekbones. Everything goes blank again, this time without me praying for it. Blank and numb.

Sometime during the night, she lets me back in. I'm shaking so hard I can barely stand. She won't even look at me; just walks right back to her bedroom and locks the door. I shiver throughout the night, hands blue, feet numb. Something's wrong with one of my toes. No matter how much I curl my body tight beneath the blankets, it feels like the skin will never ever be warm again or like the emptiness inside me will ever be filled.

When I wake up, my head sweats. Louie moans for something to eat. Where is Kitty? My big toe hurts. It's turning dark shades of blue and purple, and the nail looks like it's going to fall off any minute. Frostbite toe. *Push on, push on.* To the kitchen to feed the boys—but first to the cupboard beneath the sink where Kitty keeps her bottle of whiskey. Seagrams 7. It's nasty but feels so warm going down. I'll just have to get used to the taste.

Kitty is cracking up. She hears things, sees things, is crazy mean one minute and crying like a baby the next. She took a pair of scissors to all the clothes she ever made for me because I wanted to go to the seventh grade dance *with boys*. *Over her dead body!* Now she's an artist, Cleopatra again, painting hieroglyphs and crazy symbols only she can understand. When I ask what they mean, she grabs my arm and presses her nails into my wrist, holding too tight like she wants to pull me into something, leaving marks on my skin and shadows under my eyes. I stare right back into the sting in her eyes and it scares her. I'm learning how to fight.

I stole money from Kitty's purse again, but this time it wasn't to buy food. I ran away, took the bus to Nonni's. She opens the door and shakes her head when she sees my crazy outfit, mumbling under her breath, *"Come sei qui?"* I have on my mother's clothes: the same white blouse I wear to school with long lacy cuffs that hang too long for my arms, a brocade skirt suit rolled at the top, and my Hush Puppies. One Sunday morning, I dressed Louie up in his best clothes and rubbed away the food stains on his little bow tie with a washcloth. We walked to Mass at Saint Martin's Church, me wearing one of my mother's brocade skirt suits. Well, you'd think two zebras were gallivanting through the pews, the way people stared and whispered. Hypocrites.

After Kitty tore up my clothes, I mended them using big Frankenstein stitches and fabric scraps but ended up looking like Judy Garland when she plays a tramp. Kitty doesn't notice when her clothes go missing, since she hardly wears them. But Nonni notices Kitty's lace sleeves dipping into her chicken brodo as I drink from the china soup bowl. She rolls the sleeves for me.

Nonni is kind. She wrings her hands, telling me to pray to Madre del Nostro Signore Gesù Cristo, Holy Mother of the Lord Jesus. Smelling like garlic and bleach, she lives to cook, to clean, and to pray. Nonni is the one who took me to Holy Name Church when I was little, the same church where I was baptized. She goes back to the old country every few years with her friend Assunta, and they stand for hours in a huge crowd at the Vatican waiting for a blessing from il papa. She brings back medals blessed by him; for me, a little gold Holy Spirit dove in a starburst of fiery beams. Her hands smelled like Clorox and dough when she clipped the catch around my neck, and the sharp clean smell was comforting. Except sometimes it feels like the dove is pecking at my heart. Maybe it's because I haven't been to confession since my First Communion, and boy, am I a sinner. I sin and sin, and maybe that's why everything is breaking.

Nonni pins a lacy handkerchief to my head, wraps herself in a black shawl, and off we traipse to Holy Name on Broadway. The bells toll the hour, the bells that make me ache to find a friend who loves churches like I do. Nonni holds my hand. We're an hour early for Mass. I don't mind. The chaos fades away inside the church, under the majestic sweeping ceiling and arches. Following Nonni, I dip my finger in the cistern, genuflecting toward the altar while crossing myself with holy water. Our footsteps echo on the stone floor in the emptiness, the absolute quiet. My eyes slowly move over the fourteen stained-glass windows depicting each station of the cross. Gesù's agonies, La Via Crucis.

Nonni pulls out her little Italian prayer book and rosary, reciting, "*O amorosissimo Gesù . . . ,*" and as she moves on to recite a prayer for each station, I stare in wonder at its image in stained glass and stop at the sixth station, where Saint Veronica wipes the face of Jesus. The sun flashes through perfumed smoke and the colors: ruby wine, emerald green, brightest of yellow gold. The brilliant purple, stinging like a crown of thorns.

I take the bus home from Nonni's on Monday morning. The house is strangely quiet. Chance sits on the couch looking lost. I knock on Kitty's door and she doesn't answer but Louie cries from inside her room. I open the door to find her lying on the bed, naked back sticking out from under the white sheet. She's making jerky movements where my eyes can't reach, peeking over her shoulder at me with crazy looks like she's terrified. Of me. What is she doing? What's making Louie cry in the corner, rocking and holding himself tight, hiding his face?

She trembles. Out comes a wild sound from somewhere deep in her throat, like the wail of an animal caught in a trap: "Go away, leave me alone! I'm leaving you all! Go!"

I walk slowly toward what is hidden from my sight, Kitty twitching in weird spasms on the bed. She's carving at the inside of her arm with a metal cheese grater, the box type with four panels. I open my mouth. Nothing. The scream inside: a ruby cutting through a heavy curtain, bursting into a million dark flowers.

I take a deep breath and pull the metal box from her shaky hand. Like a bird, she pecks at the fresh cuts on her arm with her fingers, eyes darting back and forth.

"Mom, stay right here. It will be okay . . . just don't move."

In the kitchen, I open the drawers, remove the knives, forks, and sharp instruments, and wrap them in a paper bag. It's too late to call Joanie. Kitty might try to finish what she started, and we need help now. *Push on, Maddie.*

I stand on the neighbors' doorstep with Louie and Chance by my side. A deep breath. I knock. An old woman with a kind face answers the door.

"Hey, kids, you live next door, right? You need to borrow something?"

I think I interrupted her family's dinner. I'm ashamed to ask for help, ashamed of what I need to say. I stare at her feet.

"My mother is having a nervous breakdown. Will you please help?"

Joanie takes care of us, bringing us meals until the day Kitty gets released from the hospital. When she comes home, her eyes don't shine the way they used to. A strange gray dullness has replaced her shiny greens. She moves like a robot, repeating over and over how Dr. Etchy freed her from the nuthouse and how funny it was, but I don't get the joke. Joanie says they gave her electroshock therapy, and it makes her shuffle around the house like a creature from *I Walked with a Zombie.* She cooks meals, cleans up, wears clothes, but sometimes I don't think she's even breathing. She hardly speaks but she reads a lot—mostly her favorite poet, Kahlil Gibran. Sometimes she gazes at us without blinking. Her mouth is parched, and she licks her lips constantly. I write her a little poem: *Cottonmouth cottonmouth, girl in disguise, whatever happened to those emerald eyes?*

She holds her book out toward me, saying, "This is real poetry. Read it, Maddie."

Then she reminds me of the secret: that I was born before she married Big Al. I'm a bastard, just like her. She touches my cheek. I want to cry, because she never touches me, and it feels like she means to be kind. I beg her not to tell anyone I'm a bastard. Kids pick on me enough as it is.

She promises, placing her hand on top of my head like she's a priest, blessing me. I don't think I've ever seen her so sad and sweet. So different. Like it's not even her in there.

"Read this poem out loud for me? I want you to memorize it. Think of it when you want to remember me, Maddie. When I'm not around."

I read it to her slowly, stressing the words without understanding what they mean. The power of the poem scares me. Poems can do that sometimes.

I know this feeing, this something in the air like seeing the future open. Like a mystery. What will happen to Kitty? To my brothers? One thing I do know: my life will not be like anyone else's, will not be an ordinary life. It will be an exciting life. A great adventure. But . . . there will be danger, said the poet.

Kitty's eyes sparkle green again today, as if she's woken up from years of sleep. She hands us washed and ironed outfits for the first time in ages. When I ask her what's going on, she just smiles sadly and nods, "You'll see."

A caseworker from social services shows up without warning. Kitty says to pack light, so I grab some clothes, my blue binder of poems, and a few books: Edgar Allan Poe, *100 Classic Poems of All Time*, and *Lives of the Saints*. Kitty gives me the Kahlil Gibran book wrapped in a piece of mohair from her fabric collection. Louie asks where we're going. "Somewhere fun!" I answer. I decide my brothers will be safe, because there can only be so much cruelty in the world. Only so much.

The caseworker Miss Fortunato is dressed in a groovy orange pantsuit. She takes my mother aside for a whisper, then returns tilting her head, giving us the once-over. Says she'll leave us with our mom for a moment. She carries our belongings to her station wagon.

Kitty is very still. Peaceful. When she finally speaks to us, it's as if we're strangers.

"You all need to go away now. You'll be fine, I promise. I'm just too sick to care for you, and your father is, well, he's never around, is he? I'm sorry, kids."

A smile flickers around the corners of her mouth.

Feeling like a flock of butterflies waiting to escape the net, I tell her I understand.

The four of us walk to the caseworker's station wagon. Kitty takes our hands—Louie's and mine—and I hold Chance's.

She's beautiful in the sunlight, standing there, wearing her favorite Jackie Kennedy–style skirt suit with a matching pillbox hat in pink mohair. Miss Fortunato compliments the outfit. Kitty tells her the hat is a Halston knock-off, and the suit, a Chanel copy, something she whipped up from a Butterick pattern. It's the same suit Jackie O. wore when she crawled onto the trunk of a Lincoln convertible, trying to catch pieces of her husband.

Kitty leans in to kiss my cheek.

"Dreams die so new ones can be born, Maddie."

Then she turns and walks to the house. She never looks back. It's the only time I remember her holding my hand.

PART II

Defeat, my Defeat, my deathless courage,
You and I shall laugh together with the storm,
And together we shall dig graves for all that die in us,
And we shall stand in the sun with a will,
And we shall be dangerous.
—Kahlil Gibran, "Defeat"

5
THE POET KILLERS

I'm wearing an itchy plaid skirt because a staff member at the Metzenbaum Children's Center said looking pretty is important when meeting new family. Miss Fortunato walks me up the rosebush-lined steps of my new home. A thorn bites my leg.

I wipe at the scratch as Mrs. Willard opens the screen door.

"Madeleine! Welcome home honey, I'm your new mom!"

She bends down to give me a peck on the cheek, and I shrug away.

"You're not my mom, and call me Maddie. Please. "

Kisses from strangers are not my cup of tea and Mrs. Willard is a stranger. Mom? Never! But I force myself to smile and fake shyness, considering this foster home might be a nice place to live. Her daughter, Susie, is in the seventh grade at school, same as me. Susie's popular with the boys in junior high. Word travels fast in our neighborhood, so everybody knows I've been given up by my parents. I wonder why the Willards asked to foster me, since Susie and I were never friends.

The Willard house is a white bungalow with green awnings and is two stories tall. Bigger than the houses I've lived in, but not by much. Mrs. Willard (Debbie, she says I can call her, since it's a NO to 'Mom') smells like baby powder. She's wearing a muumuu, with her hair tied up in a ratted bun. The living room is neat but shabby. There are grease stains on the arms of the plaid couch and chairs, and the brown shag rug looks like dead grass. The Willard brothers sit stiffly on the couch watching TV.

"Maddie, this is Ralph and Tommy. Boys, this is your new sister!"

They don't look up at me, eyes glued to the screen.

Miss Fortunato says Louie and Chance were placed in the same foster home, but that the family didn't have room for a third. Good for them, I figure. At first, the two Willard boys seem tamer than

Louie, but the moment Miss Fortunato's car drives off, they leap up and start running around like monkeys sprung from a cage.

Tommy is a mangy little hamster walking upright on hind legs. This morning he grabbed the milk carton, turned it upside down and started spinning, spilling milk all over the kitchen screaming, *"Look at me, look at me!"* You'd think the Willards had buried Tommy in a hole in the backyard for years or something, the way he craves attention.

Ralph has a pompadour. He looks like a melted Ken doll, his hair flaking all over his bowling shirts, walking with his arms held out a foot from his body trying to act tough. The brothers are always fighting. When Ralph gets caught doing something dumb, like lighting Tommy's hair on fire, he'll blame it on evil little Tommy.

"Tommy had a bug on his head! He told me to burn it off!"

That's about as clever as Ralph gets. Foster father Arnold whacks a wet towel over Tommy's smoking noggin, gives Ralph a look, then walks away.

The only things Ralph reads are his *Jughead* cartoons, which he scatters all over the living room along with his smelly bowling shirts and socks. He does it right in front of me because he knows I'll have to pick it all up while they watch TV. Susie is taller and much larger than me all around, and she walks proudly, big breasts first. I've always found her pretentious: running with a fast crowd, doing nasty stuff with boys behind the gym. Now we're sleeping side by side; her in her pretty white provincial twin bed flecked with gold, and me in a foldout cot.

"You keep all your stuff over on that side, okay?" says Susie. People often do this, make demands disguised as questions. As if that makes the order more polite, or pleasant even. She acts all prissy and says, "Look how pretty my things are!" There aren't any drawers for my clothes, so I slide my bag of stuff under the foldout.

I brought books with me, but I'll miss the *Collier's*. I have the blue notebook where I keep lists, poems, thoughts, and drawings written or drawn on thin typewriter paper, the best kind of paper. A gift from Joanie. I write in careful, delicate script, feeling every word as it moves from my head to the pen. Writing is like singing: a private thing for me alone.

Mom wouldn't let me bring her old Bible with the red leather cover, even though I've never seen her read a page of it. It held a curl of gray hair belonging to my great-great-grandmother, a Micmac Indian who smoked a pipe. Kitty doesn't know I swiped the lock of hair. It rests safely inside my notebook, which I hide between the foldout's mattress and metal grating.

The Willard house was tidy when my caseworker dropped me off, but I quickly realize it was an act. The boys run around like wild animals, throwing everything they can get their hands on everywhere—crusts from their sandwiches, comic books, dirty clothes, and underwear—just for the fun of it. Debbie seems tired all the time and clearly can't be bothered to pick up after them. When all six of us are at dinner, I'm the last one to be passed the plates. The blood children get to go out and play after dinner while I do the dishes and clean. There are always tons of dishes. You'd think a tornado spun across the table every night. Debbie and Arnold are all smiles, winking at each other and at Susie like they're sharing some inside joke. Dinner conversation consists of Debbie and Arnold yelling at the boys or talking about nothing. They are the most boring people alive. It seems like Susie's in charge of me, barking out orders like I'm her maid. "Don't forget to take out the trash." "You missed all the pans. Doing the dishes means the pans too." "Make my bed for me, pleeeeze?"

An order is an order. Adding *please* or a question mark at the end doesn't mean a thing. I know how to do all this stuff because I've been doing it for years for my own family. But Jesus, come on. My mother was *sick*. The doctors say she is schizophrenic, the worst of all mental illnesses. And aren't these people being paid by the state to keep me? I'm no fool. On the way to the Willards, I asked Miss Fortunato how this foster thing works with money, and she acted like it was a crime to ask, then ignored me—but I wouldn't let it go.

"Don't I have a right to know about my own *life*?"

Finally, she admitted the state pays the families a monthly stipend for each foster child.

"How much?"

"The court's business isn't your business. All that should matter is that you're being taken good care of. You should be grateful."

"Come on, tell me. How many clams do I go for?"

She seemed amused by the clams comment, one of my Jimmy Cagney favorites, but she didn't answer. Gave me a smirk, then turned up the radio. Maybe if the state paid Kitty to take care of my brothers and me, she wouldn't have gone crazy.

Ralph brings home an Arby's roast beef sandwich and sits in front of me, chewing with his mouth open.

"Mmm, you want some?" he says, mouth full of mush. Then he throws the wrapper on the floor and stares from it back to me.

"Pick it up."

I ignore him. He repeats it louder, "*Pick it up, pick it up.*" Like a good Cinderella, I don't want to end up out on the street, so I obey. As I walk to the kitchen to throw the wrapper away, Ralph trips me. I break the fall with my hands. If my eyes had teeth, they would rip his face off.

I'm trying to read Poe's "The Premature Burial" on my foldout bed and in flounces Susie, disturbing my peace.

"It's dishes time!" she says with a dramatic sigh. "I'm gonna look at *Teen* magazine and listen to Nancy Sinatra."

She drops a 45 onto the record player and bounces on her fancy bed, a princess piglet who doesn't deserve to hear Nancy sing "Sugar Town." I used to like that song. The Willard boys are outside tearing up the neighborhood before it gets dark, maybe torturing the neighbor's pets. I heard Tommy say that Ralph stuck a firecracker up a cat's butt once. Reprobates. Debbie and Arnold are curled up on the living room couch watching *The Monkees*. Susie joins them, but I know the program will be over before I've finished in the kitchen.

I hope Jack isn't on KP duty in Vietnam like I am at the Willards'. If he tries to write me a letter, will I ever receive it? And where is everybody? I haven't heard from Kitty, Joanie, or Grandma, and I don't know what's happening with my brothers. Only that they're together.

I plunge my hands into the warm, sudsy water. Through the kitchen window, birds fly in formation, an arrow of wings moving through the pink-streaked sky.

Life goes on with the Willards, an army drill of dishes and housework and dishes again. At school I can hardly concentrate. Susie told the other kids that I'm her foster sister, and now they avoid me as if it's my fault that my parents threw me away. It's not like I had many friends in the first place. Roseanne is the only girl who dares to come near me. She has weird teeth like mine, and her glasses are too big for her face. She's the teacher's pet, the first to raise her hand with an intelligent question or a correct answer. I was that kid once.

Roseanne and I eat lunch together. Sometimes I share the peanut butter and jelly sandwiches I make myself in the mornings. I assume she's poor, because she doesn't always bring a lunch and her clothes are kind of shabby. Debbie prepares good stuff like tuna salad on rye or deviled eggs for Susie and the boys. I ask her why I'm the only one who gets PB&Js, and she tells me she's got to keep the household economical. I open the dictionary and get angry. It means "being efficient with money," like not spending it needlessly. In other words, spending it on me would be a waste.

One day at lunch, Izzy Treadwell comes up to our table and asks if she can sit with me and Roseanne. I nearly fall out of my chair. Izzy is one of the coolest girls at school. She reminds me of a boy, the way she moves with a funny little strut like Scout in *To Kill a Mockingbird*. She wears her hair shorter than the other girls, chin-length with bangs, and doesn't rat or stiffen it up with hair spray like the greasers. I hear she's the only girl in a family of boys, like Susie, but I hear Izzy's brothers are incredibly cool. Especially John, who's in the tenth grade. He plays the drums (!) and is on the high school basketball team.

Izzy has freckles. And a smart mouth. Once, in history class, she asked the teacher, "If we fought the English for our independence, but it was the French who helped us, why do we speak English and not French?", then looked right at me and smiled. I almost fainted.

She always has a smirk on her face. Like this whole thing—school, boys, history—is just a big joke, and none of it bothers or interests her in the least because she knows too much. Her clothes are excellent: checkered shirts that button down the front, poor boy turtlenecks with suede skirts, Hush Puppies, and knee socks. When she sits at our table with her bright green eyes, a hot flush races up my neck. Her eyes are almost as green as Kitty's.

"Hi. You're Maddie, right?"

"That's me."

"You live with Susie Willard?"

"Yeah," I sputter, blushing. She sits down next to me.

"How can you stand her?" she asks.

I pretend I have a noose around my neck and jerk it skyward, making a face and a choking sound. Izzy cracks up. She holds her hand out for me to shake. It's warm and strong, like a boy's.

"Look, there's Susie trying to get Sam's attention. He thinks she's gross."

Susie traipses past Sam Dubrowski, the football player, holding her lunch tray beneath her bouncing boobs, showing them off like two fat cream puffs.

"What an idiot," I say. "She hides her used Kotex underneath her bed."

Izzy's eyes grow huge. I don't tell her that I'm the one who has to pick them up.

"You're kidding me! What a skank!" Izzy laughs and turns to me. "I'm Izzy. You want part of my ham sandwich?" she asks.

"I'm not hungry, thank you. Want some peanut butter and jelly?"

At that moment, Susie walks by our table and jerks her head up into the air when she sees me with Izzy. Izzy nudges my shoulder. I'm trying to copy the way Izzy grins, like she's up to devilish mischief.

It's a good way of smart-ass smiling because it allows me to keep my lips covered over my buck teeth. When Susie is out of earshot, we explode laughing.

"Well, I gotta split. See you around, Maddie!"

"See ya."

Izzy pauses, looks at me hard. I hope she doesn't see my face melting off.

"You have hazel eyes, but they change colors. Cool!"

That night when Debbie and Arnold read our report cards, Debbie reprimands the whole table and says that because of lousy grades, we'll never get another allowance. The kids all start yelling about the unfairness. My grades are terrible but better than the rest. I'm tempted to say, *Hey, I've never gotten an allowance! And what about school clothes? Where is my mysterious stipend?*

"Everything was fine until *she* got here!" barks Susie, eyes shooting at me.

"What do I have to do with your grades?" I cross my arms and scowl.

Arnold slams his hand down on the table. "Enough!" he yells, and everything gets quiet for a minute while he shifts his look around the circle. "I'm taking you all to Tinker's Creek tomorrow so you can think about being better in school. Good grades next time. Or else!"

"Way to go, Dad, way to go!" shouts Ralph, who flunked nearly everything. What an unlucky bunch of brats, being rewarded for stupidity.

That night before the trip, Susie gives me the silent treatment, staring daggers. Better than the usual. Every night she goes on about which boy flirted with her and what she's going to wear to school for the whole week, a day-by-day wardrobe list. "Will these yellow earrings match my patent leather hip-hugger belt?" And "Will you iron my pleated miniskirt in the morning?" I know if I don't say "How cool!" or do what she says, I'll find another page ripped out of my book of poetry classics. The last time she was mad at me, I found a handful of pages torn out that included "O Captain! My Captain!"

The Willards run around in a tizzy, getting ready for the picnic at Tinker's Creek. I'm searching for my pedal pushers and madras shirt when Debbie appears in the bedroom.

"Honey, you need to stay here and clean up the kitchen. It's a mess."

Debbie calls me "honey" only when she wants to tell me something disappointing.

"It's okay, Debbie."

I shrug hard, the air leaving my shoulders, pretending I'm devastated. I kind of suspected this might happen. Secretly, I'm thrilled at the chance to be home alone for hours.

Debbie closes the bedroom door and whispers, "Susie's a little, well . . . she's sensitive. It's better this way."

"I can go another time. I'll study after I clean up. I'll do better."

Susie bursts in and grabs one of her silly-looking troll dolls, the one with the wild fuchsia hair she calls Connie Ann Fanny. She cuddles that thing like a pet. Still with the silent treatment, she aims her snout up in the air. I try hard not to crack up laughing.

"Don't you dare touch any of my stuff while we're gone."

I fold my hands like an angel:

"I promise."

The front door slams, the Willard station wagon pulls away, and I get to work on the kitchen at full speed so I can have as much time to myself as possible. Once the room is spotless, I make a sandwich with thick pieces of goose liver and lettuce topped with mustard, pour a Pepsi, and sprawl in front of the TV. A fantastic movie starring Marlon Brando is on, about a Mexican hero named Zapata. He rides a beautiful white horse and helps poor people fight the bad guys. I am mesmerized.

Hours go by quickly while I copy out a poem in perfect script alongside my drawing of Zapata's white horse. I place it carefully in the blue notebook, between the poem about Kitty and my drawing of the human heart. It's a handsome addition to the collection, which includes "Ode to Edgar," "The Monkey Boy (Louie)," and

"Josephine in Shadows and Light (Grandma Jo)." Someday I'll be a famous poet and live an elegant life, drinking martinis. Surrounded by movie stars like Tallulah Bankhead who'll ask for my autograph while showering me with praise.

It's dark now. The Willards can't still be at Tinker's Creek. Maybe they all went to Arby's for dinner. I celebrate finishing the poem with another ice-cold pop and lie down on my foldout, wishing I could listen to music, but I don't dare put on Susie's record player—she could walk in at any minute—so I lie there, and it's quiet, and I wonder where they all went—my real family, that is. Why doesn't anyone call or at least try to visit?

Uncle Jack is in Vietnam, so he has an excuse. The last time I saw him was right before he shipped off to a place called Nha Trang. He told me about epiphytes, another name for orchids. There are lots of orchids in Vietnam. I'm glad he has something pretty to look at in the midst of all the war's terror and ugliness. Most epiphytes live on air and just need a surface to cling to. They're self-reliant—don't need much water or food to survive. And still, so beautiful.

"Just make sure you get enough light," he said. "It's one thing most epiphytes can't live without."

Listening to the crickets outside the window, I imagine hearing their song while riding a majestic white horse through the night. I'm a boy in high boots and old-fashioned brown trousers that puff out at the thighs. The war is over. My white shirt billows like a freedom flag. I have led the poor people to victory over their cruel landowners. I'm on my way into the village, so tired I can hardly go on, and there she is, my beautiful wife, waiting to welcome me. Her silky hair falls all around her shoulders, shimmering eyes smiling just for me. I sweep her up onto my horse, and we trot slowly and safely home—a place filled with light, where we can stick.

Izzy walks me to class whispering gossip in my ear, and I recite lines from poems to impress her: *In Xanadu did Kubla Khan / A stately pleasure-dome decree*. Even the other kids at school treat me differently these days, like maybe I'm not such a creep. And it's all because of Izzy.

She sits at our lunch table most days now, which makes Roseanne blue because we ignore her. I feel bad about it, but Izzy is just so cool and not interested in Roseanne at all. Today Izzy brought a brownie, and Roseanne is upset because Izzy didn't offer her any. She gets up and says, "Excuse me," all snappy, then walks away, giving us both dirty looks. Quite bold for Roseanne.

Izzy says she collects stamps for a hobby (but I shouldn't tell anybody because the other kids will think it's queer) and wants to show me her collection.

"I have stamps from all over the world. As soon as I'm old enough to leave here, maybe I'll join the air force. Be a pilot, like Amelia Earhart. They never found her. Maybe she's still alive, stranded somewhere on a desert island like Robinson Crusoe."

Here comes Susie, dressed in a skintight poor boy sweater. She bumps my chair as she walks past.

"Her boobs look like lumpy potatoes. Maybe she stuffs," says Izzy.

"Susie's twins, Tweedledum and Tweedledee."

Izzy laughs so hard she nearly chokes on her Hawaiian Punch. I hand her a napkin.

"Can you keep a secret? I don't just read poetry, I write poems."

She doesn't react. Uh-oh. I stand up like I have to get going. Then . . .

"Can I read them?"

"Sure! But will you promise not to tell anybody?" She crosses her heart.

"Tell me about at least one," she says.

"I wrote a horror poem."

Izzy smiles. "You sure are strange."

She says it like she means strange is good. Putting her chin on her palm, she waits for me to begin. I clear my throat.

Four seasons, bloody and bright.
Season of rapture, season of night.
Season of red like a riding hood cloak,
Season of horror —

"Um . . . sorry. I forgot the rest."

I can't go on because the poem is about my mother hurting herself and the words choke up in my throat.

"That's brilliant! When can I read the whole thing?"

I could throw myself off a roof from the excitement. For the very first time, I have made a friend, and it's hard to hide how I feel, like there are clouds beneath my feet. I'm beyond-the-moon happy, because no matter how rotten it is at the Willards', Izzy wants to read my poems and hang around with me.

Back home at the Willards', I hear the song "Reach Out in the Darkness" coming from the bedroom, which means Susie's home. I want to fetch my blue notebook, to rehearse my poems for Izzy in private.

Tiny pieces of ripped paper are scattered all over the bedroom rug. Standing over the mess is Susie, her face red as a boiled beet. She's crying. Ripping my blue notebook to shreds.

"You told someone about my Kotex, you little bitch!" she screams. "How could you do that? My family took you in when nobody wanted you! Everyone thinks I'm a skank now, and it's your fault!"

Susie keeps tearing the pages into pieces. I can't move my feet, can't breathe.

"No," I say. And it's all I can say. "Please. Don't."

Everything happens so fast. She's picking up the little pieces, huffing around the room like she's gone crazy. Holding up the lock of my great-grandmother's silver hair, she laughs and says, "You freak!" as she runs past and into the bathroom with me after her, grabbing at her hands, but she's much bigger than me, so much stronger. She throws the hair and the pieces of poems into the toilet. I try to grab her hand as she flushes the toilet, cackling like a crazy witch.

"There go your stupid poems and hair, right down the drain!"

The pieces swirl. I'm paralyzed. I want to beat her face in, but I can't move. My eyes. My throat. Everything, frozen. Something is wrong with me.

Susie yells, "I hate you, you skuzzy little bitch!"

Debbie rushes in. "What's going on in here?"

I stoop to pick up two scraps of paper. The words *violent* and *pearl* are all I can make out. Susie starts to cry, telling her mother I ruined her life, when I'm the one who just died. My mouth moves but my eyes can't blink.

"Susie flushed my poems down the toilet."

I'm somewhere else, who knows where. Staring at *pearl* on the paper.

Debbie grabs Susie's arm tight. "Did you do that?"

"I flushed her stupid poems! She told the girls at school nasty things about me!"

Debbie drags Susie out of the bathroom and slams the door while I collapse down the wall, wishing I could disappear for good. I hear a voice—Jimmy Cagney's. He flickers on my eyelids, talks to me. *There you go,* he says, *with that wishin' stuff again. I wish I had a wishing well. So that I could tie a bucket to ya and sink ya.*

It's all mixed up. I don't know if Jimmy's talking to me, or if I'm Jimmy, talking to all the devil people.

How much time has passed? Debbie is here again. I'm still sitting on the bathroom floor with *pearl* stuck like glue in the palm of my hand. Debbie's hands are balled up on her hips, like she's had enough. Like I am nothing but trouble. She sighs.

"You should go to bed now, Maddie. Susie will sleep with me tonight."

As she leaves, she looks at me curiously.

"Honey, you shouldn't have done that to Susie, told those kids. Now go to bed."

After every Willard in the house has gone to sleep, I visit the bathroom and open the medicine cabinet. Kitty is talking to me now, telling me to *pick up that bottle of aspirin and shake one out, pretty little white thing. A pearl!* One at a time, I swallow the pills until I have taken maybe twenty or something, to calm the hive of bees inside my chest. I bring the bottle into Susie's room, lie down on the fold-out, and take more. Why did Izzy tell the girls at school what I said about Susie? Why are people so cruel? I don't want to think. I try to write but my hand shakes as I scratch out some words on a ripped piece of paper: *and we shall be dangerous.* There's a ringing in my ears growing louder and louder. The pitch is too high. Sharp. It cuts. Why this sound, when I asked for it all to fall silent? I want to sleep, but the ringing won't stop, won't let up. The ringing makes my head feel like it's about to cave in on itself. I'll take more pills to escape this sound.

I wish I had a wishing well . . . Jimmy Cagney screws up his face and and tap-dances away as sound pierces my brain. Well, now I'm the only one who can do anything to hurt me. I'm going to dream forever and never wake up. My heart pounds loud and slow, and the room turns hazy gray . . . slipping down into black.

I wake up on the bathroom floor over the toilet bowl, spewing my guts out. Blood comes up, streaking through the white foam while the room spins. I see five toilet bowls and retch again, missing all the toilets. Susie stands over me with a bottle of something in her hand, looking really upset, with Debbie next to her shouting, "Give her more ipecac, make her drink it! Hold her head!"

"Oh, it's so gross. I don't want to touch her!" Susie yells back, forcing a bottle to my lips. She makes me drink the poison. My guts explode again, frothy white stuff with more blood, like some demon hand is reaching down my throat trying to rip my stomach out through my mouth.

Between retches I manage to mumble out, "Please, take me to the hospital."

They lift me off the floor, placing my arms around their shoulders. If I had an ounce of strength in me, I'd punch their lights out, but I'm too weak, can hardly walk. They lay me down on Susie's princess bed. The high-pitched evil ringing is driving me crazy. Why are they still here, these awful people? So thirsty. Want to sleep.

When I wake up, it feels like late morning. Debbie is trying to feed me chicken noodle soup and crackers, but I can't take the smell of the soup, so I eat a few crackers and try to keep them down. The ringing grows softer now. They didn't take me to the hospital. Never even called a doctor. That's okay, I'll be better than fine soon enough.

Debbie decides I should go back to school two days later. Feeling like a wet noodle, I board the bus with a plan. The bus stops two streets over; I get off and run like hell in the opposite direction through the streets of Parma, past ranch houses and lawn sprinklers and bungalows, until I can't run anymore or my lungs will cave in. I stop at a corner phone booth and dial the operator.

"Please connect me with the police," and when a guy from the police station answers, I say I'm a runaway and am about to throw a brick through somebody's picture window if they don't pick me up.

When the cops arrive, it's time to lay down the law. My law.

"If you take me back to that foster home, I will kill myself. And I will tell every teacher I know at school that I told you, Officer Krupke, and you, Officer Bozo, exactly what I would do. It'll be your fault."

The cops shake their heads like I belong in the bughouse with my mother. Who cares what they think? In the back seat of the cop car, I'm like my hero Jimmy. Down, but not out.

A nurse checks me in at Marymount Hospital and starts asking questions, and the last makes her face twitch: "Did anyone mess with your privates?"

"No," I tell her.

Then I confess about the aspirin. She presses her fingers firmly on my wrist and checks her watch, looking concerned. I make up a few beatings by Ralph because I know ripped-up poems and housework will not spring me from the Willard House of Mean. A doctor pulls the curtain aside as the nurse tells him, "Her pulse is beating faster than a hummingbird's."

I shrug off her hand, eyes glued to the floor. They pull the curtain closed around me and whisper on the other side. The doc returns.

"You could have died. Please don't ever do anything like that again. We're going to do an X-ray of your stomach, and for now, I'll give you something to soothe the ache."

He places a kind hand on my shoulder, then disappears as the curtain whooshes closed again. I can hear bits and pieces while he and the nurse whisper: *"Run some tests . . ."* *"Beatings . . . suggest removal . . . Family and Children Services."*

I have a little talk too, with my hero Jimmy.

I said my prayers, Mugs. Said 'em my way. And I won. See?

6

SAFE

I'm staying at the Metzenbaum Children's Center when Miss Fortunato tells me she got a call from the Treadwells, a family interested in fostering me. They are here to see me.

Oh my God. The Treadwells.

"Do they have a daughter named Izzy?"

"Their daughter's name is Isabelle. They say you know her from school?"

"I don't think that's a good placement for me."

"Why not? They seem like a very nice family."

This can't be happening. If Izzy can turn on me like that, tell the girls what I said about Susie . . . I could have died. Because of Izzy, I didn't want to keep going, to push on. She taught me that no one can be trusted. No one. Izzy is dangerous.

"I prefer to stay right here in Metzenbaum."

"That's not possible, Maddie. Metzenbaum is a temporary placement center, and the Treadwells are here to meet you. Cheer up!"

"Great. That's just great."

I fold my arms over my chest to show her I'm not going anywhere if I can help it.

"You have to give people a chance, Maddie. You had one bad experience. It doesn't mean every placement is going to be bad."

I gave Izzy a chance, and she betrayed me.

"You don't know the half of it."

Miss Fortunato walks away in a huff, like she always does when I get mouthy. I follow her into the office and there's Izzy Treadwell with her mother. I can't even look at her.

"Are you doin' okay?" Izzy sounds sincere, but I'm not buying it.

"Yeah, I'm fine," I tell the floor.

"Maddie, this is Mrs. Treadwell," and I look up into one of the kindest faces I have ever seen; it's calm and lovely. Izzy's mother holds her hand out for me to shake, and I can smell something very delicate, like the roses in Grandma Jo's garden.

"Hello, Maddie."

Her eyes are so kind. She's pretty. *Life* magazine sophisticated, but not too girlie and not too much makeup, with a beautiful haircut that frames her face just so. She wears a breezy summer outfit with a pastel flower pattern. I can see where Izzy gets her good looks. Mrs. Treadwell smooths her skirt before she sits—a true lady.

"I guess you didn't have such a great time in your last home. I'm sorry to hear that."

"Sometimes stuff happens. I'm okay."

I cut my eyes at Izzy when I say it, and she looks away.

"Maddie, Izzy wants to tell you something."

Izzy faces me now, looking all sorrowful. "I didn't tell the girls what you said about Susie. It was Roseanne. She was jealous we became friends, so she did it to cause trouble. You know I would never tell your secrets. Never! I promise I'll never betray you. I swear."

I want to believe her and I do. Why can't I look anyone in the eyes?

"That's okay, Izzy, forget it. I didn't think you told anyway," I lie.

She comes over and gives me a hug. It's an awkward hug, like when a boy gets forced to hug a girl, but it's a real hug, I think. There's water creeping into my eyes, so I shut down the pipes. Mrs. Treadwell leans toward me.

"I've talked it over with my husband, and we'd like you to live with us. For a while, at least, to try it out. It'll be up to you, Maddie, your decision, and if you like, you'll be welcome to join our family. You'll share a room with Izzy. We have two other boys who would never dream of being mean to you. And guess what? I'm a pretty good cook too! What do you say?"

I try not to squirm while Izzy nods her head, eyes wide and grinning, like, *Just say yes, stupid!* Mrs. Treadwell is so sweet, with that beautiful smile.

"Can I see my brothers sometimes?"

"Of course!"

"Then yes, I'd like that very much."

Mrs. Treadwell gives me a hug, I hug back, and Izzy hugs me again too, more excited this time like she's in a rush. All this hugging makes the blood rush to my face.

"Thank you, Mrs. Treadwell."

"You're welcome. You can call me Marie."

While Miss Fortunato talks to Mrs. Treadwell, I walk Izzy out to the Metzenbaum common room. She takes in the picture.

"Wow, all these kids don't have families?"

"Yeah. That's Scotty over there. He used to be my boyfriend when I was here the last time, but now he ignores me."

Scotty is dancing with a much smaller girl to "Tighten Up," by Archie Bell and the Drells. He notices we're watching and starts showing off, doing little James Brown spins. This is the only time he's not shy—when he's dancing. He has on checkered pants and looks really cute, skinny legs working out in all the right moves.

"What happened to his thumbs?"

"He was born like that. I think it's why no foster families will take him. I never cared. He's the king of the dance floor."

"Did you make out with him?"

"Nah, we just danced. He has soul for days."

"Do you like soul records?"

"Aretha is the best!"

"You are gonna love our house. My brother John loves Motown records and soul music. He just bought a great record by Sly and the Family Stone."

We sit down on a bench. Izzy gets real quiet.

"Did Susie beat you up? Is that why you ran away?"

"No way, I could take her! She ripped up all my poems and flushed them down the toilet. What a scag."

I act like I don't care about the poems.

"Oh, man. That really sucks." She looks down at the ground.

"It's okay. I'll just write more."

Another lie. I don't feel like writing poetry much these days.

"Where did you go when you ran away?"

"I ran to a phone booth and called the cops."

We both crack up.

"What does everybody at school think? Did Susie tell them stuff about me?"

"She told her creepy friends you were nothing but trouble, a real JD. But we all know she's the one who's bad news. Don't worry about it."

"A JD?"

"A juvenile delinquent!"

I start singing the Officer Krupke song from *West Side Story*, and, of course, Izzy knows the words!

The Treadwells have a gorgeous split-level house with a grand living room that opens to a dining room. There's a huge kitchen and bathroom on the ground floor, four bedrooms on the second level with an open staircase, and best of all, a rec room in the basement with wood paneling and two couches, a big stereo, a bar, and John's professional drum set and rehearsal space taking up a corner. The house is like something straight out of a magazine, ultramodern and supercool. Kitty would flip if she saw this place. One wall in the living room is a huge wallpaper photograph of a forest in the autumn—it's so realistic, like you could walk right into the scene and feel the pine needles under your feet.

The kitchen has black and white tiles on the floor, marble counters, and shiny modern appliances, and it even has a dishwasher. Everything in its place, and a place for everything. The furniture is so pretty, you're almost afraid to touch it. Marie laughs and flops daintily onto the couch to show me it's okay, it's comfortable. There's one whole wall of books in the living room, most about psychology. Freud, Masters and Johnson, Kinsey, Helen Gurley Brown and *Sex and the Single Girl*. I pretend I don't see that one.

"Think of it as your own personal library," says Marie. "How about this one?"

She pulls out *Don Quixote*. I run my finger over the raised leather, feeling the tumble into a rabbit hole filled with gold.

Marie's voice is husky—from smoking I bet, which she enjoys very elegantly, like a movie star with graceful hands poised just so. Her shoes look like ballet slippers, and she wears black slacks that zip on the side. She has a slow, relaxed smile; kind and intelligent eyes; and a graceful step when she walks. What a difference from my own unkempt mother. Kitty moved like a bird that bashed its head into a window while trying to fly off to who knows where. Kitty. I wonder where she is now.

Izzy's bedroom is the opposite of Susie's. Sunlight streams through windows, casting patterns from the trees outside onto the bright yellow walls. There are two single beds with plaid bedspreads in lemon yellows, oranges, and browns. Each bed has a night table with a lamp shaped like a ballet dancer—but the room isn't too feminine, is more like a boy's room. A giant poster of how electricity works hangs over one bed. The poster of Herman's Hermits on the back of the door is the only clue that a girl might be sleeping in here. There's a dresser to put my clothes in and empty hangers to hang stuff on in the closet. I wonder why Izzy has two beds in her room. Marie notices me sliding my raggedy clothes into the dresser drawers.

"We'll take you shopping this weekend for new school clothes."

That night at dinner, I meet Mr. Treadwell, John the drummer, and Nick, who's in the ninth grade and is a science geek. He wears glasses, is really cute and bookish in his button-down shirts. Roy Treadwell owns a Chevy dealership and wears a suit to work. He's starting to go bald but doesn't have one of those bad hairdos, like when old guys try to grow the few strands they have long and then comb them over the shiny spots.

"You're welcome in our home, Maddie. If you need anything, just ask." He winks at Izzy and passes me the lamb chops. John asks if I like music.

"I love music. My grandma is a piano player." I suddenly feel weird about bringing up Grandma. It's hard to think about my family since they never think about me.

"That's cool. I'll play you some of my records later. Mom doesn't like the music I listen to, do you, Mom?"

"It's why you kids have a rec room! Classical music and Shirley Bassey are more my taste. I guess I'm just an old-fashioned gal."

"Marie studied psychology for years. She's the smarty-pants of the family," says Roy, looking over at his wife with pride.

Izzy kicks me under the table, rolls her eyes. "Yeah, Mom wanted to be a shrink!"

"I'll shrink your head if you don't bring us the dessert!" and Marie goes for the kitchen and Roy tries to tickle Izzy as she squirms away. It all seems so normal. Almost painfully kind.

The Treadwells don't put their elbows on the table when they eat, and they always ask if I want more of everything. We feast on lamb chops, string beans, and mashed potatoes, and then Marie brings dessert: little slices of lemon meringue pie. I stare at my plate but can't take a bite. Kitty loved lemon meringue.

"You don't like lemon meringue pie?"

"I'm full, but thank you, Marie."

This would not be a great moment to start bawling.

Roy goes off to make himself a scotch while I help Marie clear the table, and I'm proud to show her how quickly I can make it perfectly beautiful again. We load up the dishwasher together.

"Let's sit down and talk."

The small white table in the kitchen overlooks the backyard, with its apple tree and thick, beautiful peony bushes. I know what's coming. *The talk.* The kind of talk that gives me the heebie-jeebies.

"The caseworker explained your mother wasn't very nice to you, but listen, Maddie, she did bad things because she is unwell. Your father too. I'm sure he cares, but he has problems of his own."

She lights up another cigarette.

"Your mother suffered a lot. As sure as I sit here today, know that she loves you. Parents don't always know how to care for their children. When you're older, you'll understand. And you can just forget about those Willards. They should never have treated you badly."

My body is shaking like a leaf. I wonder if Marie can see the tremble. She gets me a Kleenex, like she knows I'm going to cry.

"You have such pretty eyes. Would you like a glass of apple juice?"
In between hiccups, I nod yes.

For my thirteenth birthday, not only did Marie bake me a chocolate
cake, but we went clothes shopping, and Izzy came along to help
pick out clothes. I got a yellow raincoat that flares out at the bottom,
a navy-blue winter coat with brass latches on it, and lots of poor boy
turtlenecks, corduroy hip-hugger pants and skirts, and a brand-new
pair of Hush Puppies loafers with fancy stitches. Red high-top Keds
and a pair of jeans that zip on the side. Izzy and I hate skirts. We
never wear them at home, too girlie. Plus, I have lots of new underwear, socks, and a pair of flannel pajamas with spaceships on them.
I prefer boys' pj's. Marie doesn't seem to mind.

Izzy introduces me to her friends, and they treat me like I'm one of
them, probably because Izzy is so boss. Susie turns away every time
she sees me, and she's no longer part of the in crowd. There's only
one girl who still hangs around with her, Cheryl. Nobody can stand
Cheryl except for the boys who want to do things to her, and even
they can't stand her. Sometimes I catch Roseanne the rat staring at
me, but she knows better than to come near.

A boy named Bill has a crush on me. Izzy thinks he's cute, but boys
don't interest me much. I lead Bill on as if I like him too, but it's just
a game to prove that I'm just as cool as the other girls. Even though
I don't like boys, my new brothers are fantastic. We talk about music
and science, which you never can with the other schoolboys, who
only think about sports or mechanics or doing nasty stuff with girls.
Izzy couldn't care less about boys. She prefers her stamp collection.

At night, in the dreamy glow of the fish tank, we sit on our twin
beds and read books or giggle. We play-wrestle sometimes. She
blows raspberries on my stomach, and I laugh like crazy, then do
it back to her. She loves it. I don't like Izzy in a romantic way, feel
she's more like a sister, and I never want to kiss her like I do the girl
of my dreams.

Izzy tells me about the other kids in school, like, "This one's going
with that one," and "He's a good dancer, but he's dumb as a rock," or

"She's a math whiz," and "That one's a skank." Who drinks and who smokes pot, she knows everything. On Saturdays, we hang out with John in the rec room, the best time of all, because he plays amazing records by Sly and the Family Stone, the Yardbirds, the Kinks, Stevie Wonder, and Aretha Franklin.

Sometimes John plays the drums along to the records, keeping a soulful beat. He has an acoustic guitar and is teaching me to play bass on the bottom strings. When I strap on the guitar and play along to "Little Bit o' Soul" next to John on the drums, it's like we're in a real rock 'n' roll band. We saw Sly and the Family Stone on *Kraft Music Hall*. There were two girls in the band, a trumpet player and an organ player; the first time I saw women play rock instruments.

Sometimes Izzy invites her friends over—Janet, Shirley, and Samantha Tamorini (a total fox) and we dance. Izzy's friends at Hillside Junior High are fantastic dancers. Izzy won't be your friend unless you can dance your butt off. The Four Corners, the Boogaloo, the Cissy Strut—we know all the dances. We watch *American Bandstand* on Saturdays, but the host bugs me. He reminds me of a Ken doll come to life, that Dick Clark. The white teens on his show dance kind of goofy and can't hold a candle to the black singers and groups performing: Smokey Robinson and the Miracles, Gladys Knight and the Pips' "I Heard It through the Grapevine," and the Delfonics stepping to "La La Means I Love You." The other day I got the nerve to sing "Chain of Fools" by Aretha for Izzy and John, and they couldn't believe what came out of my mouth. Thank you, Grandma Jo!

Izzy has been bragging about me to her friends at school, saying my voice is unreal, telling the kids I can sing like Aretha Franklin, which is definitely not true. I can only wish. The cool girls don't sneer at me these days, but I have nothing in common with them. Avoiding the in crowd I stay mostly to myself or hang with Izzy. I can concentrate again, and my grades are inching up. At home I read books like *Great Expectations* (I'm Pip, waiting for Estella). Maybe there's something terribly wrong with me because I don't really like the kids at school. In books, I find mirrors. And in the mirrors, it's always boy characters looking back at me. The boys. Always having the adventures.

Marie helps with homework, math and Latin. Nick helps with science, explaining atoms and protons and the like. He has an incredible electric microscope in his room, and absolutely everything he places on a slide reveals a miniature universe, bursting with life. A hair, a piece of skin, an ant. When Nick describes something he thinks is particularly amazing, he calls it a "miracle of nature."

I make a vow that I will do the very best I can to stay here with the Treadwells and not mess this up in any way. With luck, maybe they will adopt me one day. It's a luck I'll have to make.

John brings home the summer sounds of 1968, all the latest records. Steppenwolf has a song about drugs where the singer actually swears: Goddamn the pusher. *Aretha Now* is the best album of the bunch and crazy fun to sing along to. On songs like "Think," sometimes I sing Aretha's lines, other times I echo her words along with the background singers, *Freedom!*

When Izzy hangs out at her friends' houses, I usually don't go along, since it's nice to be alone and read or sing to myself. "(Theme from) Valley of the Dolls" makes me think of Kitty. Such a ghostly song. Marie said I could read that book, and now I get why Kitty loved it. She's kind of like Neely, goofy from all the "dolls." I see Kitty in my mind's eye, calm and quiet, walking near the sea in another land. I sing, guiding the song's words along from deep inside of me. Sadness rides the notes moving through while I pretend to remember Kitty hugging me. Why didn't she? I guess that's just how some mothers are.

Marie gives me a copy of *Jane Eyre*—maybe because Jane spends time in an orphanage, and Marie knows my mother is crazy, locked up now like Bertha at Thornfield. I ask her about mental illness. It can happen to anyone, she says, at any time, triggered by chemical imbalances in the brain, or drug abuse and alcoholism, or even childhood traumas, which makes me nervous. If that's the case, I'm in big trouble.

Weeks later, Marie tells me Louie and Chance have been moved out of their foster home because the people there mistreated them. Louie now lives in a children's home called Bellefaire. It's a group home for kids who have problems, she explains, and Louie needs attention because he's hyperactive. Chance has been placed with a nice Italian family.

"Can I call them?" I ask, and she gives me their phone numbers.

The woman at Bellefaire tells me Louie's having recreation period. Marie gives her our telephone number. I wait a whole week and he never calls. I decide to call Chance, but it takes me longer because I miss him more. I overheard John talking to Izzy about what happened to Chance. His last foster family (he's been in two already) was poor and hardly fed him. The father was a pervy creep, and the oldest boy in the house was a sicko. This boy took the family cat, spun it around by its tail, and then locked it in a room with Chance. The cat scratched Chance's little face to ribbons. One of the neighbors saw Chance outside with his face torn up and called the police, and they took Chance out of there. God made man and the Devil in His own image. But where does the love of God go when these things happen?

Marie can tell I overheard the story. I tell her I want to find that family and break every one of their bones.

"Both of your brothers are in good places now, trust me. I promise," she says. "Revenge, especially violent revenge, is wrong. It doesn't solve anything. Remember this. What's in the past is past. It might not make sense to you yet, but you'll grow up and make choices, instead of having choices made for you. So will your brothers. Think. What do you want your life to be?"

I can only hear one word repeating in my head: *safe*.

7

SISTER JUDAS

Izzy has invited six girlfriends over for a slumber party, says it's something girls do in junior and senior high. I'm thinking it'll be like the telephone scene in *Bye Bye Birdie*, but instead of being in separate rooms on telephones, we'll be all together gossiping with records playing and plenty of dancing. Everybody will bring their pajamas and blankets or a sleeping bag.

We prepare all afternoon, making little ham sandwiches with Marie, icing the Cokes, putting out bowls, plates, cups, and napkins for potato chips and pretzels. We have John's permission to play his records, with one rule: only Izzy and I can touch them. Marie tries to look all stern when she tells us to make sure we don't eat and drink too much or we'll get sick—she will *not* be cleaning up after us.

When the girls arrive, Samantha Tamorini makes an entrance, dropping her peacoat to show off her fluffy orange nightie. It's short and low cut like something Ann-Margret would wear. The first record on the stereo is "Chain of Fools," and we start dancing the Four Corners. Samantha watches me, her fluffy number billowing out around her hips when she dances. Izzy puts on the 45 of "M'Lady," by Sly and the Family Stone, and we get into it immediately, singing along: *Bum bum bum bum bum*. I bend down and stick my butt out with a wiggle on the funny part of the song that sounds like a kazoo. Samantha giggles, makes a beeline for the bar, and holds up a rum bottle, waving it at Izzy.

"Can we have some of this?"

"We've gotta be careful. Just a few sips, or my ma will know."

Samantha pours out a giant glass. Izzy is not happy.

"Don't worry, Izzy, watch!"

Samantha fills the bottle with water, back up to where it was.

"Look. You can't tell the difference."

I take a big gulp to show off. It tastes sickly sweet but feels nice, all warm going down. A slow record comes on, "La La Means I Love

You," by the Delfonics. This song gives me goose bumps, thinking about a girl I might love that much one day. Izzy takes Janet's hand and says, "Let's pretend we're with the boys!" and starts slow dancing with her. As if Izzy is ever with boys. Janet giggles while Izzy pulls her in close. Izzy is such a natural at being a boy. Everybody couples up except for Marsha, who goes out with Bob Ebersole, the best dancer in the high school. She hogs the rum bottle while we dance. Marsha is a total greaser chick, a blonde with black roots, and she rats her hair into a beehive, long in the back like Ronnie Spector from the Ronettes. She wears short, tight black skirts with fishnets and thick black eyeliner. Marsha is Marianne Faithfull, Petula Clark, and Dusty Springfield all rolled up into one—the most fabulous girl in school. Even cooler than Samantha, who is now walking toward me.

Samantha takes my hands and puts them on her shoulders, then places her arms around my waist and pulls me in tight, gliding straight into the rhythm. Her thigh moves between mine; we dip and bend. The Bee Gees and Samantha's leg stir up butterflies in my stomach. I've never felt this way with a boy. Does this make me a homo? I'm slow dancing with Samantha Tamorini, a major fox that all the boys are totally gone over.

When my mom and Uncle Jack used to talk about sex, I'd strain to hear every word. They'd discuss who had sex appeal. Kitty would say, "Oh, he is sooo sexy!" about Jeff Hunter and George Chakiris. She also liked guys with sandpaper faces, like Harry Guardino and Richard Burton. Jack thought Ava Gardner was the tops. Big Al would say, "That Tuesday Weld is a sex pot!" Put all this together: the butterflies in my stomach plus Samantha's brown eyes looking at me that way, plus the way she moves her hips, and it's a simple equation. Samantha Tamorini equals sex pot. And she's putting her moves on me.

The rum makes me feel warm inside and out. Janet wants to hear another slow tune. Pretty nervy of her. I bet everyone else does too, but we're too scared to say it out loud. We return to our original slow dance partner like we're couples. Are all girls really lezzies? I wonder, looking around at everyone swooning. Do we just pretend to like boys when we really want to be with each other?

All the couples slow dance to Lulu singing "To Sir with Love," including Samantha and me. We're like a group of little rivers flowing into one another. I wonder what Marie would say if she walked in on us.

It's like I wished her to the top of the stairs.

"Girls! It's almost one in the morning, time for bed! At least turn that music down!"

Samantha didn't bring a sleeping bag and neither did Janet, so some of us double up. Guess who is sharing with me? I'm feeling good—tipsy, as Kitty used to say. Samantha gets into the sleeping bag. It's impossible not to touch her. She smells so good, like Jean Naté and rum. At first, we're just lying there kind of stiff-like, and all the rest of the girls are giggling and whispering away in the dark and someone yelps, *"Don't! It tickles!"* Then I hear Izzy blowing a skin-fart on Janet, followed by a squeal. Ever so quietly, with the sleeping bag barely rustling, Samantha takes my wrist in her hand and places my arm around her silky waist.

My heart stops. She pulls me on top of her, into her body, pressing her breasts against mine—hers are quite a bit larger—and it all feels like some unknown force fills my body. Weak yet filled with power, with fire. She whispers into my ear, "I dare you to kiss me."

I don't know what to do. I mean, I do, but I'm petrified, so I press my lips very softly to the skin of her cheek and leave them there for a few seconds, then turn away slightly. She turns my face back to hers and puts her lips on my lips and presses softly and firmly . . . keeps them there, then pulls away a little bit, then presses harder, moving her head around a little while she kisses me, like I've seen people do in the movies. I follow her moves, her lips. She stops for a minute, then whispers in my ear again: "Let's French. Just copy me."

When she whispers like that, I can't help it—all of me rises and rubs up against her like a cat arching its back in reverse. She rubs back, and the whole front of my body turns into an animal that hasn't eaten in days. She opens her lips a little. I copy her, butterflies banging away in my stomach. Even though we're so, so quiet, I'm afraid the other girls will hear us, hear my heartbeat, speeding up and pounding louder than John's kick drum.

Samantha is an excellent kisser.

She slips her tongue in, a little bit in between my lips, soft and lazy- like, and I hear church bells, and something stirs between my legs, a feeling I've never felt before. It's my first French kiss. No wonder I've always had a thing for France.

I look over at Izzy and Janet, but everyone must be asleep. They breathe softly, nothing like the way Samantha Tamorini and I are breathing right now.

Suddenly she's filling my mouth slowly with her tongue. My body rolls and winds on top of her, she holds me tighter. I can't help but push my body into hers. It's like we're slow dancing in a horizontal position, because my leg is between hers and I can feel her thing up against my leg. Everything is hot. I'm rubbing mine slowly on her thigh while our tongues play lazy games with each other. The pace grows quicker, I pull my face away and try to breathe . . . my body, a burst of starlight exploding beneath the skin.

"We need to stop. Someone might hear us," I whisper in her ear in between breaths, and she lets out this moaning sound. The sound makes me weak. I whimper like a stupid puppy.

"Okay. Let's stop," she says.

My heart freezes. We're breathing hard, still trying our best to be quiet. Samantha Tamorini is holding on to me tight and warm, and her heart is pounding against my back. Her heartbeat. A miracle of nature.

I remember watching a movie called *The Children's Hour* with Kitty. The movie was so terribly sad. Audrey Hepburn plays Karen and Shirley MacLaine plays Martha, two teachers at a girls' school. One of their students, a girl with the Devil in her, gets mad at them and tells everyone they are "lovers," the very worst thing women can be with each other. The Devil girl ruins their lives. In the end, Martha confesses to Karen that it's true, she does have feelings for her, but Karen doesn't feel the same. But wait. Maybe she does and can't admit it? Because who wants to admit to a life where you know you'll be treated like a monster? Martha feels sick and dirty for her feelings of love, and it's so horrible, the sadness of it. Karen goes off for a walk to think. Then this look of wonder comes over her face, and she starts running toward the house with a tender smile, because maybe she does feel something for Martha. But it's too late. She opens Martha's door to discover Martha has hanged herself.

The kid who hardly ever cries started crying through that terrible scene. I couldn't stop. Kitty hugged me then, and my mother *never* hugged me. She told me how cruel the world is to homosexuals and I should be careful. It's like right then, she knew who I really was.

Whenever I see a romantic movie or hear a love song, I think of Samantha Tamorini. I'm always the guy singing and she's the girl. Heathcliff and Cathy, Warren Beatty and Natalie Wood, Tony and Maria. "La La Means I Love You." Of course, you never see girls kissing girls in a movie or on TV. Girls don't serenade girls. You never see guys making out with guys. Bugs Bunny can dress like a girl and smooch on Elmer all he wants, because people think it's funny. As if homo stuff is a joke. The unfairness of it! I know in my heart that if girls being with girls feels this good, it must happen a lot.

Back at the Treadwells', I play bass on the bottom strings of John's guitar to James Brown songs, while he plays the beat and Izzy plays the tambourine. I think about Samantha Tamorini in an orange nightie whenever I'm alone. Us slow dancing in between the sheets. School starts in September, and I'll get to see her again.

Sarah Vaughan is singing "Ain't Misbehavin'" from the stereo while Marie reads the *Plain Dealer*. She's been very upset about Bobby Kennedy's assassination. American heroes keep getting shot by weirdos who seem to hate goodness and equality. Marie takes all these murders to heart. Like Kitty, but less hysterical.

"They killed Malcolm X for telling the truth too! For saying the troubles in this country are not just about color, Roy. Do you understand the implications of it?"

"Who are 'they,' Marie? You act like it's some sinister conspiracy." Half asleep in his recliner, Roy swirls the ice around in his scotch.

"*They* are the people behind the scenes running the country, that's who. The same people who had Jack Kennedy and Dr. King killed because they are afraid of a social revolution."

"Marie's a true radical."

Roy winks at me like he doesn't take any of it seriously. Marie is right. Big things are happening in this country, important things, but why do our leaders keep getting killed for following the same lessons Jesus came here to teach?

Roy takes another drink.

"It's over my head, ladies. Good night." Roy gives his cubes another swirl, gulps, and heads up the carpeted stairs.

"That man hasn't a clue! Sometimes I think he'd be happiest if I didn't care about anything but him." She starts thumbing through the pages of *The Autobiography of Malcolm X*.

"Is that what you're reading?"

"It's what started this argument. Would you like to read it when I finish?"

Big Al once bragged about his Italian friends taking over a church at the top of Murray Hill Road, in Little Italy, when Martin Luther King Jr. planned a freedom march up that hill. The Italians went into the church bell tower with machine guns armed and ready, pointed down at the marchers. I wonder if it was true. He liked telling this story. Laughed about it.

Kitty was different. She cried when she watched black people beaten by policemen on television. When those little church girls were killed by a bomb in Birmingham, she locked herself up in her room and cried for days. The news of those little girls was so heartbreaking. How could men be so cruel? It made me think of what happened to Anne Frank, the truth growing bigger in my head about how evil can come for anyone, without a reason.

Once when Al was going on about "the shines," Kitty called him an ignoramus and threw a plate at his head. Too bad he ducked. Kitty had crushes on black guys like Jim Brown and Sidney Poitier, and there was the Cleopatra thing, her thinking and wanting to be black. In the Malcolm X book, I discover he had a mother with mental problems too. It's like all the evil happening in this world entered the souls of many of the mothers, whose minds blew apart from the ugliness of it all.

Samantha Tamorini is my Dulcinea. I will destroy windmills for her! She is passing me love notes in English class. All the girls pass each other notes, but Samantha's are long and filled with cute little sayings scribbled around the edges like in *Mad* magazine. Things like *I dig you, little fox*, and *You're so fine*, next to locked hearts with our initials in them.

Today's note says: *You have the prettiest eyes. They're so green today, like that sweater you're wearing. Want to come for a sleepover at my house on Saturday night?*

I raise my hand to go to the bathroom to read and blush about this in private.

Samantha's mom greets me at the door, a sweet Italian lady with a giant beehive and a printed dress screaming with French poodles. She orders us a pizza. We eat in Samantha's bedroom and listen to *Tommy*, by the Who, while lying together on her bed checking out the liner notes, pretending we might not even kiss later. *Tommy* is kind of boring, so Samantha puts on "I Heard It through the Grapevine," and I show off my Gladys Knight and the Pips moves.

Her mom bangs on the door and tells us to turn it down. An excuse to change into our pj's separately in the bathroom, me first, into my spaceship pj's, and here she comes in a cool nightie. It's pink. You can see through it. Too bad she has on a bra and panties underneath.

I usually hate pink, but it looks good on Samantha. What a knockout. She knows it's having an effect on me. She opens the bedroom door and yells, "Mom, we're going to sleep now, don't bother us!"

My nerves are a wreck. I can't wait until we climb into that bed. Samantha puts on Tommy James and the Shondells' "Crimson and Clover." It's swoony and romantic.

She smiles softly, opens the covers, and says, "Okay, we better get some sleep."

Yeah, sure. Sleep. I crawl in; she crawls in next to me and turns on her side away from me. Bummer. I lie on my back, afraid to move because I don't want to bump into her while Tommy James sings about a *sweet thing* with that spooky echo in his voice. She suddenly turns back toward me, right on time to the record. It's like Samantha planned every move to the words of the song. On her side facing me now, she says, "Take off your top," and I do.

"It's hot in here," I say, with my eyes closed.

"I know," she whispers. She peels off her nightie and asks me to unclasp her bra. I fumble a bit because I don't wear one yet.

She kisses me. It starts up and gets crazy real fast, and I'm feeling funny down there, like I don't know what to do to ease the aching. She's on top of me and it's making me crazy, all this rubbing and aching and kissing. I roll over on top, pushing against her. She's making the sounds again. I whisper, "*Shhhh.*" It'll be death to us both if someone hears.

She tells me to kiss her breasts. I do, and her nipples grow hard like jelly beans.

I start to suck lightly, feeling powerful because I'm making her squirm. Sucking a little harder now, wondering if milk will come out while she twists her body beneath me. It's scary, these feelings. Like some kind of animal hunger losing control. I want to use my hand. I start.

The fear stops us both.

Suddenly we're just lying there, breathing like we've run a race in the Olympics.

"Let's go to sleep," she says. I try, but can't sleep at all. She rolls over, and I'm listening for her every breath through the night.

Izzy's been busy with her crowd of girlfriends. She always invites me, but aside from Samantha, most of her friends bore me with their talk about boys, or the coolest fringe jackets and moccasins and hippie clothes and paisley prints. All boys and clothes. I start hanging out with Marsha the greaser and her boyfriend, Bob. Marsha flunked a couple of grades, so she's back with us in seventh even though she should be in ninth. No one puts her down for this because she has an amazing attitude, like she doesn't care about anyone but Bob. Bob is a junior in high school and an amazing dancer. Ever since Marsha heard me sing at John's basement party, they keep asking me to hang out.

One Saturday night, Marsha calls and asks if I can meet them down the street. I tell Izzy I'm going out, and she shrugs like she doesn't care, but I think she's a little jealous. They're waiting for me in a superbad 1967 GTO convertible, a most incredible car with some strange bald guy behind the wheel.

"Maddie, this is Steve. We hang out at his house sometimes. He's cool," says Marsha. Steve nods, and I get in on the passenger side. He says he's an old friend of Bob's.

Marsha jumps in the back with Bob. She's already a little drunk, giggling as she passes around a bottle of whiskey. Three swigs later I'm feeling tipsy myself. Steve turns up the radio for Dusty Springfield's "Son of a Preacher Man." Marsha and I sing our lungs out (she has a great voice!) while we cruise around the empty Flats downtown, our voices echoing through the steel-and-concrete shells of burned warehouses.

Steve says we should come over to his place to drink and listen to records. I can't help wondering why this Steve character, obviously way older than us, wants to hang out with teenagers. Steve is small for a guy. He's not bad looking, I guess, and he dresses okay. He seems quite proud of his house and his stuff, but he's twitchy, like Kitty gets after popping her "dolls." He runs around pointing out bowling trophies, his security cop license, his uniform. His pill bottle. Marsha and Bob take one each and ask if I want one. No way!

Steve comes out of his bedroom grinning. Holding a gun. He explains it's a Smith and Wesson .38 Special and shows us the bullets in the barrel. This is getting way too creepy for me, but Bob and Marsha seem impressed. Marsha takes me aside and says, "He likes you!" but, "He's got a gun, Marsha!" She laughs it off: "He wouldn't hurt a fly!"

Five minutes later he's trying to kiss me, telling me he'd be a fantastic boyfriend; he has a good job and his own house, and he'll take me wherever I want to go and buy me anything I want. *Hold on, buddy, no way!* I won't let him kiss or touch me, and thank sweet Jesus, he doesn't force it.

We drink cold beers, but I take only a few sips. Beer reminds me of Kitty. And I don't want Marie to smell alcohol on me. Steve is acting weirder by the minute, jumpy and paranoid. He peeps through the closed curtains, saying someone is after him. Bob and Marsha laugh and play along: "It's the FBI! The cops are gonna bust you for giving drugs to minors!"

Steve doesn't find this funny. The phone rings, he answers, mumbles something, and starts scratching at his thigh. He looks at us wild-eyed. "We have to get outta here!"

He shoves the gun in the waistband of his pants, and we all jump into his car. Marsha giggles as Steve drives like a bat out of hell. Bob is laughing and yelling from the back seat, "We are fugitives from the LAW! Drive, Stevie McQueen, drive!"

"Pictures of Matchstick Men" is on the radio as Steve screeches to a stop at the side of a road lined by deep woods. It looks like Bedford Reservation, this park I visited once with Joanie. Steve jumps out of the car and says, "They're coming! You're underage and I'm gonna get busted if we don't run right now!" Bob and Marsha can't stop laughing. It's contagious. I crack up too. Suddenly everything clicks into super-speed as we start running, and I'm starting to think this might not be a game, that whatever is going on is serious.

We're running through the woods beneath a full moon, can hardly see where we're going. I don't hear any cars, no one seems to be after us, but we keep running. Marsha trips and thinks it's hilarious. Steve turns away, freaking out and running even faster now, and—

BAM!

—a gunshot goes off.

Bob and I hit the ground next to Marsha. Silence, except for our breathing.

Marsha speaks first.

"Is someone shooting at us?"

"I think it was Steve. Fuck," Bob whispers. "I'll go check."

Bob gets up slowly. Marsha and I hold on to each other for dear life. From a little way off, we hear Bob's voice.

"Oh shit shit shit, Steve, are you all right?"

And then a weak reply: "I think so."

Marsha and I follow the voices over to Bob, who's crouching over Steve. He's lying in the dirt.

"I shot myself in the stomach," he moans, holding his hand over the blood, a dark spot spreading on his T-shirt.

Marsha starts pacing. Her eyes are frantic. This is too much.

"Oh my God, oh God!"

Bob snaps at us to keep calm, says he'll run and call for help. Marsha drains the last of the Jack Daniel's, hurls the bottle into the woods, and digs in her purse.

"The cops are gonna be here any minute! Where's my gum? Here, take a piece."

I'm ready to bolt, don't want to be part of this, but it's too late. If I run now, I will be lost in these woods. I think of the Treadwells having to fetch me at a police station. Marie and Izzy will be so hurt. Oh God, I get that sinking feeling in my stomach, and I'm trying to tell this Steve guy everything's gonna be okay, but I don't want to be anywhere near him, I don't even know him. Even if he is shot, I'm furious. He's gotten us into an awful mess. What if he dies?

It seems like forever until Bob returns with the cops and an ambulance, sirens and flashing cherry-red and blue lights, the works. They load Steve into the ambulance. The cops take us off separately to ask what happened. I tell the truth. I ask about Steve. The cop tells me he doesn't think he'll die, but I should be worried about myself right now.

When Marie and Roy arrive at the police station, I tell them the whole truth and nothing but. Even the drinking.

Marie's voice shakes.

"Never, *ever* go drinking with anyone again, especially with a stranger! It could have been *you* getting shot. You're only thirteen, for God's sake! Alcohol is for adults, and sometimes even adults can't handle it. If you want to drink when you're twenty-one, fine, but not until then. Promise me, Maddie."

I promise, feeling rotten about upsetting her. Roy hardly speaks. When we get home, Izzy is waiting. I can tell I've disappointed her. A lot.

"I'm sorry, Izzy."

"Why do you wanna hang around with Marsha and Bob? They're losers."

I promise Izzy I won't hang out with them again. And I make a vow to myself to get over Samantha Tamorini, to never drink again, to never even think wild thoughts. I want to stay right here with the Treadwells and have a normal life. If that means being saintly, then so be it.

Monday at school, everybody in the cafeteria seems to know about the shooting. It must be the most dramatic thing that ever happened to anyone around here. They stare at Marsha and me with awe, then look away when we look back. It feels good, like we're different from the rest. Characters from a movie or rock 'n' roll stars. The attention makes me feel mysterious and unique. It's so much better to be feared, to be treated with respect, instead of bullied and looked down on. I pass Samantha a note in the cafeteria that says, *It was an accident, but the secret is . . . I'm the one who shot the guy.*

Maybe writing this lie will make Samantha think I'm tough and kind of dangerous, but in a good way. Being nice seems to get you nowhere fast, and as Kitty's choice in guys taught me, bad boys finish first. Girls like tough guys, like Hayley Mills likes her Polish sailor, so this should work for me. Plus, it'll be like Samantha and I have a dangerous secret.

I watch Samantha read the note. The way she looks at me from across the cafeteria is downright spooky. She looks terrified. I panic and pass her another note: *JUST KIDDING!* She reads it but won't even turn her face toward me now, won't move her eyes an inch in my direction for the rest of the day. My stomach somersaults. What have I done?

A few kids strike up the nerve to ask me what happened with Steve, and I try to act cool, telling them it was no big deal: He's alive. He accidentally shot himself. I don't say much more.

The following day I get called into the principal's office. Two policemen are waiting for me. A skinny, Italian-looking cop slides a note across the desk toward me. It's the note I wrote to Samantha. *She betrayed me.*

I tell the cop I made it up, that I was playing around.

"Why would you do that?"

"Because I thought it would make me seem cool. It was just a joke."

They don't think it's funny.

"Steve is a security officer with a drug problem. He said you didn't shoot him; he shot himself. It was an accident."

"He's telling the truth! Why don't you believe me?"

"He might be bluffing to cover for you. It's rare, but even drug addicts can be gentlemen. You shouldn't have been anywhere near a guy that much older than you. Did he touch you inappropriately?"

"No! I hardly know him. Is he going to live?"

Marie bursts into the room. "Officer, that's enough now, he told you she didn't do it. It was an accident, so unless she's under arrest, stop harassing her. Come on, Maddie, let's go."

The cops know better than to mess with Marie.

"You must never lay eyes on Steve again, young lady. And you know what? You're grounded."

Marie and the principal talk in another room, and when they come back, I'm told I can return to English class. Everyone stares like I have leprosy.

After school, I'm waiting for the bus when a crowd gathers around, calling me names. *"Lezzie!" "Queer!" "Homo!"*

I flush deep red with shame. I want to ignore them, but there's nowhere to run, nowhere to hide. Their laughter is nasty and deep. It's the same kind of nasty laugh Big Al laughs when he calls blacks that awful n-word. What did Samantha tell them?

Izzy stares at me, daggers in her eyes. She doesn't join in with the name-calling but won't stop glaring. No one gets within a few feet of me on the bus, like they'll catch my disease if they come near. "*Queer cooties!*" they chant, and laugh their faces off, ugly names shooting from their mouths like knives. The shame in my heart buzzes like a hive of furious bees, and I don't know how to make the heat inside stop burning.

"*Faggot!*"

"*Dirty queer!*"

"*You're disgusting, you lezzie!*"

The bus stops at our street. Izzy stands over me in the aisle and talks loudly so everyone can hear. "Samantha told everybody you tried to force her to do dirty things. Trying to make her your girl-friend, like you have a penis or something! So that's what you were doing over at Samantha's! You freak. You freak, you fucking queer."

"Izzy, she's lying! She's the one that started it all—"

But Izzy walks away and off the bus. I follow, ten steps behind.

Izzy stomps around the house slamming doors, now pacing in the kitchen. I'm in the living room on the couch. Numb. I decide to try to tell her the truth about Samantha and head for the kitchen.

She jumps me. Knocks me to the floor and grabs my shirt collar, screaming names into my face. I try to protect myself, turn my head away from her wild rage, but she's going crazy, screaming, "*You sick queer!*" smashing me in the face with her fists. I'm trying to turn my body to stone so it won't hurt, terrified that she's gonna kill me. She wails, ramming her fists into my eyes while I struggle to get her off me, and now her hands go around my neck, squeezing, choking. I cough for breath, trying to rip her fingers off my throat.

Marie runs in screaming, "*Izzy, STOP!*" and drags her off, giving her a few hard shakes to calm her down, telling her to get her ass upstairs. Izzy shakes Marie away and bends over me, her chest heaving. She sees something that scares her. She dashes for the stairs.

Marie helps me up while I sputter for breath.

"Are you all right? I am so sorry!" Her face turns pale. "My God, your eye."

She takes me into the bathroom and presses a cold washcloth on my eyes and face. I can tell something is very wrong. Everything hurts. I look in the mirror: the white part of my left eye is filled with blood—deep blood red flooding out the white. Marie asks if I can see through it. I can, but it's blurry, pounding with ache. Like something has changed and I might not ever see from my left eye again.

Marie calls the doctor.

"It's a broken blood vessel—it's only temporary. The doctor says it should be back to normal within a week. If you can see, you'll be fine. You have to tell me if you get dizzy or have a headache," she says. "Why don't we go to the emergency room right now? Maybe that's the best—"

"No, please, I'll be okay."

I don't want to cause any more problems for Marie, who's been nothing but kind. She fusses, gently placing the cold washcloths on my face and eye. She looks at me so tenderly.

"I'll deal with Izzy," she says. "Relax, and I'll make some tea."

Roy comes in from work and whispers with Marie in the kitchen. They approach me together, both wearing that pity look. Roy squats down to my level. His face is kind.

"Are you okay, kiddo?"

I'm still shaking, but I nod yes.

"Roy's going to take you out for a little while so I can talk to Izzy, okay?"

Roy drives us to his local bar. He orders a ginger ale for me, a scotch for himself. He doesn't quite know what to say but tries to tell me, in his own kind way, that what Izzy did was very wrong, she will be punished for it, and the day will just fade away. Neither Marie nor Roy has asked me about the lezzie thing, but the unspoken curse of it hangs there beneath the words.

I'm blank. A big numb zero. I fill up my insides with Jimmy Cagney. Hated, on the run, guilty by all counts. *Hang me, why don't you mugs? If you can catch me. But you never will. Watch this ghosty girl disappear.*

Roy is talking to me, but I can't make out the words.

"I have to go to the bathroom."

He pats me on the shoulder, smiles sadly. "Hurry back. Your ginger ale will get warm."

The EXIT sign glows red over the back door of the bar as I head for the bathroom.

EMERGENCY, the door reads. It's open a crack. I push. No alarm.

The air hits my face as I run toward the light.

8

BAD EYE GONE

I run, heart pump pumping, not knowing in which direction I'm heading, sprinting for my life. Slicing through the air at the speed of light, like a quarter horse oblivious to everything but the wind rushing past my ears. I burn away Izzy's beating, calves bursting into flames, heart on the brink of exploding.

Jack used to talk about the North Vietnamese winning the war. He said they'd win because they're small and speedy, almost invisible, and before you can cock your ear toward what you hope is the wind rustling the bamboo behind you, there's a machete at your throat. I figure they can't be so bad, knowing how to escape death like that and turn the tables.

I slow down to catch my breath, slapping my hands on my thighs. Head hanging, chest heaving, I gulp down big pockets of air. I look around, and here comes that familiar feeling I get sometimes, the *where am I going?* feeling. Will I have to call the police to pick me up again? Or do I really try to make it on my own this time? Go downtown and make friends with strangers? Maybe hippies? I can't call my family, because if my family wanted me, well . . . they had their chance. I'll see if there's anyone cool looking who can take me in. Maybe I can clean, earn my keep somehow. As long as it's not perverted, like whatever they made my brothers do in that creepy foster home. I'll see if I can scrounge up someone friendly.

Grandma Jo gave me a book once. An old fairy tale she picked up somewhere that told the story of a bird who saw things perfectly in balance, one eye seeing the good and the other, the bad. The bird lost its "bad" eye by looking too deeply into the well of wisdom. I didn't really get that part and don't remember most of the story, except for the loss of the bad eye, which made the bird unable to detect danger. The bad eye was green and eventually became an emerald in a ring worn by a woman who had lost her children. So many lost precious things and people. People like poems running on a River of Lost Memories. Maybe there's a river like that running through every story.

I try to convince myself everything will be fine. Sometimes this works, especially when I think of Harry Houdini, the great escape artist, and Joan of Arc. Puffing out my chest, I imagine broken chains dangling from my wrists. I'm clad in armor—the flexible kind you can run in—and am invincible. I love how some animals carry built-in ammunition to keep danger away, like skunks. You learn to work with what you've got. My heart is a fist of bees, a muscle like no other. Will it learn to defend and attack to keep me safe?

I hear hippies hang around on Public Square downtown, and hippies are, after all, about peace and love and good vibrations. If what I see on TV and read about in *Life* is true, then maybe I can join up with some hippies who'll take me in. I hold out my thumb and hope I'm not pointed in the wrong direction.

A banged-up Chevy Nova slows to the curb. The woman driving is funny looking; her hair is ratted into a towering crow's nest. I lean in the car window, and the stench of hair spray nearly knocks me sideways. She looks amused when she asks where I'm going. Her car radio is blaring that song "Magic Carpet Ride."

"Downtown, Public Square, please," I say, and like I've just cracked a joke, she cackles with that deep sound that old boozy smokers have.

"I look like a taxi, huh? Get in!" she says. "You shouldn't be out here hitchhiking like this, girl. You're no bigger than Jiminy Cricket!"

"Is he the one that sings that stupid song 'High Hopes'?" I ask, and she thinks that's the funniest thing she's ever heard. She nearly chokes on her Winston Menthol.

"Frank Sinatra sings it better!"

She gasps like a fish sucking for air. Maybe it's the cigarettes. She looks me over.

"What happened to your eye?"

I make up something quick. "I was bending down to tie my shoe, and my little brother opened the door at that very minute and banged the doorknob straight into my eye. It doesn't hurt, though."

"Poor kid! I hope you called the cops on whoever did that to ya."

I'm no kid. I'm a pirate without a patch. A prizefighter. But she knows I lied, and gives me the tilted head of pity. There's nothing that makes me more squeamish than the tilted head, that look in the eyes.

"You need to go to a doctor," she says. "How old are you?"

"Old enough to take care of myself."

I'm in no mood for the third degree on top of the pity. I'm not about to admit my age. She'd probably drive me straight over to the police station.

She's way too nosy so I keep talking.

"I'm going downtown to meet my uncle Dickie in front of the May Company. He works in the men's department, and he's taking me to the doctor to see about my eye."

"Ah, too bad I'm not a fella. Maybe I coulda got a discount on some duds!"

She grins beneath her Aquanest. I watch her face screw up into serious concern as she listens to a newscast on the radio. Something about another student riot. When we reach Public Square it's around six o'clock, and a spring wind has kicked up, blowing a few stray newspaper pages around the few dozen hippies hanging out at the Soldiers' and Sailors' Monument. You can spot the salesclerks on their breaks from Higbee's and the May Company. They are stylishly dressed, sitting on the benches around the square, far from the hippies, who climb around on the monument all scruffy and starry-eyed, playing weird little flutes and drums. Some hang signs on the soldier statues that say stuff like OUT OF SOUTHEAST ASIA NOW! and FIGHTING FOR PEACE IS LIKE FUCKING FOR YOUR VIRGINITY. Wow!

We pull up in front of the May Company opposite the monument. My driver cranes her neck out the window and yells, "Dirty hippies!"

A few of them give her the finger. I'm mortified.

"Where is this uncle of yours? Is he here yet? Is that him?" she asks, checking out a shabby-looking man stuffing himself from a bag of doughnuts.

"No way! I told you, he's clean," I say, insulted. If only she knew how handsome Jack really is, especially in his MP uniform. "I don't see him, but I'll just go in the store and meet him in there, thanks!"

I leap out of the car and wave to Miss Aquanest from the curb, then turn and bolt toward the revolving doors of the May Company while she yells out behind me, "Be careful, kid!"

A good ten minutes go by while I pretend to know what I'm doing while riding up and down the escalator. Figuring Aquanest must have taken off, I head back out to the street and the square, my good eye scanning around to see what's happening.

I spot a hippie guy in an army jacket who doesn't look very old. The guy wears a colorful paisley scarf tied like a headband, so his hair is kind of dissected midway on his head, puffing out on either side of the tight fabric. His army jacket has cool patches on it, peace signs and a dove and a patch that says MIA. He reminds me of photos I've seen of Jimi Hendrix, handsome with a sweet expression. He's short, only a head taller than me, and since I'm only four foot ten, I guess he's shrimpy. I sit a distance away from the hippies and act real cool like I'm just hanging out too. And since I have on bell-bottom jeans and my hair is parted in the middle, I think I might fit in. The soldier smiles at me, a lovely sort of smile, so I figure, what the heck. I go up to him and say, "Hey," and he says, "Hey," back. He asks me why I'm downtown and not at home. I tell him, "Because of my eye," and he asks me, "What happened?"

I tell him the lie about my brother. He looks at me and grins like he knows it's not true. Then he asks how I got downtown. I tell him I hitchhiked, letting him know I can take care of myself very well, thank you.

He gets quiet. I take a chance and tell him I like his hair. He nods, doesn't say anything. I tell him the way the scarf cuts his hairstyle in half reminds me of paramecium—when you cut them in two, each piece grows its other half back, like magic. This doesn't go down too well, judging from the way he screws up his face.

"Where do you live?"

"On the east side. Where do you live?"

"Around," I answer.

Then he asks me how old I am. It's irritating. Why do people feel they need to know my age all the time? I ask him precisely that, in the nicest way possible, and he doesn't laugh at me. He just nods and grins, which I consider a good sign.

A wild teenage hippie girl is climbing around on the statues like a raggedy ballerina. She hangs a FUCK LBJ AND LADY BIRD TOO! sign around one of the horse's necks, and all the hippies start applauding and wolf-howling. The annoyed salesclerks pack up their lunches and leave.

The soldier asks me my name; feeling free, I tell him it's Bird.

"Bird?" He smirks, like it's a joke.

"Yeah, Bird," I say proudly.

He nods now, like he respects my confidence. "Okay, I hear you, Bird. You play the sax?"

He laughs, I shake my head no. What's so funny? I wonder.

"Bird is cool. My name's Albert."

This is too much. He's got the same name as my dad, Albert. Umberto in Italian. I tell him that. Then I say, "I hate LBJ," and he smiles and says he does too. He tells me he just got back from Vietnam, where he was almost killed. His eyes are kind of sleepy and sad when he says it. He seems sweet—shy, like me. I imagine he must have been so scared over there. I want to be his friend.

"Do you live in a commune?"

He lights up and says, "Yeah, I live in a big commune with lots of musicians and artists."

I'm genuinely impressed. We watch the girl on the horse wave her fist around in the air, starting a chant. The other hippies join in—"Hell no, we won't go!"—and a cop car pulls up, which makes me nervous. If I get up and run, I'll draw attention to myself. So I try to sit still, but my leg starts wiggling a mile a minute. Two big cops climb out hitching their pants up. I wonder why cops always do this, as if their pants are loose when those uniforms are always sausage-skin tight. They walk toward the hippies, thank Jesus, and that's when Albert says, "Let's get outta here."

"Yeah, I hate cops."

We head over to the Euclid Avenue side of the square.

"You ran away from somewhere, didn't you?"

I don't answer, and then I think about Albert and Jack in a Vietnam trench somewhere with bullets flying over their heads. This makes me trust him.

"I ran away from a foster home. You won't turn me in, right?"

He laughs and says, "Nah! You can come crash at the commune. It's a real groovy scene."

"Wow. That would be so cool. How many people crash there?"

"Oh, maybe twelve, even fifteen sometimes. Folks come and go. White folks, black folks, lots of musicians. We can take the bus over there."

Suddenly I get nervous—I wonder if hippies all do that "free love" thing. No stranger is going to get me to take my clothes off.

"Are there any weird people in this commune? I don't wanna do anything weird."

Albert laughs. "It'll be cool, you don't have to worry."

We get on the bus and head up Euclid Avenue. I imagine we'll end up on Coventry in Cleveland Heights, where I hear all the hippies hang out. I've never seen how real hippies live, only in magazines and on TV, and have never been on the east side of Cleveland. As we travel, I check out the streets from the bus window, recognizing the street names from the news or from Big Al. Superior, Chester, East Seventy-Ninth. Then a street sign for Hough as the light grows dusky. Dirty, roughed-up houses, some of them looking like they were burned, and broken glass in the shop windows. My stomach starts to feel tight. I hear Big Al's voice saying, *Those Hough shines are nasty. They had to call in the National Guard to try and stop them from burning their own houses down!*

I realize that the riots happened here, in this poor neighborhood that looks like it's been hit by a bomb. Would white hippies—because aren't most hippies white—live in a commune in the black section of Cleveland? Who knows? And why wouldn't they, since it's all about people being equal and loving each other?

"Albert, where are we going? What street is the commune on?"

He tells me we're almost there, not to worry. He doesn't look at me on the ride; his eyes look dreamy. In my experience, boys never have much to say to girls anyway. I'll be sure to make good friends with at least one hippie girl at the commune. The bus drops us at a corner, near an empty lot across the street from some busted-up storefronts. A lone liquor store seems to be the only business open.

"Our stop," Albert says, without a glance my way.

The houses here look like they're sagging beneath some tremendous weight. There's not a hippie in sight. Everyone on the street is black. I look at Albert and assure myself that everything's cool, knowing that when we reach our destination somewhere down this street in Hough, we'll arrive at a bona fide hippie commune because Albert is a bona fide Vietnam vet who would never lie to me.

We reach the end of the street and turn a corner. Albert walks up the path of an old brick house with a huge porch. No rainbow-colored banners, peace signs, or sparkles. No mobiles or colorfully dressed girls with flowers in their hair lounging on the steps, like in the photos of cool Victorian houses in San Francisco. A big man dressed in overalls sits on a Naugahyde chair, leaning onto the porch railing, smoking. I do not like the looks of this place, but maybe it'll be different when we get inside. Maybe the walls will be Day-Glo orange covered with flower decals like you see on the VW vans in hippie caravans. Girls with long, wavy blond hair and girls with huge Afros will be sisters together in the kitchen cooking. Guys who look like rock stars will be playing guitars, and there'll be Indian bedspreads from wall to wall.

We walk up the steps of the commune. Albert goes over to the big man and whispers in his ear. The big man glares at me and reaches into his pocket, and the sun flashes off something metal. It's a gun, slipping from his hand into Albert's.

Albert's eyes don't look so sleepy now. He holds the gun by his leg, using his thigh as camouflage, as he motions toward the front door of the house and says mean and low, "Let's go."

I look at the big man, putting words into my eyes: *Please help me.* I know he sees the plea whether he wants to or not, and is that a flash of sympathy moving across his face? He turns away, won't look at me now. I stop breathing. *Idiot,* I say to myself. *Idiot, idiot, idiot, I am.*

Albert sticks the gun against the small of my back.

"I said go."

He nudges me up the filthy stairs ahead of him. I don't look anywhere but down, past mashed cigarette butts and dust balls in the corners of the stairs. At the top, he opens a padlocked door.

This is it, the Vietnam vet's room. He padlocks the door from the inside with the gun trained on me. I can't look up from the floor, don't want this to be the last room I see before I die. Whatever death is can't be any worse than the emptiness I feel right now.

The gun is pointed at my head as he tells me to strip. I don't like anyone looking at my body. It scares me more than anything. Blankness washes over me again like a wave. I slide my jeans down into the nothingness, lift my shirt over my head because I don't want to hear the bang just yet. I realize my face is wet because I'm crying. My face, like a stone by the seaside . . . You don't ever think a stone might actually feel anything, do you? Not even the water washing over it. The gun against my ribs, stick against stone. I do what I'm told.

He makes a sound of disgust.

"Little bitch," he says. He makes me lie back on the bed, takes off his pants, and points that gun at me. I want to tell him, *I'm already dead.*

I try to cover my pelvis, but he breaks my hands away. He grabs my face, forcing me to look into the barrel of his gun.

"Bullets, see? It's loaded. You best do what I say."

I feel like I'm underwater and his voice is underwater, and I don't know where I am and nobody else in the world knows where I am or gives a damn. Nobody but Albert, the Vietnam vet who wants to hurt me, kill me. I'm a rock, I will not move. He holds the nose of the gun against my temple. Cold metal circle boring into my skin. My skin, like a spiderweb, so very thin. He jabs himself into me, and inside, a tearing pain. I hear something click on the gun. *No.* My mind screams over and over again, *No*. Then he's on me like an animal and it hurts so much. The gun, my temple, the gun. Down there.

I'm gone now. Above my body looking down, watching a ghost girl on a dirty bed, and I can hear the girl thinking, *If I do not die here, I will never ever be afraid of anything ever again.*

Letting go, lifting off, and rising up, up, and away, I'm in a flying saucer of my own design, one much cooler than the cartoon saucers on *The Jetsons*. My heart has burst open and the bees have escaped. I'm in a spaceship made of flowers, and inside the ship, my *Collier's Encyclopedia* and the books I love line the walls . . . bricks of wisdom, keeping me safe.

There's someone with me—my lonely girl. She is little but strong and proud in spirit. I'm so glad she's here. She has lips shaped like a bow and brown bangs. She wears little black slippers and a kerchief around her neck, like a sailor. She takes my hand, and my heart turns light.

"We'll go back as hummingbirds," I say to her.

"Yes, we will," she answers.

She is tender. And wise. Like me, she has seen things. She bends her head looking down toward the bed, deep in thought, troubled. Her eyes tell me someone did things to her too. Ugly things.

We fly higher until the bed disappears and we look down at Earth, an enchanted crystal ball of swirling gases and jewel-box colors. So magical, filled with strange beauty and mystery. And cruelty. Too much cruelty. What will we do with it? What will we do?

Albert rolls over onto his back with a big gust of air. I look down into my own blank eyes and make my way back inside my body. As I climb back in, I sense his smell again: sour, the scent of food gone off. He kisses my cheek like I'm his girlfriend and wipes the sweat off his neck with a pillowcase.

"I got things to do. I'm locking you in, so don't even think about leaving."

The voice of Jack is in my head, telling me that the Vietnamese would bring their own body bags with them in their backpacks when they went into combat. *Now that's what I call fearless,* said Jack. My flying saucer is my body bag.

I'm about to reach for Albert's gun.

Albert starts talking.

"You liked that, didn't you? I'll give you some more later."

He grabs the gun before I have the guts to reach for it, and he's up, pulling on pants and a T-shirt. I turn my face to the wall. The padlock on the door clicks back into place from the outside, and his footsteps fade down the stairs.

I'm frozen in place on the bed, ramming the pillowcase into my mouth when the cries come up from me. If someone hears me scream for help or even whimper, maybe that someone will want to hurt me too. I wipe my face, try my best to wipe away all pain down there, then roll up the cloth like a rope. Whatever it is scratching around in the dark, I can use the rope as a whip if it climbs on the bed to pick at me.

I look down and see a small circle of blood on the mattress.

There are other people in this house. Muffled laughter coming from somewhere below. Footsteps, and that scratching. It must be mice, or maybe worse, rats.

I start to shake, whole body just shaking like an earthquake has hit, and then it suddenly stops and the emptiness takes over again.

I don't want to get up and look for something to pee into because someone might hear me and break in. I try holding it but end up wetting the bed. The sound of the padlock being undone makes me roll onto my side and close my eyes like I'm asleep.

The smell of McDonald's fills the room.

"Eat this," he says, holding a hamburger and some fries toward my nose. My stomach spins. I shake my head no. He pulls out the gun and sets it next to the hamburger. The gun is just that close. I could blow his brains out, but it'll be hard enough to remember all this happened. If I ever get out of here, as much as I want him dead, do I want his murder in my heart too? Why is he doing this to me? Why?

Albert's clothes come off again. He lies next to me but jumps back up, cursing about the wet mattress.

"Goddamn it, you gotta pee, girl, next time, use this."

He grabs a plastic cup from the floor and waves it in my face. Rummaging around, he pulls a towel out of a pile of dirty clothes and makes me get up, then places it over the wet spot. Rolls up a cigarette and starts to smoke. I recognize the thick, sweet smell from John, my foster brother. John smoked marijuana too and gave me a few puffs once, which made me gag and feel all paranoid. Now Albert is trying to force me to smoke. I clamp my lips tight and shake my head no. He laughs and lies back down, relaxed and smoking his weed. Like we are married and do this all the time. My skin crawls. Why is he doing this? Is it because of how he's been treated by white people? What happened to him in that war? What happened to make him hurt me like this? The walls around my body grow tight as the empty feeling takes over again.

"You can't talk?"

I don't answer. Not that he cares about my silence. He starts stuff again, and I can't feel anything because I leave. This time I hover up there, looking around with my good eye for my lonely girl and the spaceship. This time I'm a bird with perfect vision in a deep blue sky, just sailing free. I want to open my wings and let the breeze carry me to my lonely girl, but the ceiling will not budge.

The next day, Albert leaves and locks me in. I'm starving, so I grab the hamburger he left the night before and gobble it down. The grease makes me gag, but nothing comes up. I look around the dirty room. Can't see my clothes. There's a black-light poster of couples tangled up in every sexual position of the zodiac. I hope he doesn't try any of them with me, because the top thing is painful enough. There's garbage in the corners: rolled-up bags, empty wine bottles, a table lamp on the floor with a red light bulb, some old pillows. Clothes thrown around, cracked plaster on the pale pink walls and ceiling, and film on the window, making the light dull and gray. I'm hurting down there, feeling like what I see around me. Lost and dirty. Lost like Albert. Like everything feels in this terrible room.

I get up off the bed and pull on the cleanest T-shirt I can find. It hangs down to my knees and at least covers up my privates. I creep toward the door and carefully try the doorknob, slow and quiet, and just a gentle pull to see if it's really locked. It won't budge. I hear talking somewhere in the house. Women's voices. I want to call out for help, but what might be lurking?

That night Albert starts straightening the place, balling stuff up and throwing it into a closet, laying out those dirty pillows on the floor against the walls. This time he's brought me a cold fish sandwich from McDonald's. I nearly retch at the smell. The most I can handle is some of the warm beer he gives me, but that turns my stomach too. He switches on the red light bulb in the lamp and turns on the radio, snaps his fingers to "Cowboys to Girls."

An older, scrawny guy and two women come in. But one of the women might be a man, I can't tell. Albert commands me to "get your ass in the corner and stay there," showing off that he's my boss. I pull the hem of the T-shirt down farther around my knees and do what he says, keeping my eyes on the cracks in the floorboards. Albert's friends sit on the pillows on the floor with their wine bottles, far away from me, and I can hardly understand what they're saying above the music. They laugh and talk to Albert like they're old friends.

I sneak a peek at the women; one of them has large breasts pressed tight inside a man's Ban-Lon shirt. Albert calls her Texas. She calls out to the dancing petite woman with the braids, "Bernice, come over here," and Bernice follows orders. Texas's voice sounds older, kind of gruff, like she smokes a lot. She looks hard, tough. But she smiles when a song comes on, nodding to Stevie Wonder singing "You Met Your Match."

"Little Stevie gettin' down!" she says, and that smile shows the woman in her.

It's like she knows I'm trying to send her signals. She looks over at me and says, loud enough for me to hear, "That your new lady, Albert?"

"Her name is Bird! Can you believe this shit? Bird! You flying yet? Where's your horn?"

Everybody laughs except for Texas. She grins, slow and catlike. I get brave and lock eyes with her when Albert's not looking at me and slowly shake my head back and forth just once, eyes pleading out a lighthouse beam. *Please, see me.* She looks away from me, taking a deep drink from her bottle. The other guy is older than everybody else and even scruffier than Albert. He just seems silly, always laughing at the slightest thing. Bernice asks Albert, "Does she talk?"

"Do I give a got-damn if she talks?" Albert says, which makes them crack up more.

Albert and the scrawny guy think this is hysterical. They laugh and laugh, passing the reefer. Texas doesn't think it's so funny, mumbling under her breath. She slides her arm around Bernice, who watches her with adoring eyes. Texas blows reefer smoke into Bernice's mouth like she's kissing her, then whispers in her ear.

I get it. They're queer. Like me.

The room begins to melt. I hold my knees tighter to my chest, T-shirt pulled over and down by my ankles like a tent. The scrawny guy stands up, stretches, and comes over to me, grinning too close to my face. I shrink further into the T-shirt.

"Boo!" I feel his breath. He cracks up.

Bernice squinches her eyes at him, real mean, and says, "Leave her alone, Reggie."

No matter how tight I hold my body, the smoky red room seeps in through my pores. Everything is turning to mush with sharp edges poking through. I close my eyes and bury my face to calm myself, heartbeat speeding as the scene drifts into its own hazy world without me.

Texas slow dances with Bernice. This doesn't bother the men; they just keep smoking, drinking. The two women flow into each other like water to the slow beat of the music. I know that feeling. They dance to the Peaches & Herb song "Let's Fall in Love," which is real pretty. I used to like singing that song.

After they dance, Bernice grabs Reggie's arm. "Come on, Reggie, let's go."

Bernice and Reggie leave, while Albert sits in the corner smoking, looking hazy-lazy. How I wish I could stand up and walk right out of here with them.

Texas yells to Albert, "Get up over here, fool."

Albert grumbles, follows orders. Texas and Albert argue quietly and then she leaves. Albert slams and locks the door and kicks at the radio.

"Fuck that triflin' bull dagger," he says. He tells me to get on the bed. I know what he's about to do next. He hurts me harder than he has so far, pointing the gun between my eyes.

"I hope you like your new house, 'cause tomorrow you're gonna clean it real nice."

I'm not afraid anymore. I'm waiting for the trigger to flip. Maybe if I knew someone was waiting for me it would make sense to be afraid. If only Big Al knew where I was. He wouldn't care; he'd be proud of the fact that he told me so about black people. But I know the truth. It's the same Devil stealing both Alberts' souls, the Devil that sends men into war to kill each other, the Devil that makes men do horrible things to women. This Devil hole I'm pulled down into when all I want is to fly up and out of this horrible place.

In the morning when Albert is gone, I creep over to the window trying to figure out if I can crawl out on the ledge and jump to the ground, but it looks so high. But a broken neck is way better than Albert and this room. I try the window. It's stuck. Tugging too hard might cause someone in the house to hear the noise. I return to the bed and think about how to safely break the glass without getting cut when I hear footsteps approaching the door.

Someone starts hammering at the lock, *bam bam bam!* Metal striking metal. Someone else wants to hurt me! I rush over and crouch in the window frame and tug and tug, using my weight to try to force it open. The door lock clatters, and I'm about to smash my fist through the glass and fly, I just don't care, when the door swings wide.

It's Texas. She stares at my raised fist, ready to smash the glass.

"Don't . . . don't do that."

Bernice creeps in behind her and closes the door quietly, finger to her lips, making hush motions at me. Texas narrows her eyes.

"How long you been locked up in here?"

"I don't know. Three days, I think."

"Did he beat you?"

She's looking at my left eye. It must still be blood red from Izzy. I don't answer. This is all Izzy's fault for killing my "bad" eye. Or is it my fault for loving girls? What's going to happen now? Hope usually never ever answers my wishes.

Bernice comes over and hands me a pair of pants and a sweater.

"Take these," she says softly. "Here . . . gimme your hand."

She pours a bunch of change into my palm. Texas motions me toward the door.

"Nobody's home, so go on, get dressed, get yourself gone. Just walk out of here like nothing's happening, everything's cool. When you hit the corner, you run like hell. We'll leave the front door open."

I wipe my face rough-like with the back of my hand.

"Thank you."

Texas nods. She turns and walks out with Bernice. I watch them cross through a patch of sunlight in the stairwell.

The sweater has a picture of mod ladies carrying umbrellas and it makes me smile. Straight through that doorway, past the broken lock and the hammer lying in the hallway, and down those stairs I walk softly on bare feet to freedom. When I reach the first-floor landing, a door opens a crack; my heart jumps as an eye peeps out at me. It's Bernice. She whispers,

"Bye, Bird."

And the door clicks shut.

I step out into the sunlight. Eyes straight ahead of me, I hit the empty porch and walk calmly down the front path to the sidewalk, walk with determination, but not too fast as to call any attention. There's no one around except for an old woman sweeping her porch across the street. She squints hard at me for a minute, like I'm an apparition. Shielding her eyes, she blinks slowly, bends down, and sweeps me away like a haunted cobweb.

I reach the corner breathing deep, taking in big bowlfuls of air. Cars crawl by, faces stare out windows as they slowly pass the ghosty girl.

Tell no one what happened, says the voice inside me. *Even if he goes to jail, he'll get out and find you. Kill you. Tell no one. Push on.*

There's a phone booth a block away.

"Operator, connect me to the police."

When the lady at the station answers, I tell her it's an emergency, I'm a runaway, and I'm at . . . Where are the street signs? I tell her to hold on and let the phone dangle while I walk to the corner to see what the signs say.

"I'm at Hough and East Eighty-Fourth Street."

"Sending a car now."

9

WAYWARDS AND WIMPLES

Cuyahoga County Detention Home is a stark, hard-edged place. Its coldness feels designed to stomp the personality right out of you, like the drugs they gave Kitty before she packed us off to the county. The drugs made her dumb and slow, a robot with no trace of chorus girl left in her. When she was doped up like that, Jack called her "Harriet Haldol." She'd give him a droopy smile and say, "They got me, brother."

I visited Kitty in the mental ward once, at the Cleveland State Hospital. An awful place. The walls here are the same sickening color of watered-down pea soup with spongy ceiling tiles and bright fluorescent lights that make people look hollow and dead-eyed.

We're guppies in this aquarium jailhouse. Attendants watch our every move through walls of extra-thick glass, in case someone decides to throw a punch to try to shatter the picture. There's a small sink, a single iron bed, shiny white brick walls, and a metal toilet in each cell. Do you need to pee or do number two? You better not be the shy type. Shyness equals constipation, and with all the bread, potatoes, and noodles they feed us, my insides have turned to Elmer's glue. No dresser, because we're not allowed any belongings besides the stiff yellow pajama-like outfit, complete with paper slip-ons to shuffle around in. The white girls here have stringy oily hair and pimply skin and look too fat in their woman-places for their ages. The black girls are either curvy and womanly or lanky and graceful, with a walk I'm not used to witnessing. It's my first time in the company of black girls, besides the ones who set me free, and I'm afraid to give anyone eye contact. They seem uncomfortable with me too—no one meets my eyes.

One girl who can't be more than twelve years old turns away each time I catch her eyes, which are full of curiosity. Her name is Mylene. I sit down next to her at rec period. Shyly, from up under her lashes, she looks at me and speaks.

"You read comic books?" She slides a *Betty and Veronica* comic across the table at me.

"Thanks."

On the cover, Veronica says, "I'd like to straighten up the mess the world is in," while she and Betty watch TV, lounging around a messy bedroom in their pj's. I point to the cartoon bubble of Veronica's words.

"Me too."

"Huh?"

Mylene's eyes read the bubble, and she giggles. She won't look me in the eye when she asks, "Why are you in here?"

"I ran away from a foster home. What about you?"

Mylene doesn't answer; she shrugs, eyes locked on her comic book. I take the hint that she's done with me and move over to a seat at an empty table across the room.

The jailhouse girls fascinate me. I hear them talk about their hair, calling it nappy, and their skin, ashey when they tease each other. Their hair has so many styles: pinned-up braids or cornrows like Mylene has, big woolly Afros, straight but tight curly at the roots, short and neat, or patchy like thick tree roots. And their moves. There is something magic and watery in their muscles, like mercury when you bust a thermometer open and let the silver stuff roll around on a tabletop. Some girls walk as if they're in a trance, angry at everyone and completely not caring to the point where picking up their feet out of a slide would mean giving in. Others have this proud, haughty walk, showing off that being in DH is no big deal, and they carry themselves very elegantly in an *I don't give a damn* way that I admire.

Mealtimes are the only moments we have contact, and after dinner, there's a brief recreation period when we can play cards or read old magazines like *Jet* and *Look* and *Life*. I try to pick up a *Jet* magazine with Cleveland's new black mayor, Carl Stokes, on the cover, but one of the girls snatches it away. So I read an old *Life* magazine with the Beatles on the cover.

We have no radio or television except on Saturdays after lunch, when the guard turns on the TV for *American Bandstand*. All the girls go dance crazy. The black girls make fun of how the white kids dance on the show. I learned to dance with Kitty, dancing to soul records by James Brown. The black girls love to show off their peacock moves, but only on songs with a good beat. I'm determined to learn their steps, every twirl, jerk, and hip dip.

A new song by Stevie Wonder comes on, "For Once in My Life." The girls do this hand dance where they spin each other, touch hands, and step in time together. One girl leads, the other follows, and it's really cute and sexy. The steps heat up, get wild, when "Shoo-Be-Doo-Be-Doo-Da-Day" comes on. You can lock a girl up in a glass cage, but you'll never succeed in killing her happiness when music like this is within hearing range. I strike up my nerve, dancing on the edge of the crowd. At first they laugh at me—a laugh that is not mean at all, is more like a laugh of curiosity. They can't believe I can dance. Not as good but at least close to it.

"Go on, girl!" they shout, and I grow bolder. But I'll never match their steps, the magic moves that seem so effortless.

This detention home is a weird train station in the middle of nowhere, and we are the outlaw wild girls rolling through. New ones coming and going every day, off to the great unknown. My court date arrives, and Miss Fortunato has either given up on me or quit. I have a new caseworker, a boring guy in a baggy suit with bad skin named Emery Richard. His hand is sweaty, shaking mine as he tells me to keep quiet in court. If I'm compelled to respond to anything, I should address the judge as *"Your Honor,"* or I'll be sorry. Even if the judge were pint-sized, sitting up there a good ten feet above everyone else in his black robes makes him seem like God Almighty.

The judge rustles papers, then speaks.

"How do you feel about staying in one place for more than a few months?" The judge's mustache twitches above invisible lips.

"Your Honor, I'd like to live somewhere safe. Maybe a university? A scholarship would be very nice."

The judge shakes his head and grins, like I'm a wisecracker. He clears his throat, calls me an incorrigible runaway, and ends his pronouncement with a hammer smack.

"I hereby remand you to the Marycrest School for Girls."

The Sisters of the Good Shepherd is a French order from the 1800s that established roots in France and Ireland before coming to America. There are two branches. The sisters in white habits teach, live, and work with the girls, while the Contemplative Sisters of the Cross, or the Magdalenes, are cloistered and wear brown habits. We see the Contemplative Sisters only at chapel on Sundays, and we're forbidden from addressing them because they've taken vows of silence. Each Contemplative Sister is assigned one girl in the school to pray for. Of course, we go crazy wondering which sister might be our very own, especially come Sunday mornings. They wait 'til we're seated, then file in behind us and sit in back pews that are positioned sideways, so they are in profile. We can never see their faces or even turn around for a peek. The Contemplatives are the forbidden. Maybe they were all once wayward girls too.

Mother Superior has the face of a hammerhead shark. She speaks with a slight Irish brogue, the kind Grandma Jo slips into now and again. Her office is a sanctuary of gleaming wood furniture, statues of saints, and a strange piece of furniture resembling a tiny pew with a red velvet bench for kneeling. Two paintings hang above a large mahogany desk: a priest holding a fiery urn and a crucifix, and a nun holding a Bible.

I sit posture perfect to impress her. After the interrogation—about my family, the escapes, and the lack of good grades—her expression flickers with a hint of surprise when I inquire about the order. She gestures to the portraits above her head.

"Saint John Eudes created the order, Our Lady of Charity of the Refuge, in France in the sixteenth century. Saint Mary Euphrasia followed in his footsteps, founding the Good Shepherd order as an offshoot in the wake of the French Revolution. Both orders dedicated their lives to the service of women and girls who were victims of life's hardships. Saint Mary was full of grace, like our blessed Virgin Mother. She had great compassion for women. And girls."

It almost slips out that I too have great compassion for women and girls. Just as the history lesson gets interesting, she changes the subject.

"As long as you follow our rules of conduct, you'll be content here at Marycrest."

"I could use the time off."

"Pardon me?"

"This is a beautiful place, Reverend Mother, thank you."

The Good Shepherd order's uniform is a white tunic and habit, white scapular, and white wimple with a black veil on top. The cross hanging from Mother Superior's beaded belt is humongous. I wonder if it also doubles as a weapon. Maybe a paddle? I heard nuns are mean. I do love a good uniform and am now wearing one myself: a white elbow-length blouse with rounded lapels and a red *M* embroidered on the left breast. A green-and-blue plaid skirt. Knee socks and saddle shoes. Despite the skirt, I find the outfit comforting.

"You will refer to me as Reverend Mother, my child. I will escort you to the Lourdes dormitory and introduce your big sister, Constance, who will look after you while you become acquainted with your new life here at Marycrest."

Sweeping her skirts out into the glossy hallway, she pauses, giving me the haughty, stern face that people in power just love to push all over you.

"All girls are required to hold to the same vow of chastity as the sisters."

If there are no men or boys around and what she means by chastity is not having sex, then she must realize she's talking about sex between girls. And if she needs to warn me about it, well, it must be happening aplenty between the waywards, and maybe the wimples too. I follow her piously, hands clasped in front. A good girl, and chaste. For now.

The grounds of Marycrest are beautiful, perfectly maintained, and oh so quiet. Along with the excellent gardening, I wonder if the silence and the nuns' constant prayers and devotions help create this grace and beauty. One would never guess such a heavenly dwelling could be home to so many bad girls. If you just happened to wander in and see us all fresh-faced and innocent in our crisp, clean uniforms, you wouldn't have a clue of what might lie beneath. For instance, the Girl Who Steals, and Lies, and Loves Other Girls.

I love the idea of wearing a uniform every day, like a costume that hides my being poor. You can't tell poverty from riches when both come dressed in a uniform. Big Sister Constance is a tall, haughty brunette with perfect posture, but I can tell she's a wayward girl, just like the rest of us, by the hint of the devil look in her eyes. She escorts me into the dormitory, walking like she has a rod screwed tightly up her bum, flicking her finger over at a cubicle to my new place of rest. All new girls are assigned to this dormitory, Lourdes, named after the town in France where the Blessed Virgin Mary appeared to Saint Bernadette. Depending on how good you are and how many merits you gather, you eventually graduate to Marian Hall and then, finally, to Regina, from where you are either released into society or confined to a habit in this convent. Yikes.

"Sister Francis will run a gloved hand under your bed for dust in the mornings. Keep it spotless or you'll do penance. The sisters will not stand for sloth. Buckets and cleaning supplies are in the utility room. Hospital corners are required on the beds. You iron your uniform blouse before you put it on every morning. Laundry on Mondays and Thursdays. Morning bell at six A.M., chapel at six thirty, breakfast at seven thirty."

"Can you please show me a hospital corner?"

Annoyed, she proceeds to teach me how to pull the bedding impossibly tight. Try flexing a big toe under those covers. Incarceration by sheet.

The dormitory windows are barred with heavy mesh screens. Golden light seeps through, falling in a grid pattern across the pale blue bedspreads, the blue-and-white-tiled floor, the small statues of

Mary on each bureau. The dorm smells like Murphy's oil soap and frankincense—clean and mysterious.

The dormitory bed arrangements feature a tall dresser set against a low wooden divider that lies directly opposite the foot of each bed. The bed on the other side of the division is placed against the dresser's back, repeating like this down the long dorm studded with L-shaped cubicles, so none of us can see each other dressing or lying down. A layout to guard against impure thoughts. The dorm is spotless; the linoleum floor resembles a mirror more than something you'd walk on. I can practically see up Constance's skirt from the floor as she marches me past the twelve beds.

At the end of the dormitory is a small room tucked into the corner of the L shape where the two dorm rooms meet. "Here is where our Sister Veronica, the Lourdes' guardian, sleeps each night. Notice that the sister can peek into both dormitories through these windows." Constance raises an eyebrow while pointing out the sliding wooden windows. Spying nuns. What is it they're watching and waiting for?

Most of the girls in Marycrest are white except for Rosa, a gorgeous Puerto Rican girl; Belinda, a cool, lanky black girl; and Shirley, a petite black girl who's an incredible painter. One of the nuns is black, Sister Betty. She plays the guitar. I wonder if she has a thing with Sister Helen, the Physical Education teacher. Sister Betty giggles like a schoolgirl whenever she plays basketball with Sister Helen, who runs and dribbles like a teenage boy in her Converse high-tops, her scapular of Jesus flying as she shoots and scores. Now I understand why these nuns are so obsessed with L shapes. Some of them are *bent.* (Jack calls homos "bent.") My eyeballs bend toward Belinda, who is extremely fine.

I adapt to life here, quickly stepping in line with the regimen, including the school marching band. I've taken up the clarinet. After finishing KP duty on the dishes, I usually race over to the practice room to work on the clarinet parts for the Sly and the Family Stone song "M'Lady" from memory. That solo part is murder! The Marycrest marching band truly sucks, but we try. Reading music reminds me of math, so I learn the parts from memory. Who on earth would be musically inspired by the likes of John Philip Sousa? We're allowed to listen to only approved musicals on the record player after dinner. The pickings are slim but many are songs I'd sing with Kitty sometimes, songs from *Oliver!*, *The Sound of Music*, and *South Pacific*. She loved musicals. Aside from our brief rec periods after supper, the silence at Marycrest feels more like a convent than a home for delinquent girls. Inside the dorm, school, and chapel, it's always extremely quiet. The nuns won't stand for what they call idle chatter. At least they like music.

Surrounded by deep woods and ravines, the Marycrest grounds sprawl over a few acres with three dormitories, a school building with a large gymnasium, and a grand colonial house, home to the apostolic nuns, the chapel, and the administrative office. The house is connected to the chapel by an enclosed hallway that branches off to the small cloister of the contemplative order. This hallway ensures the senior sisters never have to shiver on their 5:30 A.M. walk to morning Mass in the bitter winter. The lovely colonial house is the jewel of the crown-shaped campus, surrounded by a landscape that has all the peacefulness of *sanctuary*, my new favorite word. Sister Veronica takes an instant liking to me. She lets me visit the library, and it's sweet bliss to be alone with the books, inhaling pages that smell of frankincense and myrrh. *Confessions*, by Saint Augustine. *The Interior Castle*, by Saint Teresa of Ávila. *The Hunchback of Notre Dame*. An odd choice for the nuns, a happy one for me. I loved that movie.

I wondered if I might have an experience like Hayley Mills's character in *The Trouble with Angels*. She was a bad girl, in a convent school like this. Truly mischievous she was, and you never saw it coming, God tapping her on the shoulder. Directing her heart toward the Holy Dove. It happened in a flash of a moment. I secretly want God to change my life too, but at this point, intervention seems unlikely. Too many bad things have happened, and I still can't sort out if it's my fault. Or God's. Or Lucifer's.

June is glorious here, the air sweet with everything in full bloom. It's the first time I'm wide awake to the sights, smells, and sounds of nature. Today, on my way to the school building, I take a forbidden detour around the back of the nuns' quarters. Turning a corner into a wooded path behind the grand house I see an entrance to a small clearing covered by a pergola.

A statue of the Virgin Mary shimmers in dappled sunlight, surrounded by a tiny moat facing a larger pond ringed with violets. An arbor of vines filled with sweet-smelling white flowers weaves through the pergola above Mary's head. It's beautiful—a kind of beauty I've never experienced. The smell of cool green leaves, flowers, water. The chirping of birds. Mother Mary's gaze is fixed on a tiny nun in a brown habit. A cloistered nun, sitting very still on a bench with her back to me. Her posture is bent; I believe she's praying. Two small birds—sparrows, I think—perch on her shoulder. She's feeding them bits of bread. I can't tell whether she's real or an apparition as the darling birds peck from her outstretched hand like trained pets. She holds the crusts to their beaks and coos to them with a tenderness that takes my breath away.

Although I hold myself as still as possible, the nun senses my presence and turns slowly toward me. She'll be angry—I'm not supposed to be here, not allowed to look at her. Instead of chasing me away, she smiles at me with a childlike innocence, eyes shining. We stay like this, gazing at each other for a long moment. It scares me a bit. Does she want to be witnessed? Is she lonely? Like me? Her face is a mystery, a crosshatch of lines and wrinkles like the grid of an ancient map of a foreign city I hope to discover one day. Yet her eyes seem so young.

Watching her feels like I'm joined with her. On a holy journey. *Please, God. Let me stay right here inside the love in her eyes and never leave.*

I stand frozen in place, then turn and quietly walk away, not wanting to disturb her conference with the birds. I turn away because suddenly I'm ashamed to have stared so boldly at a woman so pure. Like I don't deserve it. And I wonder over a riddle: whether she is my very own nun, the cloistered nun whose duty it is to pray for only me.

What little I've heard about nuns—that they're horrid, sneering crea-tures who beat you for hardly a reason—is far from the truth here at Marycrest. Sister Veronica has mischievous blue eyes and is very kind, her pretty face brimming with joyful and secret stories. She is with us all the time: in the dormitory and common room, oversee-ing meals and recreation periods, sleeping in the little corner room between dorms, the one with the sliding windows in Lourdes. The nuns' faces stand out from their wimples as if framed and hanging in a museum. Sister Veronica's smile is cryptic, like the Mona Lisa's. I have a crush on her. I think she knows—she seems to enjoy the attention, or at least she enjoys brushing my hair. Before bedtime, when we're in the living room area playing cards or whatever, I sit at her feet while she brushes one hundred gentle strokes.

She always asks me to sing songs from *Oliver!* I'd much rather be singing the fun and mischievous tunes "Consider Yourself" and "You've Got to Pick a Pocket or Two," but the sad songs are her fa-vorites: "Where Is Love?" and "Who Will Buy?" During recreation hour, she makes me stand in front of her and the girls and sing. Her face lights up like a Christmas tree for her wee homeless waif, her very own lamb and she, the shepherdess. It's humiliating. Part of me loves it, though. I make my eyes impossibly pitiful, lacing my hands in front of me as if in prayer while trilling out the notes. When I sing, *Where is she?* about the girl I close my eyes to see, I wonder what's going on beneath Sister Veronica's mysterious smile.

Dr. Golias oversees therapy at Marycrest, and he's the only man here; the nuns run all the administrative duties. They speak of him in hushed, reverent tones, like he's the Great and Powerful Oz. I'm thinking he's closer to his name, the Goliath of the Bible. There's something extremely creepy about Golias. He appears twice a week, seeing each girl privately for lengthy therapy sessions. I've heard his rehabilitation techniques are "progressive," and I'm dreading our first meeting. We can always tell which girl he's spoken to from the flush covering her face, like she's just been force-fed a Windex cocktail.

Finally, I'm summoned to the administration house and my turn for possible torture. A large man with a Vandyke beard and furry eyebrows, Golias fills the room with his presence. He looks like a true intellectual and a weirdo with peculiar tastes. He watches me with mean, hungry eyes, in contrast with the portrait of Jesus above the desk, the Lord's sad blue eyes always watching, yet always helpless. On the other wall is a landscape painting showing the back of a tiny person staring out over a calm sea.

I sit opposite Golias in an overstuffed chair. I thought psychiatrists made their patients lie on couches, but I get it. How suspicious it might look to have girls laid out on a sofa in a convent, beneath the creepy gaze of a bearded man with 'progressive' ideas.

Lying open on his desk is a file. He reads for several minutes, then looks up at me. Back down at the pages, up to me again. I would love to grab my file and run the hell out of here while he examines me intently, as if he were deciding my very fate. I hold his gaze.

"Your mother . . . was diagnosed as a paranoid schizophrenic. She's currently at Cleveland State Hospital. What was it like, living with her? How was that for you?"

I stare him down before I answer. "My mother had no money to support herself, and my father was a bum. So she drank too much and popped pills. You'd go crazy too."

"Aha. I'm sure a lack of finances didn't help. You had a complicated relationship with your mother, did you not?"

"Yeah, I guess so. I mean, doesn't everybody?"

I thought he'd at least crack a smile, but he clearly doesn't find me amusing. Continuing to flip through pages, he gives me that piercing stare again, then slides out a stack of drawings from beneath my file.

"Let's take a simple test. I want you to look at these images and tell me what you see. Whatever comes to mind. The images are abstract, yet if you look without concentrating too hard, you're likely to imagine pictures in them. Don't think about it, just tell me the first images that pop into your mind. Let's begin."

He flips over the first picture. I see an alien creature with boxing gloves on, arms held high in a victory stance. Two other aliens sprout from its head, blowing bubbles. I tell him, "I see a psychedelic inkblot."

"You can try harder than that. I read your intelligence quotient test. You're fourteen now and that much smarter."

"What did the IQ test say? How smart am I?"

"Smart enough to use your imagination creatively. Look again."

Meanwhile, he's jotting down quick little notes. I'll try to play the game, just for fun.

He slides another picture toward me. "What do you see?"

"I see a puppy with his snout on fire. No, sorry, it's two matching guns in their holsters, cowboy style."

This makes him smile ever so slightly. He starts to scribble. Turns over another plate and waits for my description. I see two ghosts kissing and a creepy owl, but I tell him:

"Groucho Marx."

His pen freezes and so does his face. "Try and be serious, please."

He keeps flipping plates. I see ghosts, aliens, breasts, guns, and pelvic bones in the ink but keep my visions to myself, fabricating ridiculous pictures to puzzle him. Yet the inky ghosts I see don't explain how shaken up the other girls appear after these sessions. I don't get it. He's not so scary after all, just a quack with a creepy curiosity about wayward girls. When we finish, he tells me to relax and starts in on a series of questions.

"Have you ever seen or handled a gun?" This rattles me.

I tell him no. I'd rather not incriminate myself, even if the accident with Steve, Marsha, and Bob is probably in my file. He doesn't bring it up. And I sure will not tell him, or anyone, about Albert and the gun.

"Do you love your mother?"

"I feel sorry for her."

"Do you think she loves you?"

"What does that have to do with anything? Does it matter? If she loved me, maybe I'd be outside this convent instead of inside answering your silly questions."

I fold my arms tight across my chest and stare him down. He doesn't react, just keeps firing away with the questions.

"Have you ever been hypnotized, Madeleine?"

"Nope. It wouldn't work on me."

"What makes you think it wouldn't?"

"I don't believe in it."

"It's not really a question of belief."

"Everything is a question of belief."

He nods slowly and smiles, like he's figuring out every inch of my soul. So creepy.

"My mother didn't go off the deep end until she started seeing a psychiatrist. He turned her into a lunatic."

"Interesting." He closes my file and stares at me. What is he thinking?

I walk out before he dismisses me.

Dazed, I'm standing in the hallway when Sister Helen hurries past in a swish of cloth.

"Sister Helen, does Dr. Golias hypnotize all the girls?"

"I would assume he uses whatever techniques are prudent for each individual."

Her curt tone lets me know this will not be a conversation.

"But I really don't want to be hypnotized, Sister."

"You'll do what you're instructed to do. Dr. Golias is a well-respected, progressive doctor with impeccable credentials; otherwise, he wouldn't be here. Now, go to your class."

There's that word *progressive* again. Progressing toward what, exactly? I don't think hypnotism works unless you give in to it. I vow to keep my guard up.

The next time I'm called into Golias's office, he asks me to relax as much as I possibly can.

"First," he says, "you'll close your eyes. I'll be taking you through a series of exercises to guide you into a hypnotic state."

I do as I'm told, but I'm nervous. He guides me through relaxing each part of my body, beginning from my toes and moving up. I deflate my body like a balloon, in sync with each body part he focuses on. By the time he gets to my neck, I pretend to be asleep.

He arrives at my head, telling me he's going to count backward and that by the time he hits number one, I'll be in a deep and restful slumber. I fake obedience, twitching my arm a little to make him think I'm trying to lift it but can't.

"Relax and go deeper."

Let him think he has me in his power. I'll know exactly what he's doing at every second.

He talks me into a beautiful cool forest where I'm sitting alone beneath a tree. I'm completely safe, he says, at peace. I can't help but imagine what he describes, and I see myself for a moment as Puck in my natural domain, pointy ears peeking out through the finger-like leaves of a weeping willow.

"Opposite you, there's a hole in a hillside, like a cave. You're curious. What could be inside? It doesn't seem threatening. You enter what seems to be a tunnel. You begin to walk through the tunnel, feeling the darkness caressing you like a soft blanket. You see a light beckoning you from the other side of the tunnel. You walk toward it without any fear whatsoever. Now you see a figure in the light. As you come closer, you recognize the person."

Although I have my eyes closed, my senses are keen, feeling for his presence, his body approaching mine. Thankfully he's not moving.

"You're standing in the light now with this person. The person is your mother."

Okay, he's obsessed with my mother. This is getting weirder by the minute.

"Suddenly, a rage gathers force inside you. You become agitated, like a tornado out of control . . . You are so filled with this explosive rage that you want to kill her. You look around and see a large rock on the ground. You pick it up. You know what you must do."

What the hell?

"You hurl the rock at your mother's head with all your might. It strikes her. Blood begins to rush down her face. You have no pity for her. You pick up another rock and strike her again. You can't stop, you keep bashing her in the head with the rock, bashing and bashing, until her features are distorted with blood, but you don't care, you keep going."

He's crazy! What is the point of this? She better turn into a butterfly!

Clenching my eyes tight, I squirm, wanting to stop this but . . . curiosity has a hold of me.

"She's gurgling her last breath . . . You take a large knife and cut off her head. The deed is done, but now you're exhausted. So tired, so sleepy, so hungry. You begin to taste your mother's leg. You start to chew it, ripping the flesh from the bone. This makes you hungrier, and you start eating her flesh. You devour her leg piece by piece and up to—"

A steel trap snaps in my head.

"THAT'S ENOUGH!"

He leaps up from his chair.

"Calm down, Madeleine, sit back down right now!"

"I will not, you sick pervert! That's my mother! I'm not your laboratory rat, you creep!"

I want to bash *his* head in! I realize I've been screaming when Sister Frances rushes in, eyes flying from me to the flustered Golias and back.

"She's having a difficult session today, Sister. I think you should take her back to her classroom."

Golias scribbles on a pad, eyes riveted to his desk.

"You are a sick man! It's evil, what you do!"

Shocked by my reaction Sister Frances takes my arm, shakes me, tells me to calm down. Golias smirks, shaking his head like I'm a naughty kitten. He talks gently but the command in his voice makes me see red.

"Madeleine, you will not remember the last hour at all; your mind will be as blank about it as if the time had never passed. You will forget. Now take her, Sister Frances."

Sister Frances laces an arm tightly around my shoulders and rushes me out. As soon as the office door closes, I tell her what happened in a rush of words.

"Sister Frances, he's evil! He told me to cannibalize my mother and—"

"Stop it! I do not want to hear about your private session."

"But, Sister! What he's doing is wrong, it's horrible!"

"Quiet now, or I'll have to sequester you!" She's clearly upset but refuses to listen to another word as she leads me toward the school building. And in my head I recite the words I didn't say beneath the helpless eyes of sad Jesus.

Oh no, Dr. Golias. I will not forget. I will remember every word. One day, I will load my slingshot. And my aim will be true.

10

SODOMITE!

Another sleepless night, wondering about the Catholics wanting us to eat and drink the body and blood of Christ. And now the body and blood of my mother? Should I tell Sister Veronica about Golias wanting me to cannibalize Kitty?

The little dove, the Holy Spirit on the black ribbon around my neck, beckons to me. The dove seems so harmless. I see its true form now, perpetually diving downward, beak pointed straight at my heart. Ready to peck it into Swiss cheese while I dream of Saint Michael wrestling with Lucifer on a crimson bed. They fight, they dance. They can't make up their minds if they love or despise each other. Sometimes Michael has my face, sometimes my face belongs to Lucifer. I hear the swishing of skirts and fall deeper into the dreaming. Naked alabaster bodies on wooden crosses twist and turn, begging for release. I'm in the middle, a torn scarlet robe bunched around my loins.

I watch my little crippled gimp of a heart through a slice of light in his rib cage prison. My heart is a cripple named Hugo. He has a hunchback, a sewn-up left eye, a lame leg, and a pockmarked face, courtesy of the Holy Ghost dove's pecking.

Two of the ribs part like a clamshell and Hugo wriggles free, giddy little fool. Off he goes, fumbling down the road toward the holy land, aching for a wash. A baptism. To be clean once more. And then to be loved. He follows after a beautiful girl called Hulga, trying his best to keep up with her confident strides. Hulga the Rose. Hulga sees him hopping up and down, dancing on his one good leg for her attention. She stops, lifts her skirt enough to show Hugo she too has a gimpy leg; it's wooden, yet it doesn't stop her from running away from him. Dejected, he limps back into his cage.

He reads a book by Saint John of the Cross: "Do the most difficult, the harshest, the less pleasant, the unconsoling, the lowest and most despised, want nothing."

Casting one lonely eye around his prison cell, he spies his flute. Delighted, he raises it to his lips and begins to blow softly, the sound like sweet wind whistling through reeds on a peaceful night. The purest of notes make colorful shapes in the air above him, bursting into a million dark flowers pinpricked with light. Notes that bloom, dance, and pirouette above him in a beautiful ballet of music.

Enchanted and happy, he falls into a dreamless sleep. The flowers begin to descend upon him—four-petaled, white with glowing scarlet tips. Dogwood flowers. Flowers of crucifixion.

And then, a single red rose. The rose beckons. The rose comes to rest on my chest, its petals the softest of velvets. I reach for it, and a thorn opens my skin.

How tender is the rose? It all depends on where and how you touch.

It's nearly impossible to become friends with the other Marycrest girls. We can talk in the dayroom after dinner, but only under the watchful eyes and ears of the sisters. This rule seriously messes up decent conversation. Newspapers and magazines are forbidden, along with radio and TV. Except for a collection of approved books (and my secret visits to the library, thanks to Sister Veronica), the sisters keep us tamed and under surveillance, like animals in their private zoo. We are see-no-speak-no-hear-no-evil monkeys, guarded by a flock of penguins. God forbid we catch some of the wildness happening out in the streets and start a revolt of our own. Being locked up is bad enough. Having no news of the revolution outside is absolute torture.

We count on Dorothy, a senior girl from Regina Hall, for our reports about the world outside. Her brother visits and fills her in on everything, sometimes slipping her a newspaper. Stories rush through the dorms like flash floods, taking on steam from girl to girl:

— Charles Manson's cult murders Sharon Tate and other Hollywood people
— The Woodstock festival is a fantastic phenomenon
— John Lennon and Yoko Ono stay in bed for a week to protest the Vietnam War

— Astronauts walk on the moon
— The SDS takes over Harvard University
— *Oliver!* wins Best Picture at the Academy Awards (my goose is truly cooked)
— The National Guard sprays chemicals on protesters in Berkeley, California
— The Chicago 8 trial begins
— The *Cleveland Plain Dealer* prints photos of the My Lai massacre in Vietnam

I think about Jack, praying that he's safe.

Joanie is taking me on a home visit to Grandma's. It's the first time family has ever picked me up for a visit, and I'm afraid to feel too excited, since Karl might be there and ruin everything. Sister Veronica once asked me if I ever felt homesick. My answer was a headshake. Nope. Aside from Grandma's piano, no home to be sick over. I will never ask Joanie or anyone else why they don't come to visit. Only weaklings would do such a thing.

Joanie tells me Kitty is still in the hospital, and the doctors say she's a paranoid schizophrenic, a very serious disease. She's safe and is being taken care of. Karl is working a double shift today, and I can have Grandma all to myself for the entire day because Joanie has to work too. I ask Joanie why she doesn't come to visit. She looks embarrassed, says she's been working really hard and has a boyfriend now. But she thinks of me all the time. Hmm.

When we arrive, Grandma gives me a huge hug and seems glad to see me but looks sadder than I can remember. Her piano is gone. Karl replaced it with a Hammond organ, a beast of a thing decked out with colored levers for different beats and sounds: bossa nova and cha-chas played by fake flutes, strings, and French horns. It sounds dark and chintzy, like a merry-go-round in hell. Karl thinks the opposite, says the organ is perfect and more suitable for hymns. Probably reminds him of German calliope music. I can tell Grandma hates that organ. When she begins to play, her body looks different, like a deflated balloon. No bounce. Her left hand can't beat rhythms on the organ keys. You have to press organ keys, and softly. Organ keys can't swing or dance with Grandma Jo's rhythms. The piano was her joy, her life. Karl may as well have committed murder.

At least Grandma is allowed to choose which hymns to play and sing. She sings a mournful "There Is a Balm in Gilead." Afterward, we eat scrambled eggs, and she looks at me sadly, then goes upstairs to take a nap. I creep after her and listen at the bedroom door to her weeping alone in her room. The wooden floor is cool. I press my face there, singing quietly through the door crack: *There is a balm in Gilead / to make the wounded whole . . .* It quiets her and comforts me. I silently curse Karl. And curse having been born a woman.

In my bed at Marycrest, my mind's eye sees Grandma gazing out the kitchen window, lonely hands lying still among the dishes in the sink's sudsy water, all joy having drained from fingers that would never dance again, and I think, *Why didn't I help her with the dishes? Why didn't I tell her how beautifully she played, how happy she made me? How the roses in the garden danced when they saw her coming, and how it felt when she held my hand? That touch of warm beloved palm, thumb, and fingers transferring the grace and the love of music into mine?*

I pull the covers over my head like I did as a child and sing in a mournful whisper, thinking of a favorite poem. Song and poem connecting to make me wonder with a sadness overwhelming that love might never triumph over hatred. That the world may not ever fall in love with love again. But had it ever?

"Prophet!" said I, "thing of evil!—prophet still, if bird or devil!—
Whether Tempter sent, or whether tempest tossed thee here ashore,
Desolate yet all undaunted, on this desert land enchanted—
On this home by Horror haunted—tell me truly, I implore—
Is there—is there balm in Gilead?—tell me—tell me, I implore!"
Quoth the Raven "Nevermore."

I met Belinda when Sister Margaret asked us to pack up our instruments after band practice. She played oboe and wasn't bad; I played clarinet poorly, stumbling through the ridiculous marches we had to learn. One night after Sister Margaret leaves and the girls have gone, I ask Belinda if she wants to hear me play the clarinet parts I've practiced from the song "M'Lady." She grins and tells me to go ahead. I blow the introduction phrase from memory, with its cool, high-pitched squeal at the end. I can pull that off effortlessly. She seems impressed. Then I get to the solo part and mangle it. She cracks up.

"I never could play the whole thing."

"Yeah, but you tried. It sounded pretty good, for a minute there."

Her laughter sounds deep and smoky, like Dionne Warwick's. I tell her she has beautiful eyes. And she does—huge golden-brown eyes with long lashes. I've admired her from afar since I arrived here. Belinda is the only other girl Sister Veronica loves listening to. Her most requested song from Sister V. is "Sunrise, Sunset" from *Fiddler on the Roof.*

"I like your voice," she tells me, "but those songs Sister Veronica makes you sing . . ."

"I know. She always asks for the *Oliver!* songs. It's a curse."

"Or a blessing. She likes you. Twist." She giggles; I blush.

"You too! You can *really sing.*"

"I try."

I don't know what to say next. My nerves get the better of me and out comes something stupid: "What's a nice girl like you doing in a joint like this?"

She looks at me like *What on earth did you just say?* when BAM, in walks Sister Helen to get me off the hook. Courting girls is nerve-racking.

For the next few weeks we steal glances, sneaking notes to each other. Our notes are very different from the exchange with Samantha Tamorini, much more poetic. I go to the source, the Song of Solomon. *My Beloved is a bouquet of henna flowers in the vineyards of En Gedi.*

As our notes exchange hands, the touch of her fingers jolts through me.

Belinda sleeps in the other section of the Lourdes dorm. We share the same bathroom, but we never meet at shower time, are on different bathing schedules unless we have to pee in the night, and we're discouraged from rising after lights out.

The nuns allow us to have wristwatches. Aunt Joanie gave me a watch on a thin black band, and Belinda has one too. We plan to meet at three A.M. in the bathroom between our dorms to get to know each other better. On a Wednesday, when Sister Veronica will be on night watch, since she's a heavy sleeper. We figure she'll be the most lenient if we get caught, since she likes us both.

The night arrives and I can't sleep a wink, peeking at my watch 1,001 times until three A.M. Like a spy on a mission, I tiptoe on bare feet across the cold linoleum, past rows of beds filled with dreaming girls, past the nun's room, and into the bathroom, which seems to glow phosphorescent in the moonlight. I wait, my blood on fire.

Belinda appears. It's summer; we have on matching thin cotton pajamas. Pale blue, the color of hope. Belinda seems petrified and excited, just like me. I take her hand, and we creep around to the side of the door, staying near it so we can make a quick getaway if we hear a sound. We can't even hear ourselves breathing, even though our chests silently rise and fall like bellows. I put my hands on her shoulders and pull her down slowly until we're both on our knees facing each other. We move closer, watching each other's mouths. She kisses me. It's so unbelievably soft, like melting. I kiss her eyes. She kisses mine, then my forehead, and our mouths come back together again and again, and it's nothing like with Samantha. This is something pure. Holy and glistening.

I'm on top of her, moving and stifling her moans with my mouth, quieting my own. Some of our breathing escapes the net. We can't help it, our bodies like winding question marks searching every curve of flesh and bone and muscle and warm place with the world slipping away. Like it does when you pray. When you believe.

Soft lips on my ear, she whispers, "The cedars will be the walls of our house."

I whisper back, "The cypress trees will be our rafters."

Mid-kiss, I look to the side. To a foot in a terry cloth slipper. Tapping. Up the shin to the chenille robe, to the crossed arms. The stern face. Head wrapped in a white veil.

I don't know what shocks me more: her presence or the fact of seeing Sister Veronica out of her habit. How long has she been watching?

"Get up. Now."

We scramble to our feet. She glares at us like she wishes there were a convenient guillotine nearby. I'm dumbstruck but manage to mumble, "Sister, we're so sorry . . ."

As if.

"This is an abomination in the eyes of God. Get back in your beds, quietly. You'll be dealt with in the morning. I do not wish to disturb the other girls."

She grabs our arms and propels us in opposite directions.

The following day Sister Veronica wakes me at dawn, commanding me to follow and not to bother to dress. Still in slippers and pajamas, I follow on tiptoe past sleeping girls. She leads me over the walkway to the administration building, into a tiny, narrow room without a window.

There's an iron bed, a toilet, a tiny sink. A crucifix on the wall. A Bible sitting on the bed. Sister Veronica turns and leaves me there, locking the door. If I walk one foot after the other, the room measures around nine feet, long enough for the single bed by three feet. Not for the claustrophobic or the weak of heart. Not a word about how long I'll be made to suffer inside this coffin of a space. Alone with Jesus in solitary confinement, I sit staring at the cross, bolted to the wall by five screws. No telling what harm you might do with a loose crucifix.

Sister Veronica returns a few hours later with a small wooden chair. It's so strange to see her this upset, face frozen into a look of scorn. Smoothing down her habit, she sits on the chair next to the bed and opens the Bible I've been reading. Her lips look tight, hard at the corners when she speaks.

"Do you understand the magnitude of the sin you have committed?"

"I don't . . . understand, Sister. About love being a sin."

Her lips tremble. Clearly, she hears the word *love* as an abomination on my tongue.

"What you did isn't love. It's sodomy. Filth. Do you understand the sin of sodomy?"

I shake my head in the negative. I don't know what sodomy is, only that it's queer. Is it butt sex? If it is, maybe telling the truth will help. Like, *Sister, we didn't have butt sex, I swear!* But I doubt this will go over very well. Jack told me homos have butt sex, and he'd laugh about how much it must hurt, but I felt sorry for homos after getting raped because I figured it must hurt like crazy. Sex with a man hurts so much in the other hole, which is at least slightly bigger than a culo. Culos are so tiny. Jack never mentioned the word *sodomy*.

"Sister, what is sodomy?"

Her face twists into shocked confusion. It feels like she might cry as she takes the Bible from my hands, frantically flipping the pages. She reads, voice shaking. "Jude 1:7. 'Even as Sodom and Gomorrah and the cities about them in like manner, giving themselves over to fornication, and going after strange flesh, are set forth for an example, suffering the vengeance of eternal fire.' Is this what you want? To burn in eternal fire?"

The fire I feel is the sting of the bees again. She's getting them all worked up inside me. She doesn't explain what sodomy is, but it clearly equals homo for both boys and girls to these nuns. Until I can figure this out and study what the Bible says, I'll hang my head, act remorseful. Sister Veronica trembles, inhaling deep, shaky breaths. Why is she so upset?

"You'll stay in this room until you read the books of Deuteronomy and Leviticus. You will meditate until you come to contrition and full remorse over your sins and make a full confession, do you understand?"

"Yes, Sister."

"What you did is shameful and dirty. You must never do it again, or else you will lead a life of horrible debasement. You are a precious child of God. Learn how God punishes sodomites. Learn it well."

"But, Sister . . . I learned this passage from the book of Psalms for you. I think it was written by David. 'For you created my inmost being; you knit me together in my mother's womb. I praise you because I am fearfully and wonderfully made; your works are wonderful, I know that full well.' Doesn't this mean that God loves all creatures, no matter who they choose to love? Even if they are… criminals?"

"You are a tangle of wicked thoughts, Maddie. I am so disappointed in you."

Trembling, she hands me the Bible, clearly not wanting our hands to touch, like she might catch my disease. She gives me a damning look on her way out the door.

The lock clicks.

I hate to disappoint Sister Veronica, but I think I'm in love. With Belinda. This presents a bit of a dilemma.

Although I have read stories in the New Testament many times, I turn to Genesis and figure I'll have time enough to start at the beginning. I read the story about Sodom and Gomorrah, about the men who show up at Lot's place wanting his guests to come out so they can have sex with them. It's very confusing; the guests are two men who happen to be angels, sent from God to destroy the city because of its wicked ways. This Lot character is a creep, having offered up his daughters to be gang-raped. Why would the angels agree to it? Lot didn't even know if they were angels; he was just guessing, making it even more horrid. Then, to top it off, Lot has sex with his daughters and pretends to be *asleep* while he's doing it. All this wrongness gets blamed on the girls, as usual. As if you could sleep during sex. Especially with your own daughters, even if you're drunk, for God's sake. Then the children of these sinners become two great and noble tribes, the Moabites and the Ammonites.

Sister Veronica knows I'm not an idiot. Does she expect me to discuss this with her? If she does, then I'd better be prepared. There's nothing else to do in solitary except dream about Belinda and read this Bible.

Leviticus 20:13: "If a man also lie with mankind, as he lieth with a woman, both of them have committed an abomination: they shall surely be put to death; their blood *shall be* upon them."

Leviticus must be talking about butt sex. No girls with girls here. "Put to death" is a bit strong for men making each other feel good. And just a few sentences before this one, Leviticus says that both people who commit adultery should be put to death. All this violence. Others deserving the death penalty are people who work on Sundays. And we better not eat shrimp. I love shrimp. This means Kitty, Jack, everybody I know, and most churchgoers who eat shrimp cocktails are doomed as the "unclean" and should be stoned to death.

There are way too many passages in the Bible about "lying with beasts." Was there a lot of sex with animals going on back then? Disgusting. I read the New Testament now, my favorite book being the book of Matthew. Matthew and Mary Magdalene seemed to understand Jesus better than any of his apostles, even if Mary was a prostitute. Reading Matthew carefully, I look for Jesus having anything to say about homos.

Matthew 19:12: "For there are some eunuchs, which were so born from their mother's womb: and there are some eunuchs, which were made eunuchs of men: and there be eunuchs, which have made themselves eunuchs for the kingdom of heaven's sake. He that is able to receive it, let him receive it."

I imagine this can be interpreted many ways, one being that Jesus loved eunuchs and viewed them as holy creatures. Creatures that only the wise will understand. And then I remember a section called "SIN" from a Percy Shelley poem I loved, about a man named Peter and the Devil:

But from the first 'twas Peter's drift
To be a kind of moral eunuch,
He touched the hem of Nature's shift,
Felt faint—and never dared uplift
The closest, all-concealing tunic.

Did Shelley think eunuchs were sinful? Was Peter too frightened to know the truth of it?

A nameless nun brings me three meals a day, so at least I won't starve to death. Solitary confinement sets up a terrible hunger, but not for food. I read and reread the Bible. I do push-ups and run in place so my legs won't turn into noodles.

After three days, Sister Veronica enters with the small chair and sits next to the bed.

"What have you learned?"

"I'm confused about Lot. He . . . well . . . you know the story, don't you? He slept with his daughters. He offered them to a gang of rapists."

Her face flushes beet red—with rage or confusion, I don't know which. I can't cave in; I must be strong and defend my and Belinda's honor.

"Lot made sacrifices for the Lord God the Father, whose ways are mysterious. The daughters were evil. The story's point is that God destroyed the city for its sin of sodomy. Have you learned nothing?"

"But I also read about Jesus and the eunuchs. He accepted them. And in Isaiah 56—"

"Eunuchs have nothing to do with this! Eunuchs are men without . . . without procreative organs . . . do you understand?"

She nearly chokes on the word *organs*. It's no use. If she doesn't know that the true meaning of sodomy is butt sex, I'm not about to explain it to her.

"Yes, Sister, I understand."

"You are reading everything through the funnel of your own sins. I'm adding another week to your confinement. I will send in the Mother Superior to further elaborate on the abomination you've committed and what is likely to happen if you continue in your wicked ways."

"Please, I'm doing penance. I've already said fifty Hail Marys and fifty Our Fathers in contrition and haven't even been to confession yet—"

She storms out, leaving me to question what it is Sister Veronica truly feels beneath all the damnation. I saw her tenderness. I saw it, felt it. And deep tenderness is in the love one person has for another, no matter the sodomite.

When I reenter the school two weeks later, I hear whispers. Celeste is telling another girl that Belinda and I are lesbians. I hate that word more than anything. When the girls ask, "What happened?" I go quiet, won't discuss or deny it. I know the other girls have all thought about it, even if they haven't fallen in love like us. Hypocrites, every one of them, with their suspicious, dirty looks. All wanting what we have the nerve to taste.

I watch the girls in Lourdes dormitory line up on their way to morning Mass, watch the nuns walking the cloister to the chapel. All have their loneliness, their desires, folded away, tucked up into hospital corners. Afraid to look, to beckon. Walking without speaking, longing for tenderness.

The order of it. The ache of silence and shame.

11

REVOLUTION, GOODBYE

Sister Veronica has lost her affection for me. She avoids me, leaves the common room when I enter. My status with her has been revoked; no more visits to the library, no affectionate hair brushings. At least that'll be the end to the *Oliver!* songs. I guess she still cares for me by the way I catch her eyes sometimes. Heavy, they seem, with a mournful look, as if she's lost something dear. It hurts, but I don't show it. Then one day, she simply disappears. When I ask Sister Helen where she's gone, I get a cryptic answer that she's been called for another vocation and won't be returning.

I'm forbidden to go near Belinda. They've moved her to Marian Hall, and if I catch a glimpse of her every two weeks, I consider myself lucky. Truth is, without Sister Veronica and Belinda, or my secret praying nun, there's nothing left to keep me at Marycrest.

A new girl decides to be my friend. Incredibly tall, lanky, with long reddish-brown hair and glasses, Beth carries herself gracefully. She's studious, quiet, and shy. You never see her trying to befriend other girls, and she never speaks in classes except when she's called on for an answer. She has a brilliant vocabulary. I'm not attracted to her, but the solitary loners never fail to grab my interest.

Beth approaches me one day in the empty bathroom after school.

"Don't you find Dr. Golias of dubious character?"

"Most definitely. He's experimenting with us."

"I'm an epileptic, and he tried to convince me that I'm idiopathic as opposed to symptomatic. The next time they call me to his office, I'll fake a seizure so I don't have to see him. He doesn't have a clue about the disease, clearly. Fucking bastard."

"Oh wow. Do you have a lot of seizures?"

"Only on occasion. Confidentially, I need to get out of this place. Would you like to escape? If it were possible, would you?"

"You mean run away?"

"Yes. Why not?"

"I've had it with this joint. You should hear what Golias pulled on me. He tried to hypnotize me, and when the creep thought I was under, he made me brutally murder and eat my mother's leg!"

"You're kidding! Did you tell any of the sisters?"

"I tried, but they treat him like the pope."

"All the more reason to make our great escape."

I don't have to think twice.

"Let's do it."

Standing there together in the bathroom mirror, we make a funny-looking pair, grinning at the difference in our heights. Sister Claude walks in at that moment clapping her rusty hands.

"Now, now, girls, no chatting! Let's wash up and get ready for dinner."

Over the next few days, Beth and I sneak in bits of conversation about how and when to make a dash for it. A campus uprising at Kent State University over Nixon's invasion of Cambodia was squashed by the National Guard, who shot and killed four students and wounded nine others. Because of the student murders, we will hitchhike to Kent State, to be part of the revolution.

Another lone wolf I speak to is Shirley, the painter. Mother Superior has her working in the big house at least once a week. When Dorothy mentioned Kent State but couldn't give any details, I asked Shirley if she'd heard anything about it and she filled me in.

"They shot four student protesters dead. But the same thing happened in Mississippi not even two weeks later at a black college, so the news didn't talk about it. I saw a tiny article about it in the *Plain Dealer*. The police shot up a dormitory, killed two students, hurt a bunch of others. Talk about a mess. But you didn't hear it from me."

"That's crazy. What are they gonna do now—shoot everybody who protests?"

"Probably. Might be safer to just stay inside this penguin cave."

Shirley paints on a canvas with real oils, which is quite a privilege. She's working on a group of African warriors. They stand tall with their spears and shields, faces tattooed in wild patterns and colors, eyes daring you to move an inch closer. She's been at it for a whole year, and it shows; it's beautiful. Kind of abstract and in motion, like the characters are about to leap off the canvas.

Beth and I plan to do the runner. We'll break the line on our way to basketball at rec period, the safest opportunity to run for it, but it means we can't bring any possessions with us. We're wearing gym clothes: T-shirts, blue shorts, and sneakers. While we file across the campus with the other girls, we throw each other a hand signal, break the line, and bolt toward the woods like rabbits in a quar-ter-mile race. A nun shouts, *"Two runners!"* her voice already at a distance as we scramble down a mud bank toward the ravine. By the time we wade through the shallow water, we're filthy. The mud and the sun going down give us the cover we need while we run for our lives, waywards gone underground to join the revolution.

Dogs begin to bark—they've set the dogs on us? Flashlights sweep the trees above as we crawl on our bellies through muddy earth and brambles. Hearts thumping, we whisper curses at cops and nuns and all enemies of freedom!

After scrambling through what feels like miles of woods, we stop, breathe deep, and try to clean ourselves up a bit. We've lost the bark-ing dogs and searchlights, and the coast seems clear, but night is coming on fast. I go out on the road and stick my thumb up, trying to look innocent as Beth waits just inside the woods. A few cars whizz by, and finally, one stops.

The driver is an older white guy who reminds me of a car sales-man, kind of like Mr. Treadwell. He seems harmless. Could it be a trick of my bad eye gone? We'll never get anywhere if we don't risk putting ourselves in harm's way. There are two of us, so I feel safer.

"Where are you headed?" asks the old guy.

"To Kent State, back to school. Can you give us a ride?"

He looks us both over. "Have you two been mud wrestling?"

I think fast and start laughing. "Haha! We were chasing our friend's dog through the woods and finally caught him!"

"Yeah, he's back home now, but we need to get back to campus and clean up. Kent is southeast, near Hudson. You know it?" says Beth.

"I can't take you that far, but I'll get you to the 80."

He doesn't try to touch us. In fact, no driver does, thank sweet Jesus. We hitchhike all the way to Kent, desperate with excitement. On our way to be part of the revolution.

In Kent, the atmosphere on campus is broken and weird. It's evening and deathly quiet when we arrive. The revolution seems over—I think we missed it. We hang around the nearly empty campus square, feeling like maybe we should turn ourselves in, when a couple of mopey-looking hippie-type guys start talking to us. They tell us the pigs are still everywhere, watching everybody (they point out two guys in an unmarked car), and we can stay with them in their dorm room, but we have to be careful not to get caught.

This is not what we expected at all. We thought the students would be fighting even harder because of the killings. It seems they've all given up.

The dorm room has only four beds compared with the ten at Mary-crest. I will not be shacking up with these guys in their bunk beds! I paste a scowl on my face so deep that everyone gets the message immediately. One hippie sees my arms folded tight across my chest and says, "Whoa, this one's a toughie!" A guy named Tony comes over, a sweet, soft-eyed guy with long hair and a crazy mustache. He tells me he's a janitor, not a student, and he's bunking with these guys until he leaves for 'Nam. He promises me if I share his bed, he won't touch me, swearing on his mother's life. I want to believe him, but I refuse to sleep in his bed. He gives me a blanket, and I make a bed for myself on the floor next to his bunk.

We smoke pot, I get a little more paranoid, and we listen to CSN&Y's *Déjà Vu* record. The songs seem to make everyone even sadder. "Our House" comes on, and the harmonies and lightness of the melody make me feel safe enough to relax a bit. Tony is sick about going to the war, says he'd never hurt a fly and can't believe he might be forced to kill some stranger for no reason at all, or even be killed himself. I tell him about Jack.

"I hear those gooks are better soldiers than our guys."

Jack told me horrible stories about the brutalities over there, soldiers losing their minds all hyped up on speed, LSD, and blood-lust. Shattered men, Jack said. I ask Tony if he thinks MPs are in more danger than regular soldiers. He flicks a doughnut crumb off his mustache.

"War is war, and war equals death. I don't want to sound like the Grim Reaper here, but your uncle will be lucky if he gets out alive."

He hands me the other half of his doughnut.

The guys are being so nice to us, like we are actually friends and not rabbits to chase and make a meal of. Two white guys, Tony and Ben, and a black guy, Robbie, all seem like they sincerely want to help. Tony treats me like a kid sister—such a relief. That night before we go to sleep, I ask Tony if Beth and I can shower. The guys give us T-shirts and jeans and a towel we'll have to share. Tony's jeans are way too big for me. He hands me a belt so they won't fall off.

Tony keeps his promise and doesn't try to touch me, even though he sleeps in his T-shirt and boxer shorts, which makes me nervous. He stays on the far side of the bed against the wall snoring while I toss and turn on the floor, fully dressed.

I hear sounds coming from the bunk across where Beth and Rick are doing the dirty deed. She makes squealing noises like a baby piglet and my stomach churns. Why does it sound like he's hurting her? I wonder if I should rescue her, but she starts whimpering and cooing like a dove. Rick's obviously not hurting her now. I count the paisleys in the psychedelic poster of Jimi Hendrix, thinking of Albert the Vietnam vet, wondering what happened to him in the city, in that war, to turn him into such a monster. I think about my own wars and what I'm going to do with myself come morning, staying awake through the night.

The next day, after the guys leave for school and Tony for work, Beth is acting strange, like suddenly she doesn't know me. I tell her I'm going to the bathroom and she follows me timidly, not saying a word. While I wash up in the sink, she takes our towel, wets it down, and closes herself into a bathroom stall. She keeps flushing the toilet over and over. I hear her crying softly the whole time.

Tony left me a few bucks, so Beth and I go outside to try to scrounge up some food. The sky is the color of mud as students move across the campus, quiet and solemn. It's like the National Guard killed the revolution right here where we stand. The song "Déjà Vu" is in my head, matching the eerie sadness around us.

I need to get out of here.

A hippie girl walks past.

"Hey, can you tell us where to find the cafeteria?"

She points and laughs, "Don't expect much. They serve a lot of pig."

It's too early for lunch, too late for breakfast, so the pickings are slim. I grab something for Beth and meet her back outside. We sit on a bench overlooking a square of green.

"I got us a ham sandwich."

"Thanks."

She's clearly in no mood for conversation, and neither am I. A blackbird lands a few feet away. I peel off my crusts and toss them over, thinking of the tiny nun and her bird friends. One greedy bird gobbles up the crumbs, then flies off to join her flock of buddies on a buckeye tree.

"I think I'm gonna turn myself in."

Beth sighs and wraps her sandwich. She hasn't taken more than a bite. "I'll stay here with Rick."

"But you don't even know him."

"It's preferable to being locked in a convent."

"You're gonna live in a dorm room with a bunch of strange guys?"

"Rick likes me. He'll do for now."

Maybe he will take care of her, at least for a while.

"Well, guess I'll be seeing you then." I get up from the bench.

"Where are you going?"

"To hell in a handbasket!"

I do a little tap dance to cheer her up. She shakes her head and smiles, like I'm a ridiculous fool, and maybe I am. A queer, wayward sodomite, walking away across the green and into the next adventure. Pretending I don't have a fear in the world.

I hitchhike into downtown Cleveland. This time I won't be going off to who-knows-where with any sleepy-eyed strangers. At least for now, I'm free and eager to know just what's going on in the world before the cops pick me up and I'm on to the next jailhouse.

It's 1970. Soul voices preach to a beat, singing "Ball of Confusion" from a shiny red Mustang's radio. A different crop of hippies and freaky types hang around Public Square, rowdier than the crowd from last year. One stringy-haired girl clinging to a crinkled lunch bag smiles at me with eyes rimmed in dark circles. She's pretty, Italian looking. She motions me over, and I fall in with her crowd, a bunch of older teenage hippie girls and one dirty, skinny boy with acne and bad teeth who says "fuck" every other word.

They take me to a rathole apartment near the Detroit-Superior Bridge, where we sniff toluol (it's glue, they tell me) out of paper bags. This stuff is wicked. It gobbles me up, makes me hallucinate monstrous green blobs with human faces flying out of the TV set. I guess I fainted, because suddenly, the dirty boy and stringy-haired girl are pulling me away from the TV.

"You tried to punch in the TV screen, har har har!"

As I snap out of it, I look around at my new companions sitting on the grimy floor, bleary-eyed and huffing from wrinkled paper bags. They remind me of Kitty after one of her crazy fits, their pupils dull, mouths slack and drooly. Then sudden bursts of creepy energy. The dirty boy turns out to be a fuckboy. He and the stringy-haired girl have sex in front of everybody, and then he's doing it to the other girl, pumping her like a rabbit kicking its legs. Gross. They play "Space Cowboy," by the Steve Miller Band, over and over again on a crappy record player, acting like zombie morons, trying to dance with no rhythm at all. These kids are dumber than a box of hair. A twenty-dollar bill sticks out of fuckboy's back pocket as he fumbles around the room doing a chicken dance. He's oblivious. I snatch the twenty. Fuck this idiocy, for real. I'm outta here.

I go to a Big Boy restaurant, eat a hamburger, and call the cops. They pick me up, and I'm on my way back to the detention home, thank sweet Jesus. Because I'm a ward of the state now, classified by the court as an incorrigible, habitual runaway, my delinquency is carved like letters on a tombstone. I've reached the end of the line. The judge remands me to the highest-security reformatory in the state of O-hi-O: the Blossom Hill School for Girls.

12

THE DISPOSABLES

A slightly older, big-boned girl sits on a bench in the back of the transport van from DH, posing there like a royal dude. I can hardly stop myself from staring. There's a diamond stud in her left ear and a pinkie ring on the right hand to match, and I wonder if those are real diamonds. The pinkie has a long nail on it, whereas all her other fingernails are short and gleaming with shine. She reminds me of Texas. She's wearing a guy's shirt, short-sleeved with cream fabric and brown suede panels.

"What do you think you're starin' at?"

"Nothin'."

She checks me out for another painful minute.

"The name's Slick. What's your name?"

"Maddie."

"What kind of name is that? You always mad?"

She turns away, laughing to herself. I say nothing, figuring I've blown my chance at making the kind of friend that'll matter at Blossom Hill.

"You need a name that suits you."

She stares, inspects me. Stone-faced. But wait, now she's chuckling.

"You're on your way to trouble, understand? They don't mess around on the Hill. Just how tall are you?"

"Five foot and a quarter. But that don't mean nothing."

This makes her laugh even more.

"Tough girl, huh? I hear you, but we best change your name before we get an inch closer to the Hill."

She checks me out, rubbing her chin in consideration. I try not to squirm.

"L'il Bit is a good name for you. Or Shawty."

"L'il Bit will do."

I hate it, but I would rather live with that nickname than die without it.

"Now, here's what's gonna happen. I'll take you under my wing and teach you the ropes, or those studs at the joint will tear your little ass up. You play the game?"

I shrug and nod my head. I heard about the "game," which is what they call "it" inside the joint. Little did Slick know I had foster sisters and nuns trying to kick the game out of me for two years now.

"Most of the girls inside play the game, but a lot of them got a man on the outs too. Are you a stud? Or a lady?"

I put on my toughest pose and smirk. "Do I look like a lady to you?"

This amuses the hell out of her. She leans in, not wanting the driver to hear. "Okay, here's what you do. I'm gonna tell them you're my little white sister from detention home, that you're cool and not to fuck with you. I'm a repeater, been to the Hill twice already, and they regard me as the king up there. They know better than to fuck with me. Stay close, watch the way I move and talk. And don't run your mouth too much. I'll teach you how to pull a lady so they know not to mess."

I grin at her in thanks. "But . . . what makes you think I need to be taught?"

Her chest shakes while she laughs. "Ha! L'il Bit! This, I gotta see. You'll be all right."

Two weeks later, I'm strutting alongside Slick on our way from school back to Cottage Two. Slick is five foot eight, I'm four-eleven. Just like her, I hold my inner thigh with the left hand, swing a graceful arc with the right, and strut a limp on the same side.

Blossom Hill looks more like a private school than a jail. There are six white colonial cottages with pillars at the doorways placed around a center green. An administration building looks out over the green, and there's a school building toward the back of the property and a gym. It's surrounded by woods, on a country road with hardly any houses nearby. Next to the school sits a bone-dry swimming pool I will never see filled. There is absolutely nothing readable in the joke of a library. Still, I'm determined to keep myself learning at least one craft, even if it's acting. I'm thinking my talent for acting, dancing, and singing might be the only way to stay afloat here.

These girls are tough. I'm the only white girl out of twelve in Cottage Two, where they've placed me. There are a few white girls in other cottages. I see them at school but am afraid to make friends with them because the black girls might think I'm weak.

New emotions surface as I learn how to be here, to befriend these girls. I don't believe most of these girls have ever been within twenty feet of a white girl, until me. But I'm guessing the Devil ran through their families like he did through mine. I guess it's different, because I'm white. I'll have an easier time when I get out there. But only if I hide being queer. These girls won't have such an easy time because of the color of their skin.

I watch and listen. I see beauty and sadness. Loneliness. Pride. Silliness. Strength. Joy. Rage. I see a thirst underneath all, like a straw sucking for air, peeping out of the eyes of a girl here and over there. I can't seem to find the same buoys, the lights and bells that once kept me afloat through the mists. Like any lost sailor, I look for anchors. I look at Slick's hands, smooth and graceful, so perfectly manicured, unblemished and glowing. Just watching them at peace resting on her knees gives me comfort, where just the sight of Big Al's evil hands made me cringe. Big Al's hands, so cruel. Cruel as the hands that held the gun.

Rumor has it that some of the girls in here actually committed murder. I don't believe it. One girl buried her newborn infant in the backyard because she didn't have the money to feed it. Where do you turn when there's no money for food, for diapers? When you have no home, no family, no books? And no help? It's hard enough to face that kind of trouble on your own, but with a baby?

None of these girls seem like criminals; they're mostly truants, runaways. Druggies and thieves. Incorrigibles, with a tendency to exaggerate their crimes. Some assaulted teachers, and yes, others have babies they couldn't take care of. I am coming to understand how all of us have screwed-up families we never discuss because we are gangsters. We are lovers. And in the unspoken deep where the shame of seasick sailors creep, we are the disposables.

Slick tells me what brought her back in here this time: she had three girls she was pimping on the outs. Wild. Is she really a pimp? When a trick beat and bruised her bottom woman, Chrissy, Slick caught him in the act and stabbed him in the thigh with a pair of scissors, then took all his "scratch" (money). The trick reported her, and Slick was found guilty, even though the trick might have killed Chrissy. The trick walked away scot-free. So unfair. When I ask her about the other times, she grins like the Cheshire cat.

"Bit, you don't even wanna know."

"Did you ever . . . uh, beat on a woman?"

She laughs her ass off. "Nah! I treat my women right. I'm no Iceberg Slim, don't do that pistol-whippin' bullshit. We have a mutual respect thing goin' on."

The girls in here all do respect Slick. She's powerful but gentle and quiet, softly padding around like a cotton candy Romeo. But you just know if you mess with her, she won't hesitate to cut you. On the outs, Slick lived in a pimpin' world that all these baby mack daddies inside could only imagine in their wildest dreams.

Slick's protection works. The other girls pretty much ignore me, when they aren't smirking behind my back. After dinner we go to the gymnasium for recreation period, to dance and roller-skate to the same records over and over. Songs like:

— "ABC" / "The Love You Save" / "I Found That Girl," by the Jackson 5

— "Thank You (Falettinme Be Mice Elf Again)," by Sly and the Family Stone

— "Ball of Confusion (That's What the World Is Today)," by the Temptations

— "Express Yourself," by Charles Wright and the Watts 103rd Street Rhythm Band

— "Up the Ladder to the Roof," by the Supremes

Apart from Slick's blond lady, Debra; another fly femme called Trash; and Julie in Cottage Two, there are only a few other white girls here. Lizzie seems cool enough, but she lives in Cottage Six, so I never get to see her much and she doesn't come to rec periods. Jeanie in Cottage Three is cool and sassy. The black girls eyeball me with interested suspicion because I can dance, and I'm careful not to show off too much. In the beginning, I watch. The girls skate in couples with the stud skating backward, holding hands with her femme and leading her in smooth, mackin' moves around the gym. Now, I know I can dance, but this is dancing on skates, and skating backward is essential if you're a stud. The recreation crew acts oblivious to the courtship of it all. It's a high school dance for romancing couples, for studs on the cruise for their next lady and vice versa. We're not stupid enough to kiss, knowing that would be grounds for lockup. Later, I'll discover the secret spots for make-out sessions.

We prank each other to chase away the boredom. The black girls glob Vaseline all over the white girls' hair at night before lockup, and the whiteys dump baby powder in the black girls' freshly greased cornrows. It's play-war, but some girls get kind of rough with it. After supervised showers, we fill up buckets and bring them into our rooms; no trips to the toilet once you're padlocked in. Sometimes I hear a girl sobbing to herself after lights go out, especially after visiting days when no one shows and you pretend you don't care, like Slick and I do. For some of us, it's understood: the only real family we have is each other, whether we like it or not.

One night Slick slips me a dog-eared copy of *Pimp: The Story of My Life*, by Iceberg Slim. I study the book for knowledge of pimp-speak, in preparation to throw my first mack. The daytime cottage matron, Miss Smith, finds the book in my room and confiscates it. She calls Iceberg Slim "triflin'," but she lets me keep the dictionary. Slick is shy about not reading well, so some nights we sit on the bleachers for a good hour working our way through the dictionary. We have fun with it—*acknowledge, acquaint, acquit*.

"Funny how words flow together," she says with a laugh.

Slick and I get out on the floor; she takes my hands and turns into her backward dance on wheels, with me trying to follow her lead. All the girls think this is beyond hilarious. Being the femme on skates for a minute is the only way I'll ever learn how to skate backward.

"Look at Slick's sissy girl!"

"Yeah, I knew she was Slick's punk!"

"What's-a-matta, girl, you can't dance on skates? Only pussies can't skate backward!"

"You all are a bunch of got-damn fools," says Slick.

I ignore them and concentrate on the task at hand. As soon as I catch my groove, I bend my knee, scoop, bob, and dance to the music. We glide around the floor, and Slick picks up speed. She spins me around, and I try to follow, skating backward. We take it slow, and I start to lead, to catch on. The girls skate figure eights around us, trying to throw me off course.

A lanky, fly stud named Bookie skates up. Bookie's more pretty boy than girl, with high cheekbones and a super-cocky smile. She wears an apple cap cocked over one eye and is always laughing, showing off her dimples.

"Hey, l'il mothafuckah! What you got? Check this out . . . wanna follow me?"

She skates like a Motown superstar. Spinning around us in circles, she makes a kissy face at me and skates away. Bookie is clearly one girl I will need to impress.

We're given a choice between Catholic and Baptist services on Sundays—no contest as far as I'm concerned. The cooks from all six cottages come to service on Sundays, and they can *really sing*! A lot of the girls are amazing too. Of all the music I've listened to, there's nothing so grand as the sound of voices singing gospel music in harmonies. And it's not about perfect notes. It's more like a messy, glorious swell of mischievous angels hollering their ecstasy, sure to raise every hair on the back of your neck with the magic of the Spirit. Listening to this music makes me feel that if there really is a God, well then, God has to be music. I memorize the songs hard my first month of Sundays. When it's time to let the bird fly out of my mouth, I wail, *We've come this far by faith / every day we are leaning, leaning on the Lord!*

I stomp, clap, and sing as loud as anyone. I don't know how I can have lungs as big as I do when I'm such a shrimp, but they sure are coming in handy on the Hill. I'm catching the Spirit and the girls feel it. They nudge each other and raise their eyebrows, smiling and nodding their heads, as if to say, *Yeah, maybe this girl's all right.*

While Slick and I walk out of church one morning, here comes Bookie, strutting in our direction. She calls me a new nickname.

"L'il Pimpin'! We want you to join our gang, but you got to fight me first. You down?"

My mask is calm and collected. I don't want to fight her. I'd much rather kiss her, even if she is trying to be a boy. She's so damned cute. I'll show her who the real boy is.

"Yeah, I'm down. Let's go."

Miss Smith likes to doze in the dayroom after church, so we quietly pad to the end of the hallway in front of Bookie's room upstairs and face off. Bookie smiles, real slow and sweet. Just like that, she shoves me against the wall, and we set to it.

"L'il mothafuckah, I will kick your ass!" she says, but she's grinning. She can't wait to put her hands on me. The feeling is mutual. We both try not to giggle while we wrestle each other down to the linoleum play-fighting, making it look real to Slick and the other girls watching. Bookie might be head and shoulders taller, but my speed is a match for her strength, and we keep flipping and pinning each other. Now I'm on top feeling her muscles squirm beneath my body. I don't know if she just lets me win or whether I really am that strong, since this is the first time I've ever won a fight. We're breathing hard. I have her arms pinned to the floor, her skinny hips bucking beneath me as I squirm on top of her, holding her in place. She gets this look on her face like she's really enjoying it too. Closing her eyes, she moans a little.

Damn Miss Smith's timing! She's huffing up the stairs yelling, "Get your butts up off that floor!"

Miss Smith yanks us up by our collars while we try not to crack up.

On our way to solitary, we pass Slick. She pats a hand on my shoulder for a job well done. Bookie grins at me.

"You cool, L'il Bit."

"Thanks, punk."

"I ain't no punk!"

She grabs my shoulder. Miss Smith steps between us.

"No touching, you two, that's enough! Lord have mercy, you need to stop!"

Bookie and I do a little jig on our separate ways to solitary, fly-stepping for each other's benefit.

Compared to Marycrest, solitary isn't as bad here. They lock us up in our own rooms for three days minimum and bring us meals on trays, and we use buckets for toilets day and night. A cottage matron escorts us to the utility closet to empty and refill, but otherwise, we're padlocked in and not allowed to shower, which is a big drag. I have a Harriet the Spy book from the library—a huge yawn.

When we get out of solitary, having been in lockup blesses us with an extra side of cool. Bookie and her stud gang decide we should all become blood brothers and don gangster names. Bookie's boyish cuteness is crowned by her new nickname of Baby Face Nelson. Frank Nitti has a cool, smoky high voice, straightened slicked-back hair, and freckles, with a temper that can flare up like sulfur off a match. Legs Diamond has a curvature of the spine that only accentuates her pimp walk, and she's funny as hell. Dillinger is a short and wiry toughie like me, and Lucky Luciano's breasts are too big for her to be a true stud, but she refuses to be a lady and is the best dancer at the school. Slick (whose name is slick enough) presides overall in her quiet, kingly way. Our mascot is a little twelve-year-old with a touch of Down's syndrome. We all feel sorry for her and call her

Slim Goody. They call me Capone. If Big Al could see me living a true gangster life that he only wished for, with black girls, his head would explode.

The biggest drag about Blossom Hill is the two shelves of books they call the "library"—*Little Women, Black Beauty, Harriet the Spy*, and maybe twenty others. Clearly donations from a few well-wishers. I've read *Harriet* three times already, am bored to death of it, and find the Bible much more exciting with its accounts of this one lying with that one, the grisly murders, the ecstasies, the poetry. The school itself is pathetic, teaching third grade math and other subjects to girls going on seventeen. The administrators do not care about our education. They understand I'll learn nothing in school, so I'm granted permission to take the afternoons off and hang out as helper to the recreation staff.

The rec staff consists of a blond guy named Mr. Lewis. Jack would call him "loose in the loafers." Miss Donelly, a tomboy with a gap between her front teeth, wants me to call her Patty.

Patty is a jock and pretty swift at basketball, but Mr. Lewis is a candy-ass who usually wimps out and leaves us to it. When I ask either of them if they're queer, they howl with laughter and deny it up and down. Patty wears T-shirts and jeans and has long brown hair and a loud, bold voice. Blossom Hill lets us wear street clothes, and the administration allows Patty to shop for me with my stipend. I have Converse sneakers now, jeans, and cool sweaters and T-shirts— all clothes a cool teenage boy would wear. I've been begging her to bring me an apple cap. She shows up with a brown speckled one, and I wear it at a just-so angle. The gang approves.

The rec staff's most ambitious project is trying to force the girls to make papier-mâché figures and masks, but most aren't having it. On the afternoons when we're not cleaning up the gym or straightening skates in the locker room, I mess around bending chicken wire into gangly human figures with the faces of wolves. I read the newspapers first, then rip strips, dunk them in pasty flour, and smooth the pieces over pointy snouts while Patty dangles her leg over a chair and grills me about my childhood. I tell her nothing. She teases me for trying to be mysterious. How do I explain that there are stories I'm just not ready to tell? No one would believe me anyway.

Miss Calloway is the nighttime cottage matron, a young, super-fine hippie. She wears blue jean elephant bell-bottoms and embroidered blouses, is a combination of Twiggy and Julie from *The Mod Squad*, with crimped long blond hair framing a heart-shaped face. She refuses to call me L'il Bit, prefers my name and says it with a French accent: Mada-*layne*. Once, on an errand for the rec staff, I started singing "I Found That Girl" by the Jackson 5 and caught her hiding around the corner of the dining room, listening.

Our friendship is sealed the day she sees me brooding over a stack of *Jet* magazines. She pads over to me smelling fresh, like strawberries and lemons.

"Not much to read, huh?"

"If I read one more word about Billy Dee Williams, they'll have to drag me out of here in a straitjacket, I don't care how fine he is."

She knows I'm starved for good books and music other than the stack of scratchy overplayed records. Anything nutritious. Diahann Carroll stares back at me from a cover of *Jet*, and I flash back to Kitty in her makeup and wig, playing Cleopatra.

Miss Calloway is pretty. Very feminine. My type. But NO WAY. Ha.

"Janis Joplin died yesterday," she says.

I shrug, keeping my eyes down. "I don't really know her songs. The nuns at Marycrest only allowed us to listen to musicals."

"She died of a drug overdose, like Jimi Hendrix. You don't plan on doing drugs when you get out of here, right?" She laughs.

"I doubt it."

I keep my eyes down, flushing red like an idiot. That's one of the drawbacks of being white: your blush shows in full bloom. She pulls a book out of her big, overstuffed purse and hands it to me. *The Female Eunuch*, by Germaine Greer. Can women be eunuchs?

"It's about feminism. I'll get in trouble if anyone finds out I gave you this. Keep it out of sight."

"This is really something, thanks!"

I try to read the book after lockdown, but the lights are switched off at nine thirty. I tell Miss Calloway about it, and the next night the padlock rattles softly outside my room. In she comes, wearing her pajamas, powder blue with a red rose pattern. I can hardly contain myself; I feel so blushy. She turns on a flashlight and hands me another book.

"You can't let anybody see these. Seriously, I'll lose my job," she whispers.

"But where can I hide them?"

"Hide them in the common room when I'm not on duty, on the top shelf behind the TV. Or under your mattress. Miss Smith will never search either spot."

Before she closes the door, she leaves me the flashlight and says, "You can call me Myn."

I scan the book: *I Sing the Body Electric!*, a collection of short stories by Ray Bradbury. I bounce between Ray and Germaine Greer all night.

Ray says, *Grandma, O dear and wondrous electric dream . . .*

Security is the denial of life, sayeth Germaine.

The first rule of courtship in Blossom Hill is that the stud is the boss. You skate up to a girl you have your eye on and ask if she wants to be your lady. If she says yes, she's hired. And when you get tired of her, you skate up and say, *"You're fired!"* Sounds simple enough, but a lady can go off on you something fierce, depending on her temperament. My first lady is Karen, from Cottage Two, and her room is on the other side of the stairs. She's a great skater but way too tall for me to feel comfortable partner skating with. Soon enough, I have my eye on someone else. Renee is shaped like an hourglass with short, marcelled hair. It's a high-maintenance hairdo that requires her to stay tight friends with Karen, queen of the hot comb and the Dixie Peach. Karen does beautiful work on heads, but only if she likes you.

She's fond of peach cobbler, and on the rare nights when the cook serves it up, Karen can count on at least six helpings of the sweet goo by the time dinner's over. Karen wasn't too happy when she heard about Renee and me, but Renee paid her off in cigarettes and cobbler to sweeten her temper. It worked. For a while.

Renee's a fantastic slow-dancer. After showers, we all hit the rec room, where we're allowed to hang out in our nylon pajamas, play records, and eat potato chips we soak in hot sauce until our eyes tear up. The minute the night matron walks away, Renee switches her hips over. We slow dance, grinding and dipping to the grooves of Smokey Robinson or the Stylistics. I croon along to "Love on a Two-Way Street" softly into her ear. Judging from the way she fits in tight when we roll our hips together, Renee loves this as much as I do.

Karen dances over with her new stud, Dillinger, but she keeps her eyes on us. Karen calls me a punk ass. Bookie is dipping a new girl who can't believe her luck. She blushes while Bookie flirts, not knowing that Bookie goes with a fine lady named Sheila from Cottage Four. Myn Calloway sees all this Romeo-ing and lets it slide. Strange, how she never tries to break us up, even when we start to make out. She pretends not to notice and lets us get on with it.

Wednesday night, Myn returns to my room. We sneak down the dark hallway, and she quietly opens the door to the supervisor's bedroom. It's much bigger than our rooms, with its own private bathroom and a comfortable reading chair. Very cozy. I sit on the edge of the chair, not knowing what to do. Myn has a portable record player next to a stack of books on her desk. She puts on *After the Goldrush* with the volume low, telling me it's her favorite new record, and I fall in love on contact with Neil's voice.

She asks me if I want to spend the night.

"Yeah, sure," I say. Sweet Jeezus. This invitation gives me the willies.

"Well, don't be shy."

She takes off her slippers and gets in the bed. I crawl in with her, careful not to touch her. She laughs softly. I'm terrified. She strokes my hair. Just a little.

Now that you find yourself losing your mind . . . sings Neil.

I want to do things that I did with Belinda, but don't dare touch Myn. She's like a goddess. The fact that she's old but not quite old enough to be my mother makes me consider it. But I know if I touch her, my heart might explode.

"You really have feelings for other girls, don't you?"

"Yeah, I guess so."

"That's not necessarily a bad thing."

I don't know how to respond, so I change the subject. "I really love the story about the grandmother in the *Body Electric* book."

"I knew you'd like it. Anything can happen in the world of science fiction."

We lie there, me staring up at the ceiling, heart pumping, listening to Neil's haunting voice. When the album ends, the silence makes the air feel like cement. Myn gets up to take the needle off the record. Careful not to touch me, she crawls back into bed and turns onto her side away from me.

"Good night, Madda-*layne*."

I can't sleep, thinking about whether I should touch her. How clumsy I'd feel. She's a real woman. What would happen if we got caught, me here in her room? I think about telling the other girls, how impressed they'll all be, but I vow to keep it secret. Someone is bound to mouth off out of jealousy. Myn would get fired and might end up in prison. Maybe they'd lock us both up in separate wings, in some hellhole like the Ohio Reformatory for Women in Marysville. The terror keeps me awake until dawn.

When Myn shakes me a full half hour earlier than the usual 6:30 A.M., I pretend to have been asleep the whole time. She walks me back to my room and locks me in. She knows I wouldn't dare tell anybody, so doesn't bother to warn me, but she seems sad. The next few nights, she hardly acknowledges me—until a week later, when she comes to my room again, saying she has a surprise for me. We slide quietly down the hallway.

Myn unlocks Renee's door—I can't believe it! Frightened, Renee jumps up in bed, and I rush over: "*Shhh.*" Renee catches at her heart, sees it's me, and giggles softly. "Boo," says Casper the Ghost Girl. Myn closes the door behind us, locks us in tight. Renee opens the covers.

That night, because I know I'm different and will always be, because Renee is so soft and sweet and I think I might love her, I teach myself to do many things I imagine people like me, girls who love other girls, do in the sweetness of night. Things Slick has told me about. Things I'd have loved to do with Myn Calloway if I wasn't so shy.

I sing down there to her moves and moans while giving every known and unknown muscle of my mouth plenty of practice. She tastes like cantaloupe. I wonder if all girls do.

There's a bulging blister on the web beneath my tongue the next morning. Eating toast makes me wince, the crumbs, like salt in a burn. Myn smirks; I blush into my oatmeal. It isn't so complicated after all—Myn Calloway is my personal angel, loving me the best way she can.

I show my buddies the blister, but don't spill the details. Renee confirms it to her lady friends, but we tell everybody we snuck behind the curtains on the gym stage and did it standing up. Plenty of raised eyebrows as the news spreads through the school like wildfire. Bookie just will not let it be; she has to know everything. "Did you get hairs caught in your teeth? Did she cream on your nose?" I push her off, and we hit the ground laughing and rolling. Meanwhile, it seems like the ladies want me that much more, enough to tip me right over the edge into superstardom. Capone has truly arrived.

When I sing to the ladies, it's magic. I'm the supreme gangster of love. The power has me hiring and firing ladies like it's a game of dominoes, determined to have all the girls pass through my stable. I fired Renee because someone from Cottage One caught my eye.

"Damn, you are cold, Capone!" says Bookie with a grin.

Damn right I am. Renee was getting too clingy anyhow. We studs have one another's backs when it comes to our exes. Slick broke up with Trash too, and lately I find myself checking out Trash a little bit too often, although I wouldn't dare touch her. She's white—bad for my image—not to mention Slick's ex. But she sure is cute—petite and curvy with long dark hair and a bubble butt. Unusual for white girls, who Slick says have butts like pancakes. I agree.

Most of these ladies are straight on the outs. Studs like me, Slick, and a few others are different. We are what we are—queer!—and there'll be no changing inside the joint or out.

It's not that I don't think boys can be cute, but I'd rather *be* one, not *beneath* one. But sometimes I imagine being with girls like this out in the world and having some gang of bullies beat me to death for it, like Izzy tried to. How much will I have to hide? Well, the real world is far away. Right now, I'm in heaven and life is beautiful.

Bookie and I go to the administration building to speak to Mr. Summers about a talent show. Mr. Summers, principal and chief administrator, is a light-skinned guy with wavy blondish hair. He's a stylish dresser, always smiling. Lots of the girls have crushes on him. We're telling him how excited we are about showing the world our exceptional talents. We need microphones and professional equipment. *"Come on, Summers!"* we beg. He excuses himself, leaving the office for a minute. A few neckties hang on the back of his office door. We snatch the ties, stuff them down our pants, and take off. Our gang's first successful heist.

That night in Cottage Two, dinnertime is showtime. We wait until all the girls are seated before making our entrance. With a grand flourish, Slim Goody opens the French doors, head held high. She marches in clapping her hands, clearing her throat.

"Attention! Al Capone and Baby Face Nelson will grace us today with their presence. Please do not look at them unless they look at you first. Here they are . . . the honorable Al Capone . . . and Baby Face Nelson!"

Karen and Renee make little laughs of disgust as the other girls regard Bookie and I pimp-strutting into the dining room. Stone-faced. Cold-blooded. Renee cackles and sets all the femmes to giggling like six-year-olds as we approach our chairs. We don't crack; we glare forward, over everyone's heads. Slim pulls out my chair first, ceremoniously dusts it off with a napkin, then runs like a rabbit over to Bookie's chair and does the same. I don't sit until Slim's done with both chairs. Bookie and I nod to each other, straighten our ties, and bend our bodies into place—two ballerina pimps about to hold court.

That's when I see her in the hallway through the French doors: the Cottage Two counselor, Miss Hennenboch. Observing. Hennenboch is pretty and smart but is also a pain in the ass, thinking she knows what's best for everyone. She opens the French doors.

"Madeleine, get over here. Right now."

The sound of my real name cracks everybody up. Damn. I follow orders with all the dignity I can muster. Why isn't she calling Bookie out too?

As soon as I'm eye to eye with Hennenboch, she closes the French doors, but all the girls can watch us clearly through the glass as she yells at me. She hauls off and slaps me so hard, I feel the hot handprint rising on my face.

The entire dining room gasps.

She grabs my arm, drags me upstairs to her office, and slams the door. All this over a necktie? Has she lost her mind?

"Take that tie off."

"Why did you hit me?"

"Who on earth do you think you are?"

"I was just having some fun. Why didn't you yell at Bookie too?"

"I'll deal with her later, and her name is Yvonne. What's your name these days? Capone, is it?"

She snarls at me while leaning back in her chair. I hope she falls over.

"Do you think you're a man?"

"No, I think I'm in jail, trying to have some fun."

"Don't get clever with me. Do you think you're like these girls? Do you really?"

"I don't know what you mean."

"You're not like them. Do you hear me?"

"Are you telling me that I'm white? I know that."

"No, smart mouth, that you're not ignorant. You are not like these girls when it comes to your future. Not to mention your life will be hard enough without you thinking you're a homosexual. You're not queer. It's unnatural, do you understand? You'll never make it out there if you act like you are, or if you even think it."

"Are you saying these girls are ignorant because they're black?"

Her eyes are about to pop out of her skull. "You're lucky I don't slap you again! Don't put words in my mouth! Now go to your room, you're in solitary for the rest of the day. And where did you get the ties?"

I shrug, still smarting from the slap and the lecture. I can't even look at her. So what if I'm queer, so what? It's my life.

"Never mind, just hand it over."

I undo the tie and toss it on her desk. I wish I could strangle her with it.

In my solitude daydreaming, Jack comes to the rescue. He's springing me out in a blaze of military glory when high-pitched screams and a commotion jolts me out of the dream and into a sharp smell piercing the air. Something's burning. Miss Smith is jostling around downstairs, hushing everybody. Footsteps pad quickly up the stairs, and Bookie whispers through my door that Karen went off on Renee. She says Karen was straightening Renee's hair when suddenly her eyes went all voodoo. She picked up the red-hot straightening comb, grinned, and pressed it into Renee's cheek. Bookie says you could hear skin sizzling like bacon. Damn. I hope this wasn't about me. Renee will have a scar, no doubt.

It seems like the most violent events in the school go down between the ladies, not the studs. Rough stuff just doesn't happen often, but you can sense the anger sometimes, jumping just beneath the surface, like things could blow at any moment. Sometimes a brain pops and a girl might be gouged with a shard of glass from a broken plate, or bruised with a butter knife too dull to cut. That's the worst it gets. I guess that can be thought of as pretty bad.

I can't sleep tonight, thinking about a graveyard of letters with no addresses. When I'm alone, my lines get hazy. I don't know who I am sometimes, aside from hungry. Starving for so much, for the world to deliver. Tonight, I'm a sailor, kicking through a sea of letters. Wandering through tombstones bearing names I don't recognize. In another country, on to another port now: Ireland, England, France, Italy. Connect the dots, collect the hearts. I bury my head and sing a low moan into my pillow, singing for a girl I haven't met. She sings back about how she too is longing for someone to talk to.

I take off my clothes and lie across the narrow bed, shoulder blades like skinny pink wings. Wings batting like a dragonfly's in a wild garden of names. Of girls who were here before me, who've lain on this same mattress, their sweat, the music of their days, settling over their pores like a misty second skin. Little girl criminals. Sinners for having rebelled against the lack of love. Delinquents, punished for not having arrived on time or for having arrived at all. We come together here in the night, one into another like the petals of flowers mixing, crushing in tight dances. Colors bleeding over the sheets . . .

Roses. Violets. Hyacinths.
names tattooed across my body
over my skull beneath my hair
on every inch of my skin.
Mary Maria Rosa Christine
Annie Belinda Alicia Jeanne
Holy and lost.
Lost and found.

13

NINA THE QUEEN

Blossom Hill can award high school diplomas, but I bet a diploma from here isn't worth the ink it's written with. Hennenboch told me being a ward of the state can help you attend college, and sometimes the state will pay for your education. Still, it's left up to each of us to figure out how to claw our way through the paperwork, get a diploma or a GED, and try to work the system for a chance. When we leave, we're on our own. Some girls join the Job Corps. I hear others fall into crime on the outs. Accustomed to jail life, where you're guaranteed a bed and three square meals a day, some pull dangerous stunts for a one-way ticket to prison.

I'm not concerned about an education these days. I'm concerned about love. Once a month, the bus from downtown brings new arrivals to Blossom Hill from the detention home. Girls working in the administration building pound the drums, the beats reaching us quickly about each new girl's look, crime, and attitude.

I'm playing five-card stud with Baby Face after school when Frank Nitti bursts in to tell us about a new arrival. Nitti looks spooked, acting all nervous. Baby Face places her hands on Nitti's shoulders.

"Calm down, Nitti, dag!"

"What's her name?" I ask.

"Nina Charles. Wait till you see her. I wanna hear how hard you'll be laughing then."

Nitti's expression is dead serious—you'd think she just witnessed the Second Coming.

"She is the finest lady you have ever laid eyes on. And man, if you mess with her, she looks like she'll cut you and not think twice about it. You are in for a shock."

The next day, I'm at the gym with the rec staff when Bookie beckons me from the doorway with her serious face on—a rare occurrence.

"What happened? Somebody die?"

"L'il Bit, I just saw Nina Charles walk down the hallway with Summers."

Bookie takes off her cap and snatches the do-rag from her head, wipes her brow, acting all dramatic.

"You and Nitti have lost your minds!"

"She's too fine for words, Bit. We need to make a plan. Later."

She smacks me five and rushes off. I'm perplexed. How can some new girl wipe the permanent smirks off Bookie's and Nitti's faces?

Saturday afternoon, while nearly everyone else is at rec period, Bookie and I walk down campus to Cottage Four. We've decided to present ourselves to Nina with all the authority our gangsterhood commands. We walk up to the door, knock, and hear old Miss Harris, the Cottage Four matron, shuffle toward us and flip the locks one by one.

"What you all want?"

"We wanna meet the new girl. Is she here?"

Lucky for us, Miss Harris doesn't really have a clue about what we're up to. Like the rest of the day matrons, she's a kind old custodian, jangling her keys and rousting herself just enough to lock and unlock doors according to the clock.

"I'll go get her, y'all stay put."

Bookie and I wait, posing—me in striped bell-bottom jeans and a brown-and-gold T-shirt. I lay my left hand on top of my upper left thigh and lean all my weight onto the right foot while I stroke an imaginary beard. We check each other out, grinning and nodding. I hear music from the dayroom—Martha Reeves and the Vandellas, "Love (Makes Me Do Foolish Things)."

The door opens.

First it's her posture. Nina stands like a goddess, posing with one hand on her hip, her head held so high it seems as if it might float away. Her skin is smooth, and her Afro is like a soft halo around her head, browns and reds and ochers and shades of chestnut in there all woven through. A perfectly shaped 'fro, like Angela Davis's. Her cheekbones are high, eyebrows perfect, eyes almond-shaped, and lips like cherries and—

"Who are you, and what do you want?"

Nina is not smiling. The intensity of her expression shows a fierce intelligence burning like a small fire between her eyebrows.

I have never seen anyone so beautiful in all my life. I try to maintain my stance despite my terror. Bookie goes tongue-tied. I clear my throat.

"We came here to introduce ourselves. I'm the honorable Al Capone, and this here is Baby Face Nelson. We are pleased to make your acquaintance, Miss Charles, and to welcome you to Blossom Hill."

I offer a dignified nod and shift my weight. Bookie says, nervous-like, "Yeah, welcome."

Nina cocks her head a little, considering what she's just heard and witnessed. Her lips don't show the slightest curl toward a smile. She stares coldly, as if we're strange specimens, like shellfish moored in the sand and she's deciding whether to make a meal of us or fly off.

She laughs in our faces. "I'm the queen of Alexandria. What a pleasure it is to meet you! Well, goodbye for now, pimps."

And with that, she throws the door closed with a curt little slam.

It all begins with humility. Acting pimpish is clearly not the way to this girl's heart, so I search within myself and think long and hard about what to do, which track to take, which pose to strike or whether to strike at all. Word travels fast in Blossom Hill. Within hours I hear rumors about Nina, like:

— She's in because of truancy and violence, the details
of which are unknown. (I doubt the violence part. She's
refined.)

— She was a drug dealer at her school in Hough and got
busted with a kilo of marijuana. (Not likely. She doesn't
seem like the social type.)

— Something went down with a family member, but nobody knows what. (Possible.)

She's a straight-A student, skipped a grade and is now in eleventh. (Good luck learning anything in here, Nina.) She keeps to herself. The only person she speaks to is Wanda, another solitary girl from Cottage Four who is extremely sweet and beautiful in a different way from Nina. Wanda is small and wiry and wears her hair in neat, short plaits. She smiles without showing her teeth, like me, but I doubt she has an overbite. She seems like she's afraid to take up space. Wanda doesn't play the game—a bad sign. Maybe Nina is against the game. Maybe she's married. Or religious?

I decide to keep it low-key with Nina. I see her in the evenings at rec period. The first few nights, I read and stay quiet on the bleachers, just watching. Watching her walk. Her posture and the precision of her gestures give her a regal air. She's always hanging around with Wanda, sitting on the bleachers, or skating partner style with Wanda. Always with Wanda, who shows her teeth for the first time, delighted that the prettiest and smartest girl in school has chosen her as her best friend.

I imagine my position on the bleachers gives off a powerful aura. I fired my latest lady, Trina, and every time she circles past me on her skates, she scowls. Nina steals a look over at me sometimes while she glides around the gym with Wanda, but when I catch her, she turns away immediately.

Nitti, Legs Diamond, Slick, and Bookie have all hit on her in their own ways, only to get the cold shoulder. This earns her the nickname the Ice Queen. One night, while I'm dancing to "Ball of Confusion," she skates by and stops to bend down and retie her skate laces. I say to her softly, so nobody else can hear, "Ah, the queen of Alexandria."

She smiles, pulling her body up into position like a ballerina. As soon as our eyes meet, I do a smooth spin away. She snorts a little air through her nostrils, like I have a lot of nerve, and with that sly little smile skates off without another glance in my direction all night long. Nina is haughty. I admire a proud woman.

After a few of these solitary rec periods, I decide on a surprise charm attack. I rise as if from the dead to skate alone around the gym, singing along to "Signed, Sealed, Delivered (I'm Yours)." Nina's watching. I'm vigilant, refusing to look at her. Let her make up what she wants to about me. Let her laugh at me. Wonder about me. Think I'm an idiot. Hate me because I'm white, hate me because I'm acting black. I don't care what she thinks, as long as she's thinking about me.

Al Green is crooning "I Can't Get Next to You," and Nina skates alone, gliding like a swan on a frozen lake. I get my nerve up to skate alongside her. She doesn't skate away.

"Hi."

She smiles, doesn't look at me. She says hi back—sweetly, I think. The wings of the Holy Spirit flutter around my heart.

"So. What do you think of this place?" I ask.

"I never was partial to jails."

"Some people's minds are like jails. What are you in here for?"

"None of your business," she says with a smile. "What about you?"

"Grand larceny. Extortion. Kidnapping."

"Not murder?"

Is she flirting with me?

"I shot Lee Harvey Oswald, but don't tell nobody."

She goes quiet for a minute and stares at me. I guess the joke flopped.

"You are really strange."

I blush.

"Why do you act like them?"

"Like who?"

"Like these fools who think they're pimps. Your buddies."

I shrug a little. "I yam what I yam."

"Oh, now you're Popeye? More like Mighty Mouse."

"Maybe. Maybe a little of both." I keep skating, donning my best mysterious smirk. Thinking I might just fry up from the heat shooting off her smiling eyes.

"You are something else. Do you know what a real pimp does? A pimp puts a woman out on the streets, makes her do filthy things, takes all her money, and beats her. Is that the career you want?"

"It's just a game. You know, acting."

I'm a bit thrown, will never believe what pimps get up to in Iceberg Slim's book is what Slick really does on the outs. It's a game to me. An act. Nina's still smiling, but I know she's serious, testing me. Truth is, I don't know who the hell I am. I'm whoever I need to be to stay safe.

"You need to get real. If you wanna talk to me, be real. I don't play the game. Unless you missed it, I am not a child and am not no n-word. A black woman, yes, n-word, never, and I don't play with no n-words or pimps, be they black, white, or calico."

She skates off, head held high. Everybody stares. You'd think we were in a movie. I keep skating, pretending like everything is fantastic, when I really want to crawl into a dark hole with my cripple of a heart and disappear.

It comes to pass that Nina and I are a couple. It comes to pass because I drop the act whenever I approach her and speak very politely. I try to be myself. Sometimes we'll sit on the bleachers or we'll skate and talk, and she'll tell me little bits about herself and her life. When I become too inquisitive, she'll shut me up with a "none of your business" and a secret smile that means some doors might always be locked, and I'll just have to deal.

The most I tell her is that my mother is crazy and gave me up to the state. Her mother died when she was very young, leaving her alone with her father. She doesn't say much about him. She'll talk about how proud he was of her academics, how he encouraged her, but then she'll grow dark and say she hates him.

"Hell, that's why I'm in here, because of my father. He's lucky I didn't kill him."

She won't tell me why, but I can guess. The bastard.

When she asks about my past, I tell her about the foster homes, running away, Kitty and Al—but I spare the goriest details because, quite frankly, I just don't care enough to talk about it. She never digs too hard, which is fine by me. I talk about the writers I love: Edgar Allan Poe, Charles Dickens, and Percy Shelley. She tells me about wanting to be a nurse someday, how she's going to college when she gets out. She's determined. Knows what she wants. She smiles a bright, sparkly-eyed smile whenever I sing along to a record, something by the Jackson 5 like "Who's Lovin' You." But she turns cold whenever she catches me playing pimp.

Last night I hung out in Myn Calloway's room and it wasn't uncomfortable at all. Myn and I listen to groups and singers I never get to hear in the rec room. She plays a record by a white girl named Laura Nyro, whose voice is extraordinary and weirdly high-pitched. The album is called *Christmas and the Beads of Sweat*, and many of the lyrics are dark, mysterious. I want Myn to turn it up—it's so amazing—but we keep the volume low, or else, trouble.

She looks tired, dark circles under her eyes. I ask her what's up, and she tells me she's been going to school during the day, working here at night, and not getting any rest. She's about to get her degree to teach English. She'll be leaving Blossom Hill in August, just before the new school year, moving down to Columbus for a teaching job.

"I wish I could send you books after I leave, but we aren't supposed to have contact. I've got a new one for you, though."

Myn hands me *I Know Why the Caged Bird Sings*, by Maya Angelou.

I'm on an errand for the rec staff when I catch Nina walking alone down the hall. I try the handle on the utility closet. It's unlocked. I grab her hand, she giggles, and we rush into the dark closet and close the door. She smells like breakfast, like jam and butter. Smiling through the dark, she says, "You are so bold."

I lace my arms around her waist. She places her delicate hands on my forearms. I kiss her. Her lips are like cherries, smooth and firm. She presses back but holds her lips closed and gives me these short kisses like she's nervous. I put my top lip between hers and hold her bottom lip ever so softly between mine. She shivers a little. Her arms wrap around my shoulders; mine go tighter around her waist, my hands clasped at the small of her back. Her breasts move against mine, and she slides her tongue into my mouth. It's getting hot in here. She breaks away.

"We gotta go, we'll get caught."

I don't want to let go, but I do. A last touch, running my hands over her hips.

I must admit, I'm proud that the smartest and most beautiful girl in school is mine. But it might be getting under the skin of my buddies. When I'm in the gym around Baby Face, Nitti, and Dillinger, I'm still Capone and don't need to prove anything to anyone. We're still family; Slim Goody is my child, Bookie is my brother. But I'm breaking the rules because I won't talk about Nina. I keep her to myself and the gang doesn't like it. It's about walking a fine line between respect for my buddies and respect for Nina. Nina's more important.

The talent show is set for Fourth of July weekend. We'll perform on the gym's main floor, and the audience will sit in the bleachers. Everybody's excited about coming up with an act, especially because family will be invited, and we'll have a chance to prove our worth to everyone who called us worthless. I'm used to no one showing up for me. My performance is for Nina. We've put together a trio, like the Supremes or the Sweet Inspirations. Slick asks me to do a comedy act with her for that Mickey & Sylvia song, "Love Is Strange" and against all odds, I agree to play femme. The rec staff promises to help with costumes. I plan my outfit around a silly going-to-church hat and dress as Peaches. We play our roles, Slick mackin', me doing my best Flip Wilson. It's ridiculous and fun as hell.

Nina, Wanda, and I call ourselves Love, Peace, and Charity—Nina's idea. It's corny, but I take Charity because I love Shirley MacLaine. We decide to do three songs: "I'm So Proud," by the Impressions (Nina's and my special song); "Sweet Inspiration," by the Sweet Inspirations (which all three of us can sing together and do solos on); and a big production number to finish: "Aquarius/Let the Sunshine In," by the 5th Dimension. For this finale, we'll take care of the vocals, and five other girls will dance behind us. Bookie agreed to be one of the dancers. She can't hold a note to save her life, but she really wants to participate. Slim Goody, Trash, and two other white girls from Cottage Six, Ruth and Lizzie, are the backup dancers. I've choreographed an interpretive dance with moves based on routines I remember from *The Ed Sullivan Show*.

When "Aquarius" begins, we three singers will stand in the middle of the stage, swaying from side to side as the dancers walk solemnly around us in formation. The dancers hold their bodies tight, postures like real ballerinas, with high steps. I want them to glide. When I show them how to do it, Bookie cracks up, and the dancers fall down laughing, practically peeing themselves. Even I have to laugh. Finally, Nina gets serious and backs me up, saying if we all do this right, we'll be the stars of the show. My baby has my back!

After the second rehearsal, the embarrassment begins to wear off and things go a little better. Most of the white girls know it's a privilege to even share the same space with girls like Nina, so they fall in line. Lizzie holds her own and never tries to act black or be anything other than herself. I admire her for that.

Before long, the girls run and jump from the back of the line to the front, waving their arms during the choruses. Even Slim Goody goes down on one knee, arms outstretched and swaying, for the dawning of the Age of Aquarius!

Something else is about to dawn. And it has nothing to do with peace guiding our planet or love steering the stars.

A new girl just hit campus. Her name is Mary, but everyone calls her Moe. She hates white people and makes it known by sneering at us every time she glances our way. She walks around all tight, like a balled fist. A mean stud, hair peppering her head like ball bearings, and one of her front teeth is missing. The hole doesn't stop her from flashing a menacing smile at the ladies. The femmes love her. I guess they find meanness strangely handsome.

Moe takes over the scene at Blossom Hill as soon as she steps on campus. Even Slick steers clear of her. Before her heels cool from the trip in, Moe hires Karen (my ex, the hot-comb girl) to be her lady. People say Moe nearly killed one of her white teachers on the outs, and her brother was a black nationalist in Hough.

She lives in Cottage Six, which means I don't really see her outside of rec periods. But on those nights when we're in the gym, she stares at me across the room, murder in her eyes. I heed the message and steer clear.

A wave of excitement pulses through the joint when Moe puts together the black nationalist drill team, a last-minute contribution to the talent show.

Mr. Summers demands that at least a couple of white girls be included. Because Trash and I are the only two white girls with any rhythm, we're in. To add insult to injury, not only are we in, but because we're both shorties, we will be leading the two columns. Having us twerpy white girls leading her team annoys the hell out of Moe. I can understand why, since it really is a black thing, but you don't say no to Mr. Summers.

Moe plays it cool with us at first, especially since Summers usually attends these rehearsals. What can she do, really?

She teaches us the steps, barking out the commands as hands clap and heels slap down in fierce rhythms, echoing through the gymnasium. I can pull off the steps, and Trash isn't a slouch either. Summers is so impressed that he buys the drill team uniforms: black trousers, black berets, and bright yellow short-sleeved shirts. We think we're extremely fly, but probably resemble a hive of mackin' bumblebees. Moe is the drill sergeant marching up and down the line, giving a talk to the troupe about posture and neatness, black power, dignity, and pride. Gangsters start giving the power sign, greeting each other with:

"As-salaam alaikum!"

"Wa-alaikum salaam!"

One day, when Summers isn't supervising, the tone of her talk changes.

"Us African people gotta rise up to whitey and take what's ours. Remember this: no white person is your friend. You are a fool to ever trust a honky. When you look at a honky, you better know that their daddy or granddaddy tortured and bound your ancestors in slavery, their great-granddaddy raped your black grandmother. You can never trust white devils."

Moe narrows her eyes at Trash. Trash's eyes dart around in a panic. Then Moe walks toward me, stares me down in a long moment of silence. Before Moe breaks her stare, she aims and spits. The spit hits one of my shoes. Not a peep from the drill team. Everyone is petrified. Right now, all I want to do is kick Moe's ass from here to Detroit. Big Al was racist, but he never hurt a black person, he would have been too scared. I am the descendant of folks from Sicily and Ireland, and those places did not have black slaves, as far as I could tell.

"Liar." I say it under my breath. I can't help it, the word sneaks out. And Moe hears it.

"What the fuck did you just say? Little white bull dagger, did you just call me a liar? Bitch, come right up to my face and say it again."

Just as Moe calls me out, Mr. Summers appears, possibly saving my life.

14

DEAD GIRL WALKING

Nina tells me she's leaving Blossom Hill. First, the news about Myn. Now Nina?

"They're releasing me so I can finish senior year on the outs and get a proper diploma."

I play it off like I'm happy for her. And I am, really. But what about . . . us?

"Will you go home to your father?"

"There's nowhere else to go. He's coming to the show, that son of a bitch. Ha!"

She turns away, smoothing the hem of her dress. Nina always makes this short laugh, one syllable—"Ha!"—air hot from her nostrils, when she talks about her father. It's like she's pushing out something she can't control, and it becomes funny instead of angry or sad. Still, the anger beneath is not to be mistaken.

"What about your people. Will they be at the show?" she asks.

"What people? I told you, my mother… she gave me up." I laugh a little because it's no big deal.

"Every one of us has people, no matter how they treat us."

I want to hug her and tell her she's my person, and I feel like it's what she wants me to do but instead, I fake a stomachache and say I should get back to my cottage. She drops a single on the record player, "If I Were Your Woman," by Gladys Knight and the Pips, and she's standing there with this strange smile, singing along to the record while I walk away. She sways, lost in the music. Is she singing this song to me?

Whenever I feel lonesome, I think of snow. Leaving the gym, I pretend I'm walking through a snowstorm smoking a Kool with that song in my head. Why did she have to put that record on? And what'll

I do here without Nina? She'll leave, like Myn Calloway. Like everybody else. And I'll never hear from her again.

In Cottage Two, the other girls are upstairs getting ready for bed. I can hear them laugh and screech from outside the front door. Myn Calloway lets me in.

"Can I hang around downstairs and listen to some records? Please?"

She can tell I'm upset. She pulls out a cigarette, my ration for the next day.

"You really should be upstairs getting ready for bed, but fine. Keep the volume low. I'll come back for you."

Off she goes, swooshing her elephant bells along the steps, smelling like Love's Fresh Lemon. I sit in the dark smoking my Kool, but I don't feel like putting on a record. I've heard these 45s a million times. Myn returns.

"What are you doing sitting in the dark? Being mysterious?"

"Yeah." I laugh. "I'm bored with our records."

"Listen to this new one."

She puts an album on, Carole King. I like the song about the earth moving but that song "Home Again". It's too sad. Damn.

Myn decides to get serious. "You're gonna be okay when you get out of here. Better than okay. You'll see."

"Thanks."

I take a long drag and stare out the window at the imaginary snowstorm. How can I know what I want when I don't know who I am? I can't even cry. Even when I try these days, it doesn't work. I get up the nerve to tell Myn I'm gonna miss her. She cuts the deck and we play gin rummy long into the night.

It's showtime! Nina is first up, singing "Sweet Inspiration." That's my baby! Visitors filling the bleachers give her a round of applause to spur her on. Summers has set us up with a real microphone, and Nina wields it like a professional, doing little graceful steps and hand gestures while she sings. I get nervous, so Dillinger steps in for me on backing vocals. Nina is singing her heart out, and people in the audience start to clap to the beat of the song. Wanda and Dillinger sing whoops and backing coos. The gym is huge, so the voices echo over the record player and sound fantastic.

Out of the corner of my eye, I catch Moe arguing with Mr. Summers by the side of the bleachers. He's getting more agitated. Finally, he just waves his hands in the air and walks away from her in a huff. Moe stomps into the locker room, fuming.

The show goes on. I sing "I'm So Proud," and we get a massive round of applause from the families and friends. I can see Nina's father in the audience, a tall, handsome, mean-looking man, sitting alone in a nice dress shirt and slacks. He doesn't clap or smile, just nods his head to the beat for Nina's song.

No one came for me as usual, but I'm happy to be singing. Myn Calloway is here, sitting in front like a Greek goddess in a white high-waisted hippie dress cheering me on.

When it's finally time for Nina and Wanda to back me up on "Got to Be There," I'm a nervous wreck, but I still sing my heart out on every word, opening my chest to let it rip on the highest note, nearly falling over on the last spin. People start clapping before I finish the song, and my heart feels like it will burst.

That's when I notice Moe stomping back and forth between the bleachers and the locker room which serves as our dressing room. I'm headed back there with Love and Peace when Bookie grabs me aside.

"Moe is hating on you, Capone. Watch out."

This is not exactly what I want to hear after singing my heart out and feeling the love.

"What else is new, Bookie?"

Now it's Moe's turn to shine as she directs the drill team. The sound of rhythmic steps echoes through the gym like syncopated thunder, the applause following like a rainstorm. Moe is proud, taking the props and bowing. I hear she wanted Trash and me dropped from the team at the very last minute. Summers wouldn't have it.

After the show, all the girls hang out with whatever family showed up for them. There's cake and other refreshments. And for me, many smiles and people coming up to say, "You can SING, girl!"

Best of all, Myn is by my side like a proud big sister.

The next day, I skate up to Nina, still high from the show. Moe watches me as she rounds the gym, partner skating with Karen. They laugh when they pass us, and Moe makes a kissy sound at Nina. Nina lets go of my hands and skates away. Completely confused, I follow.

"You mad at me?"

She shakes her head in disappointment, says,

"*Why* are you mad at me. Girl, speak properly."

"Okay… you seem mad. Why?"

"Moe is out to get you, and I can't be around it. Sorry. I'm leaving soon and don't need trouble."

I look over at Moe; she stares back with her usual evil. I guess I shouldn't have called her a liar.

"So that's it?"

"That's it. This game shit is done."

Nina skates away. Conversation, over like a slap. I try to act cool, shake my head and laugh a little, like she just said something funny. But when I turn my head, there's Moe, huddled with the others across the gym. Watching.

Word travels fast about Nina firing me. A real stud *never* gets fired—we're the ones always doing the hiring and firing. At least Nina isn't going with anybody else. I know her enough to guess that she'll stay single until she leaves.

Moe has pretty much taken over our rec nights, skating around with Karen like they're the king and queen of the Hill. Moe's in deep now with my buddies, and they're all freezing me out. Slick, ever faithful, says I'd better be cool because Moe's the real deal, a killer with a rep. I bluff, saying I'll kick Moe's ass into a lump of ground chuck.

The window of my room faces east. Blue-white light from the full moon bleeds through the crosshatched metal gate on the window. I do push-ups and practice my left hook in the stainless steel panel of a mirror, searching for clues, praying I'll survive Moe's hate.

I've become the enemy because they're all scared of Moe.

My eyes search the steel mirror. One well-angled kick from Moe's skate and my head shatters like a snow globe. No, she'd never be that gutless, she's too proud. She's at least forty pounds heavier than me and taller by a foot. But I've got the speed. I've got the spark to cause the explosion that'll force her down in the first round. I still have Slick, no matter that the rest of the gang thinks she's old and played out. And Slim Goody still smiles through heavy-lidded eyes and says, "Hi, Daddy!" whenever she sees me.

Nina is not about to make a fool out of me, and the same goes for the gang and Moe. I will not cower in a corner like sad-sack Eeyore in *Winnie-the-Pooh*. I'm tired of it, tired of being picked on, tired of the burning feeling in my chest. I will be victorious.

Marvin Gaye sings "That's the Way Love Is" while I skate the gym, nose wide open for a new fly girl named Niecy Johnson. Little Niecy is just my size, a perfect match in curve and roll, with a big freedom 'fro and a way of shifting her weight when she's near me that signals a come-on. She approaches the bleachers, looking me up and down.

"Whatcha reading, baby?"

That's all I need to hear. I tell her to meet me in five minutes behind the heavy velvet curtain on the gym stage. Nina's watching us; she swings her head nose-first to the sky.

I see Niecy take the stairs to the stage, wait a minute, then follow when I think no one will notice. She stands there smiling sweetly at me in the dark. I take her gently in my arms and whisper in her ear, *"Baby, huh?"* as she moves herself up against me.

A hand grabs the collar of my shirt from behind and wheels me around.

"Who the fuck you think you are, rubbing up against my cousin? L'il Pimpin', my ass!"

It's Moe. Niecy ducks behind her. I've been set up. Moe's hands shake as she grabs and holds tight to my hair. I stare her straight in the eyes, grinning like I don't care when inside I'm jelly.

"Bad luck for her, being related to you."

Moe's eyes go the darkest yet as she yanks hard on my hair, holding tight. It feels like my scalp will burst blood, but I don't flinch.

"Bitch, you are finished, you hear?"

Patty calls out that rec period is over and to put our skates away. Moe lets go of me and walks away with Niecy running behind.

That night I look around my room, taking in what might be my last sorry memories. The tatty wooden drawers built into the nook with the steel plate bolted above, the photos torn from magazines on the walls. Angela Davis giving a power salute. Bob Dylan looking like a girl in his *Highway 61 Revisited* days. Sonny Liston splayed out on the canvas with Muhammad Ali towering over him in a victory stance—first round, first minute. Jack smoking in his MP uniform with *Nha Trang, 1968* scrawled in blue ink on the border.

I imagine a blanket of flowers covering my bed. I want to lie there and dream, but tonight is for finding courage, for practicing left hooks in the mirror. I inspect my face in the half-light so that I might see clearly. See that I'm ugly. Know why I work so hard to make up for it. Know that I'm wearing a mask. Knowing I have to hide what's beneath as best as I can.

So that I might be dangerous.

The next night, I walk into the gym, cold and ready as I'll ever be. None of the gang meets my gaze except for Slick. She shoots me a bolt of courage and a power sign. I salute back as Moe strolls over to me.

"You ready to throw down? Act friendly while we go into the locker room."

Moe throws an arm around my shoulder so Patty and Mr. Lewis will think we're just going in for our skates. We slide across the gym, everyone's eyes on us. At the back of the locker area, we face off as the gangsters file in.

They watch. Traitors. Moe punches me in the chest. I'm made of steel. She spits, it hits my cheek. I pretend it doesn't faze me.

"White little bitch. Did your mama love n*gg*s too?"

Nobody insults Kitty, even if she is a lunatic. And nobody is ever gonna kick my ass again. Everything turns red; something inside me screams murder.

I pull my right fist back like a bow and throw every pound of my body weight into a punch straight at Moe's face. She flies back against the locker. My dukes are up in a boxing stance as her hand touches her nose in disbelief. Suddenly she's on me, catching me square on the jaw with her fist. I punch her hard in the stomach, kick her leg out and knock her down.

We're on the floor, rolling and punching, and I'm fighting with all I have but Moe is winning. Her forearm presses on my throat. In my mind, the words of Kahlil Gibran echo with the sound of my mother's voice: *Defeat, my Defeat . . . in you I have found aloneness / And the joy of being shunned and scorned...*

"Enough! What the hell is going on in here?"

Mr. Summers and Patty drag Moe and me apart. All you can hear is panting, heavy breaths. Patty pulls me to my feet.

"Who started this?"

Summers has a hold of Moe. We don't look at each other, mouths clamped tight. I can hardly keep my balance.

"You know this means solitary for a month. L'il Bit, Moe, I'm taking you to the infirmary. Then you're both going straight to the hole."

We file out into the gym: the warden, the traitors, Moe, then me. The girls gather around to watch the procession. It feels like the longest walk of my life but I'm still breathing, still alive by some miracle of God. Or the Devil. My forehead is trickling blood, face numb, body shot full of pain. Still, I hold my spine erect and keep moving. Nobody speaks. A few girls flash Moe the power sign, and she gives them a victory smile. I keep moving forward. Shaking, I hold myself steady, hot face swelling. I will not turn my head, even when I hear Nina whisper, "Pathetic," as I pass her.

Push on. Moving forward through faces, none offering an anchor. Except for Slick. She stands apart. I see what I think is a tear in her eye, a tiny prick of light. I steer my hope toward that light to wash away the violence wanting to burrow inside me. The ugly, twisted thing that could grow into a hydra, casting its shadow over any truths I still cling to in my soul.

In solitary, again. I punch a fist into the wall so many times the knuckles bleed and bone peeks through. The only time I feel anything is when I try to sing, but my voice cracks, flooding like a leaky boat. I can't get through a single line without the notes burning my blood. Blood like lava, like hot poison seeping through me.

Nina leaves Blossom Hill the day after I'm released from solitary. Myn Calloway tells me what time she'll be walking up the campus from Cottage Four toward the administration building, and I make sure the rec staff sends me on an imaginary errand.

The day is dark with heavy brown rain clouds gathering overhead. The smell of the electricity in the air raises the hair on my arms; lightning pierces the sky off to the north. *One one thousand, two one thousand,* I count for when the thunder will crack. Then I see her up ahead on the walkway, head held high. Suitcase in one hand, she glides over the sidewalk as if she's never even touched ground here, never cared about anything but her freedom.

I call out her name, just as the first few fat drops begin to spatter down, smacking the cement like a toy drum. She turns, smiles for an instant. Cocks her head to the side in that pigeon-like way. I doubt she's crying, but I'll never know and am happy for the rain, the rain in my eyes, the rain that's falling harder now.

She turns away and keeps walking, slow and steady to the rhythm of the rain, through a curtain of water and onto a new stage of her very own.

Slick told me she was going to do a runner because her lady was emancipated. She took off right on the heels of Nina leaving. I became solitary without the confinement, the loner white sheep of the school. Fine by me. The gang in my cottage tried to get me out of myself, to buddy up again, figuring I'd learned my lesson. But they'd never let Moe, the Supreme Pimpin' Being, find out they even talk to me. Punks.

Moe didn't win that fight and I didn't either. I wonder if Moe understands, like I do, how we both lost. Pride is the biggest sin of all.

I'm somewhere else these days—or my body is here, but I'm gone. I've lost interest in it all, in skating, in mackin' on the ladies. Patty hated doing it, but the rec staff banned Moe and me from the gym. Most nights I stay at the cottage reading. I have the books Myn gave me, and the writing grabs my heart. Two women, black and white, writing about racial stuff, about women. Writing honestly and showing the hurt through the beauty of how they put words together. As long as I keep my thoughts and the books secret, as long as I don't act proud and remain invisible, I'll make it through to emancipation.

Andy Warhol has become my new fascination. I read about him in *Life*. He paints pictures of Campbell's Soup cans and rich people are stupid enough to buy them, believing it's great art. Myn and I had a good laugh about his con before she left. Andy and his entourage wear striped T-shirts and sunglasses, are ultra-skinny and very cool. But they listen to that crazy group, the Velvet Underground. A friend of Jack's, a young priest who hung out at that club La Cave in downtown Cleveland, gave the record to my mother right before the state took us away. One of the only things Kitty and I had in common toward the end there was how we both couldn't stand the Velvet Underground.

I'm seventeen, on the brink of emancipation. The administration must figure out what to do with me, since I don't have a place to go. Kitty's friend Hugh Harris has started showing up to see me.

Hugh is a lovely guy, chubby and scholarly, with an agreeable mustache. He's extremely good-natured and sunny. If a bomb blew him to smithereens, his ghost would probably appear to tell you, *Oh well, tomorrow's another day!*

Hugh is married, and he works in a high position at NASA, which guarantees my immediate respect. He met my mother at the halfway house for battered women where he volunteers. It pains him to tell me this, how she ended up homeless, but the bad news is followed by the good: Kitty's okay and she sends her love. She's safe—in a new hospital, for the time being. She asked him to come see me and to tell me she loves me. It's hard to hear.

Hugh asks what I'd like to do with my life. I want to be an artist, and he brings up the Cooper School of Art in Cleveland.

"Cooper might offer you a scholarship, but you'll have to take the GED test and pass."

I find this very amusing. GEDs are for dummies and high school dropouts. I never dropped out; Blossom Hill wasn't equipped to teach me. Not to be arrogant, but I'm too smart for a GED.

"Can't I show them my drawings and take art tests? I'm sure they'll let me in."

Hugh has a kind, good-natured laugh, like I'm being charming when I'm not trying to be.

"You'll still have to take the GED. That's how life works. You have to follow the proper channels."

"Do you think Andy Warhol followed the proper channels?"

"Well, he did pave his own road, but I believe he attended art school. The most accomplished artists learn the rules before breaking them. I read that he was an illustrator for fashion magazines before his, um, abstract phase."

"I bet he used an overhead projector to paint the soup cans. We have one in the rec office. How much of an education does it take to copy something?"

"Well, I guess it's what and how you copy something that's important, don't you think?"

I like Hugh because he doles out advice like he's telling me something I already know, which makes it easier to take in.

I wonder if Andy Warhol gave up on being loved like I have. Or if he didn't care and being worshipped by strangers was enough. If that's what fame is all about, is fame enough to wish for in a life?

PART III

To find relief in what has been,
we must make ourselves eternal.
—Violette Leduc, *La bâtarde*

15

WALTZING THE GI BLUES

The bastard with the oranges broke my watch. Eddie, his name is, slipped it right out of my apron and bashed it on the table until it exploded into tiny bits of flying metal. I'd taken it off so it wouldn't get splattered with paint. It wasn't worth much, but didn't it start something, all the guys whooping and scrambling for the innards while I yell for Harvey—*where the hell is Harvey?*—and instead, here comes old Dr. Katz, rising out of his wheelchair to reach for a teeny spring bouncing across the table. Now they're all at it, ripping the place apart.

Dr. Katz shouldn't even be in here with the Vietnam vets. Now he's sprawled across the floor, plaid bathrobe up around his waist, whining in his childlike voice while the orderlies yell for order and wrestle the guys back into their seats. I try lifting Katz up by his armpits. It's useless. The man's legs are deadweight. All this nuttiness because of Eddie the bastard.

The Brecksville VA Hospital is right down the road from Blossom Hill. Mr. Summers worked out an arrangement for us girls about to be "emancipated," whose families don't want us, to get us working so we can support ourselves upon release. Summers drops us off and picks us up every day in the school van. It's not dangerous, not like we're alone with any of the veterans. Orderlies and attendants are here all the time. What makes me nervous about working in a hospital for crazy vets is the possibility of running into my uncle Jack in a wheelchair, looking as if his very soul just flew off, a look so many of these guys have in here. Jack and I have been out of touch since he left for Vietnam, and this hospital is not the place I want to reunite with him.

Lizzie works here too. The nurses keep her busy cleaning bedpans, serving food at mealtimes, and changing sheets. She enjoys calling herself a "nurse's aide" and is happy knowing she'll have a nice little stash to start her new life with. She curses about the bedpans, and who can blame her? I work in a more sanitary position in the Occupational Therapy Department as an assistant, but it can get crazy in here.

The other guys in morning OT call Eddie "the bastard" not because he was born out of wedlock like me but because he's a jerk, always stealing the other vets' favorite treat; oranges. The Tasmanian Devil bastard peels them in a fit so fast that a guy can't grab it away before it's down his throat, him mugging at you while drooling orange juice. Jimmy Clancey says the bastard "burned all his fuses on speed in 'Nam" and tells me you could get any drug your heart desired over there. Well, it seems the go-pills never left Eddie's system. He is a speed demon. On rare times, I'm able to grab his attention long enough for him to sit still and work, and he'll draw molecules and atoms with dots so fast and intricate, it makes your eyes cross.

The OT room is enormous, with two walls of windows that open at narrow angles covered with heavy screens inside and outside. This prevents the guys from punching the glass into smithereens or from trying to stuff their bodies through to freedom. The room is filled with light—a combination of sunshine and the fluorescent tubes on the ceiling. The tubes also have thick screens holding them in. The OT supervisor Mr. Trafalgar tells me, "We had a tall fella who'd reach up and grab a fluorescent tube and crack it across his knee to hear the pop, the explosion. The guys would freak out. Many of these vets can't handle any noise that reminds them of combat. We had to build cages over the lights."

Jimmy Clancey points at the bulbs. "Jailed, just like the subjects of their illumination," he says.

Trafalgar is an easygoing type with pasty skin, greasy slicked-back hair, and black-rimmed glasses. I like his cool glasses and the fact that he talks to me like I'm an equal and not a teenage jailbird. When I first arrived, he showed me the kiln and took the time to demonstrate how to use it, which he says we can't do unless an orderly is present, in case somebody decides to get buggy, open it, and jump in when it's fully fired.

OT has everything you can imagine for the guys to make art. Paints, plenty of paper, and easels. A wheel for throwing pots. Simpler crafts for the vets who are severely disabled. Long tables are strewn with all sorts of projects. Intricate and strange drawings, like the bastard's tiny worlds of crazy. Small sculptures made of Popsicle sticks and rubber bands, pipe cleaner statuettes, and clay monstrosities.

Trafalgar gives me the lowdown on the vets and what to expect. It'll be Korean and World War II vets in the mornings and the Vietnam guys after lunch.

"For the most part, the morning patients are fairly tame, but there are a few wild cards who'll get ornery on occasion. Some of these guys haven't been around women for years, aside from the nurses in the hospital, so if they make advances, decline politely to avoid provoking them. If they start pulling any crap, call for help. There's always an orderly within shouting distance. Harvey over there... he'll look out for you."

He nods over at a humungous guy in a white uniform who gives me a big smile and a wave. I wave back.

"The Vietnam vets can be more trouble. Psychedelics make some men go to places of no return. It's best to avoid talk about combat or anything military. Change the subject to the crafts at hand. Keep them focused on the projects, don't get sucked into any strange conversations. Always be polite, and never ever argue back if they try to pick fights. Just calmly walk away. We have books with examples of what to draw in case their imaginations blank out on them. Clay to work with, a bunch of projects in progress. Look around. You might find some interesting."

We stroll around the tables. I spot an urn decorated with headless horsemen.

"Most of these guys love occupational therapy. Art is their favorite time of day."

Jimmy Clancey is an Irish hippie with an ambling walk and stooped shoulders, a full beard, and a mustache. Reddish-brown curly hair and piercing blue eyes that light up when he smiles, and the dimples in his cheeks are a joy. Harvey told me Jimmy was one of the most decorated soldiers in the hospital. He freaked out when he returned home, burned his uniform, and then tried to kill himself. Not once but many times.

"Jimmy was awarded a Purple Heart," says Harvey, "but he won't talk about it."

I'm helping Jimmy with what I thought were vases, but discovered they are hookah pipes when he asked me to help him drill holes in the sides. After a couple of weeks of working here, we become friendlier and start to talk about stuff we're not supposed to talk about.

"Can I see your Purple Heart?" I figure I may as well ask. Maybe it's the one thing he decided to hold on to.

"I threw that heart away."

He shifts in his seat, head down at the table. His eyes scan around, like maybe he'll find it right here in the OT room. Sometimes he calls me Storeen, which he says means "little" in Irish.

"But why? Isn't the Purple Heart the highest award you can get for courage in battle?"

Jimmy rubs his eyes when he smiles. "Being wounded has nothing to do with courage. If I had an ounce of courage, I'd have wasted the pigs in power who sent us all over there to kill and be killed in the first place. That would have been courage. The other stuff was just survival. Don't ever let any government man make you think killing people is a good thing, that it will ever keep anybody safe or free. It's a lie. Pigs, they are. All that killing just to fatten up some rich fecker's wallet."

He places his hand on my shoulder, but quickly removes it and gets back to work, sliding a woven tube through one of the hookah holes. Workers and patients aren't allowed to touch.

Jimmy and I become good buddies. He loves Jimi Hendrix and the Moody Blues, and he's painting the lyrics of "Dr. Livingstone,

I Presume" with glaze around the base of one of his hookahs. The words lace through a jungle scene filled with parrots, elephant-eared plants, and a giraffe, which he paints with the tiniest of brushes. When I ask him what he likes to smoke in these pipes, he laughs and tells me he doesn't smoke anything, just enjoys making objects of beauty for others to appreciate. Jimmy has a brother who brings him all the accessories he needs to finish the job: the hoses made from multicolored string and mesh, the smoking tips, the brass bowls, and the screens. Jimmy's brother takes the hookahs, urns, ashtrays, and leather belts and sells them, keeping the money in a special savings account for Jimmy. The hospital doesn't mind, probably because Jimmy's work is so gorgeous.

We experiment with colors and shades of glazes. When we return the next day and open the kiln to a shimmering ocher-and-green-glazed urn we've made with our own hands—or, I mean to say, Jimmy made and I assisted with—well, he's ecstatic and so am I.

Sometimes he'll talk about the war, both of us going silent whenever anyone comes close. He gets this haze in his eyes and his voice grows soft when he starts, talking of severed limbs flying through the air, corpses so burned from napalm he didn't know if they were our soldiers or the Vietcong. How sometimes, if he looks out the window right here from the hospital, the parking lot turns into a sea of purple-and-green corpses, which is why he has to take his meds like clockwork or his vision goes screwy. He says he took a lot of LSD over there. It made his brain explode from the inside out, right along with the bombs. He calls his brain "a kaleidoscopic volcano in hell."

He says he feels bad about telling me things a young girl shouldn't have to think about. It's okay by me, especially if he needs to let it all out. I'm an adult, I tell him, with a job now. "You can always talk to me, Jimmy. I've got stories too."

I tell a few stories about my life that equal war in my book. Somehow in the telling, they always come out funny. I guess I'm trying to make Jimmy laugh, but he just smiles at me like he pities me. And I let him do it, only him.

I tell him about the time I ran away when I was thirteen because my foster sister beat me so bad that the blood vessels in my eye burst, just because I loved a girl. The truth tumbles out before I can stop myself. Jimmy doesn't blink. So I tell him about the Vietnam vet I met downtown on Public Square who said I could stay at a hippie commune and how things turned evil. I guess that's why I'm not scared anymore. I shouldn't tell Jimmy this story, but I can't help myself. I want him to know how brave I am. Like him. Like we've both been to war and survived. I watch his face. He's real still. He takes a deep breath. His chest shivers.

"I guess we both deserve Purple Hearts, huh, Storeen?"

I nod yes and go quiet while we place the finished hookah in a glass case.

The next day, I ask him to tell more stories. I'm so curious.

"There were little children who would beg to do dirty things with you. For food." Jimmy grabs his head in his hands. "Get back!" he yells, like he doesn't want the horrors to come out from where he's been hiding them. He pounds on his temples and cries out, "I'm sorry, I'm so sorry!" and I feel like such a creep, asking for stories that make him freak out like this.

I try my best to comfort him: "It's all over! The war's over, Jimmy. You're safe now."

But I know the truth. For some people, the war will never be over. Jimmy knows it too. I feel awful while Harvey wraps an arm around Jimmy's shoulders and takes him away, still pounding on his own head.

In the mornings I meet with a vet named Dr. Katz, a prominent scientist who made an unknown critical discovery and went completely nuts during World War II. Trafalgar pushes Dr. Katz to the table in his wheelchair, a small, pudgy bald man with glasses thick as the bottoms of pop bottles.

Dr. Katz's head rolls toward one side. The meds make him talk with a lisp, his tongue lolling around in a big hump. Even though his words come out mushy, the tone of his voice is sweet, kind of feminine. He's always careful to say "Please" and "Yes, miss, I would like that," and "You look lovely today." Things that take the focus off how horrible someone can appear, how you can be scared by looking at what you really think the inside of yourself may look like too. When the orderly first introduced us, Dr. Katz held out a clammy palm. "It's a great pleasure to make your acquaintance, Maddie." He had a wicked little gleam in his eye.

"I hear you're a very important scientist, Dr. Katz."

"Oh yes, a nuclear physicist! Not that anyone would be attentive to that fact here, but perhaps I will elucidate upon the subject for you sometime, my dear. Would you like that?"

"I would. Very much, Dr. Katz."

Dr. Katz can't do anything too crafty since his motor skills are not up to scratch, so Trafalgar suggests Plasticine flowers. You bend wire into the shapes of flower petals and leaves, dip the shapes into a series of multicolored cans of translucent Plasticine, then carefully place the flowers on racks to dry. Voilà! The flowers harden into what Dr. Katz calls "objects of obscene beauty," until he screws one up and flies into a pouting rage, complaining that this "exercise is . . . ludicrous! And the plastic solution reeks!"

The poor old geezer. Once an important scientist, now confined to a wheelchair spending his days dipping Plasticine flowers. I hold his hand steady while he tries to shape another petal.

"Plasticus, plassein. . . Oh, this is pathetic!" He starts to smile, then flips into a rage and throws down the wire. "Why do they have me doing asinine tasks? Would I do it if it weren't for the fact that they'd keep me locked away in a padded cell if I didn't? Infantilizing me like this!"

"Now, now, calm down, Dr. Katz, let's make a flower and talk, and you can tell me all about atomic particles. Or the nature and history of words. Whatever you like."

He gets this dirty little gleam in his eye and his hand turns cobra, striking in between the buttons on my uniform, trying to cop a quick feel.

"Hahaha! I gotcha. Let me see, Mommy!"

"Hey! Knock that off!" I snatch his hand away while he giggles, drool spilling over his tongue. "If you do that again, I won't be able to work with you ever again, Dr. Katz!"

But he tries it repeatedly. It becomes a ritual of him reaching, me knocking his hand off and scolding, and him giggling like an idiot. Not a complete idiot, because Dr. Katz is, in truth, a genius. And when he isn't being gross, he amuses me.

The next time I see Jimmy, he's happy and relaxed, like all his edges have been steamed and fluffed. We set to work on studding a brown leather belt with his astrological sign, Scorpio. We work quietly together like this for a minute, listening to Emerson, Lake & Palmer's "From the Beginning" on the radio, and he turns and says, "You and me, we have communion, Storeen." He turns away, shy-like. Pushes another stud through the leather.

"We do, Jimmy."

"Communion has nothing to do with a—a wafer, or the body and blood of someone who forsakes you just like his father forsook him. Forsaken and forsook are we! But in communion, together."

His blue eyes twinkle. The Irish in him reminds me of Grandma Jo. I miss her so.

"Jimmy, you are a very cool dude."

He's right. Communion has nothing to do with anything other than being here, like this, with a guy called Jimmy Clancey. I look around and the coast is clear, with no orderlies in sight. Rising, I curtsy to him formally, like the lady I ain't.

"Sir Jimmy, would you like to waltz with me?"

Jimmy grins, jumps up, and places one hand lightly on my waist, holds my other hand out. We don't know what we're doing, but I bet he's seen this dance in a few TV shows like me, so we fake it. Off we go, waltzing away. He guides me around the floor, ONE-two-three, ONE-two-three . . . We wind through the vets at their tables working on their projects. The ONE-two-three doesn't match the rhythm of the song, but who cares? We laugh as the other guys seem happy to be watching our little show. One of the guys rolls himself over to the radio and turns it up while we glide across the floor laughing. Jimmy spins me around. It's fantastic to dance like this, and it makes everyone so happy. Me too. It's like we're in a movie.

We pass bastard Eddie, and he starts banging a paint pot on the table, banging away all excited and silly like a damn fool. Jimmy gets this strange expression on his face, and his body bends and crumples away from me into a heap on the floor. He's holding his ears, screaming, "STOP, stop it, hold your fire, I'm not the enemy, help me, Jesus!"

Harvey rushes in with two orderlies, yelling toward me, "He's flashing. Get out of the way!"

Jimmy flops like a fish out of water there on the floor, eyes wide, lids stuck to his forehead. I'm scared, but I bend down over him; I want to help, want to sing that Jimi Hendrix song into his ear, the one he loves about an angel coming to soothe him, but Harvey yanks me by the arm, up and away. The orderlies tie Jimmy with white belts and take him out, screaming and kicking and everyone watching in shock. Eddie slinks off to a table in the back, head down back into his dots. Two more orderlies arrive to help settle the room. It takes a bit for the other guys to calm down and return to their projects, but soon, all seems back to normal. The air feels still and rough. No smoke, but I swear I smell sulfur. Like the war has left its trail in the air.

I'm packing up Jimmy's supplies, placing them neatly on his shelf. Thinking I'll make a sign with his name in blue glitter letters. That'll be nice. Blue, like his twinkling eyes, to hang in the glass case above his jungle hookah.

16

THE GOOD, THE BAD, AND THE LONELY

Six months pass of me being a responsible working stiff. I've learned to hold a job without getting fired, earning money for the work I do, and it's good work, helping the vets. Mr. Summers drops me off in the morning and picks me up at night, Miss Smith feeds me breakfast, lunch, and dinner, and the staff washes my clothes. All I have to do is show up at the hospital in my creepy pantyhose and uniform and be kind to the vets.

Hugh Harris says soon it'll be time to get my own place, and because Blossom Hill has been banking my salary for me, there's enough money to do just that. Hugh is looking for an apartment in Cleveland. He asks where I'd like to live; I tell him near West Twenty-Fifth Street. I like the Euclid-Superior Bridge and often imagine crossing it into downtown. I hear there are gay bars downtown.

We're driving across the bridge onto West Twenty-Fifth Street in Hugh's Buick Skylark. Turning on West Twenty-First, we pull up to a dilapidated two-story house in a row of old houses with burned-out lawns. It's a wooden house painted with what must be ten layers of paint, the faded colors peeking through like peelings on a scab. Both levels have small porches. The only joy about this place are the Christmas lights hanging across the upstairs porch.

Chirpy as always, Hugh announces, "This is it, your new home."

I don't want to disappoint him by grumbling about the house and its look of poverty. I jump out and grab my suitcase, all smiles. "Let's see the inside. Do you think it has a fridge?"

"Oh yes, it has everything. I made sure."

Hugh pulls a large box from his car, and we walk onto the porch past a living room chair with its stuffing hanging out. I'm spooked. It reminds me of a porch from another lifetime. Hugh fumbles with the lock, and the door swings open to what looks like the second most depressing place I've ever laid eyes on. It stinks like mold and gas. Hugh is embarrassed.

"I'll call the gas company and have them come out to make sure there aren't any leaks."

The living room floor is a strange pattern of black linoleum with confetti-like squiggles, and walls that were once yellow are now a grayish mustard color, streaky and sad. The windows are greasy with dirt. A wooden chair with a ripped Naugahyde seat is the only piece of furniture in the room.

Hugh smiles, doubt twitching the corners of his lips. I'm tempted to say, *Gee, thanks, this is the best you could do?* I can't be an ingrate. He's the only person who showed up to help me. Not that I need anybody. I'll be perfectly fine on my own.

"It's only thirty-five dollars a month. We've got you all paid up through the summer, and if you stay at the VA hospital, your salary will be more than enough to fix this place up a bit. I'm giving you your savings from work. You have $956 left."

"That's a lot of money! It's all mine?"

"It certainly is. You worked for it. Please be careful and spend it wisely."

Hugh clears his throat as he kicks a wooden molding back into place. He walks me into the kitchen, where whatever linoleum once lived here has been torn away to expose the crusty wood beneath. The kitchen is painted Pepto-Bismol pink, and there's grease splattered all over the walls around the stove, which thankfully isn't too filthy. The old fridge is another story. I open it, and whatever remains of something that's been in there for years nearly jumps out at me with its smell. At least there's a Formica table and two chairs in decent shape, no missing legs.

"Don't worry, I brought you some cleaning supplies too. And here's a radio."

"Great! Can we turn it on right now?"

As Hugh takes things out of the bag, I search for a radio station and find sweet Al Green crooning away on "You Ought to Be with Me," which cheers the atmosphere immediately.

"There's a lot to do, you know," he says. "You'll have to open a new bank account so you can write checks and pay bills for the phone, gas, and electric. I brought you a frying pan, a saucepan, a plate, and some silverware, but you'll need other kitchen things and some furniture!"

Even though the place is a dump, I'm suddenly excited by all the possibilities, like the fact that I can cook and eat whatever I want. But I'm truly on my own out here, without friends, without knowing how or what to cook. Without a washing machine. Without connection to anything or anyone.

"I brought you a sleeping bag until you can buy a bed, and there's a Salvation Army right around the corner. Here's your Social Security card and a number for the phone company. If you go down there and show them one of your pay stubs, you can have your own phone. You'll be an upstanding member of working society now, with all the responsibilities."

I start to laugh. Hugh knows how silly it sounds, especially when describing me. I stand there in the middle of the room and take it all in, a bit dazed and speechless. His eyes go soft. Uh-oh, here it comes.

"We both know you're capable of this, right? You're going to be just fine. You have a good job, and your supervisors think you're great. After you pass your GED, I'll help you get into art school. You might want to start thinking about that. It's why I found you a cheap apartment. Art students don't live in palaces, you know. They spend their money on supplies."

"Hugh, they should just let me into Cooper. I don't think the GED is necessary to prove you have talent as an artist."

At this point, it would be nice to hear something a bit more inspiring than "You're going to be just fine." If there's anything I hate more than pity, it's more pity.

"We've already had this discussion. You know what you need to do if you want to apply to Cooper." Hugh hands me an envelope. "My phone number is in there too, in case you need help with anything. Buying furniture, things of that nature. I can help."

I'm nervous that he's about to hug me, and he does. It's awkward. He leans down and hugs from the shoulder, careful not to touch me with anything but his arms and shoulders.

"I think I'll hit the library and see what I can find out about the GED."

I figure this lie will make him feel good, and sure enough, he lights up. I should not be lying to him. He's too nice of a gentleman.

"Great! Okay, help me get the stuff from the car."

As soon as Hugh leaves, I take a deep breath, exhaling and blowing away the fear. What am I worried about? I have a job, cleaning supplies, and best of all, I have music and can turn the channel and listen to whatever I like on the radio. I'll call the VA on Monday morning to say I'm sick and might need a few days off. There's just too much to do. My home should be in order before I show up for work. After all, I've never taken a day off so far or ever been late.

The Salvation Army is around the corner from my house on West Twenty-Fifth Street. I buy a big lamp for the kitchen. The base is a tangle of bent rods, and the large green shade with an amoeba print reminds me of Kitty. I also buy a smaller lamp with a black ballerina on the base to set beside my sleeping bag for reading. I need clothes too, so I pick up a pair of black square-framed sunglasses, some Cub Scout uniform shirts, a pair of white chinos, and a black-and-white-striped T-shirt. I'll be as cool as the Warhol crowd. The best score is a boy's suit in brown pinstripes. The pants are too long but the jacket fits perfectly.

A magical jacket hangs on the wall over the cash register, an embroidered Vietnam combat jacket that says WHEN I DIE I'LL GO TO HEAVEN BECAUSE I'VE SPENT MY TIME IN HELL, with a map of Vietnam and Cam Ranh Bay embroidered on it. It's beautiful. I can't take my eyes off it, but I don't understand why VIET-NAM is hyphenated.

"Either buy that TV or you'll have to leave, son."

I nearly jump out of my skin. The guy who runs the shop is standing behind me—*is he talking to me?*—but I'm nowhere near a TV. He's talking to a mean-looking guy with a long scraggly beard and tattoos who is fiddling with the tubes on a TV set.

"Shut up, old man! I'll do what the hell I want! I was in Vietnam!"

"No need to get mouthy, son. No enemies here."

The shop guy walks away, and the scary vet glares at me, then continues messing with tubes and wires. If Jack comes home in one piece, I hope he doesn't return mean as a rattlesnake like this veteran. Knowing now what the war can do to a man, I wonder if maybe Jack has forgotten me. Or maybe I'm just the very last thing on his mind. There are more important things to think about right now, like how I'm going to travel by bus to work, open a checking account, and do the million other things I have to figure out to become a fully functioning member of society. Ha.

The man who runs the store is the only one left in the shop now. He has a scruffy, grayish beard, but I can tell he's not that old; he just seems kind of tired. When I ask him the price of a lamp, he says he'll give me a deal. Then he stops and looks me over. Nods his head.

"Some of these poor men come home after being in combat and think they can bully the rest of us just because they had a hard time. It's a damn shame."

"They're not all like that."

He chuckles. "You new around here?"

I decide to put on my best Oliver Twist face and tell him I just moved in around the corner and have a whole apartment to furnish and hardly any money to do it.

"Call me Lenny, and welcome to my junkyard treasure chest."

Lenny shows me a boxy couch in a nubby beige material with a matching chair. It isn't seedy, just used. Not the color I had in mind, but it'll serve the purpose. I bet I can lay the sleeping bag on it and use it as a bed until I get a proper brass one, like in the Bob Dylan song "Lay Lady Lay." Lenny asks for fifteen bucks for both the couch and chair and says his helpers will carry it over to my place for an extra buck.

I get another matching set of lamps for a couple of bucks and a blond coffee table the next day. I hit the hardware store and buy paint and brushes, a saw, Elmer's glue, and six light bulbs: two blue, a yellow, and two white. No red, thanks. Red is for whorehouses. I buy eggs, milk, tuna, mayonnaise, coffee, and ten rolls of heavy-duty aluminum foil at the grocery store.

The first Saturday in the new house is spent drinking cup after cup of coffee, scrubbing the kitchen floor with Murphy oil soap like we did at Marycrest, and bleaching down all the sinks, the stove, the fridge, and the toilet, like Nonni on a cleaning streak. The toilet doesn't flush properly, which means I have to fill up a bucket to flush every time I go. At least now I don't have to use the bucket as a toilet.

The oldies station on the radio is playing "Workin' on a Groovy Thing," by the 5th Dimension as I prepare dinner: bread in the Sally Army toaster and perfect soft-boiled eggs that Miss Smith taught me how to cook, right down to laying the newspaper on top of the pan. Too bad she didn't give me the recipe for making a good cup of coffee. I always seem to make it too strong, even with milk. I have a cup of Lipton tea and sing along to the radio while sawing the legs off the couch and chairs. Low is the way to go for a bachelor pad. I stay busy gluing aluminum foil to the walls until two A.M. The music on this station has turned to mush, so tomorrow, more of my savings will disappear into a record player and some records.

Whoever lives upstairs is blasting Barbra Streisand. She has a voice like no other and is quite the comedienne. I respect her, because not only can she sing like an angel, but she has a colossal honker and still made it to stardom, where it seems beauty means everything.

I go out on the front lawn to get some air after all that bleach. It's Saturday night and my neighbors are having a little party upstairs. The Christmas tree lights on the porch are on, and shadows dance on the porch ceiling. Maybe it's a bunch of secretaries or college girls? At least three or four. I can tell by the silhouettes. It makes me feel lonely.

I don't have any friends on the outs, and fat chance I'll be calling Big Al or even Aunt Joanie or Grandma. Or anyone else in my family. They haven't tried to contact me, and they must have known I was getting out. Or maybe they didn't. Who cares?

Maybe I'll be friends with Lizzie from Blossom Hill, when she's emancipated. I heard Slick ended up in Marysville. Mr. Summers predicted she'd probably end up there but I never understood why. No matter what Summers or anyone else said, I still refuse to believe Slick had one bad bone in her body. She may have been a pimp, but the thought of her raising a hand to a woman, well, I could not see it. Kick a trick's ass? She'd do it in a minute to protect her ladies. Slick's toughest bark was a purr. If women want to give her money, how does that make her a criminal? I'm sure she didn't force anyone's hand. Maybe she'll get out soon and I'll run into her when I finally go to a real gay bar downtown.

Asking about Nina, like where she might live would not have been cool. The administration staff wouldn't even hint at the idea that love or even courtship happened between girls in Blossom Hill, no matter how obvious it was. They allowed the "game" to go on, as long as it was never discussed out loud. They figured that as soon as we were on the outs dealing with real life, we'd drop the game and get boyfriends. I'm sure many did. Maybe Nina too. Not me.

So, I don't dwell on being alone out here. My living room is covered in silver wallpaper now, just like Warhol's Factory. By the light of the ballerina lamp I read *Sailing Alone around the World*, by Captain Joshua Slocum, which begins, "In the fair land of Nova Scotia, a maritime province . . ." Lulled by the idea of Grandma Jo's people traveling by boat from Ireland to Halifax, I begin to fall asleep on my very own couch in my own home, with giddy squeals and high heels dancing to Barbra Streisand over my head.

"Lenny, do you have any record players for sale?"

He pulls out a brown portable Magnavox hi-fi, the kind where the turntable folds down from the front with speakers folding out on the sides.

"It has a new needle and a sweet sound. Wanna hear it?"

Lenny keeps used records and 8-tracks behind the counter. He plays the soundtrack album for *Breakfast at Tiffany's*. Lenny's a square! But the melody of "Moon River" can't be denied. It drifts through the store and it's a killer.

"The sound is excellent. What other records you got back there?"

"A music connoisseur, huh? All right, how about this?"

He puts on Isaac Hayes's *Hot Buttered Soul*, "Hyperbolicsyllab-icsesquedalymistic."

"Now, this is more like it! How much?"

"Fifteen dollars and I'll throw in this record."

"Come on, Lenny, everything is fifteen dollars around here. That's highway robbery! How about you keep the record and give it to me for ten? That's all I've got."

He shrugs, walks away. I really want the record player, but I don't know what to do. Being nickel-and-dimed doesn't sit well with me. The world owes me for what I've been through, and I'm looking for a payday.

"Let me think about it." Lenny blows the dust off a Supremes album. "What about your folks? Why don't you ask them to buy it for you?"

I can't tell him about reform school. Too complicated. So I make up a lie, which might as well be true. "My parents died in a car crash last year."

"Lord, girl, I'm sorry to hear that. Tell you what. I'll give it to you for ten."

I nod my head down at the floor, as if the memory of my parents has me tongue-tied when it's really the lie that trips me up. Lenny shifts a box of 8-track tapes from the counter to a shelf and back, giving me side glances. Swayed by my orphan angle, he loads the record player onto a wagon. Not one look of pity. Smart man.

"Go ahead, wheel it home. You can pay me in installments."

Lenny is super kind.

The next day I head to Public Square on the bus, where the May Company beckons. I blow most of my savings on black cotton underwear, socks, a nice tight pair of boy's jeans, and a sparkly red pullover. The rest of my cash is spent at a fantastic record store on Public Square called Record Rendezvous. I buy Roberta Flack's *Quiet Fire* and *First Take*, Janis Joplin's *Pearl*, Santana's *Abraxas*, and a Bob Dylan record. I love Dylan, but everyone at Blossom Hill hated him, and I was dying to hear his records. I pick *Blonde on Blonde* because it's a double album and the picture on the cover is blurry, very artistic. I also pick up Aretha Franklin's *Aretha Now*. You can't have a record collection without the Queen of Soul. And because of Andy Warhol, I buy *the Velvet Underground's Live at Max's Kansas City* to go with my silver apartment. I figure that, like whiskey, I should get used to the taste.

After the spending spree, I'm getting nervous about money and realize I never called my supervisor at work. Sitting on the couch listening to Bob Dylan singing about a sad-eyed lady, I check out the bus schedules Hugh Harris left. Getting to the VA hospital in Brecksville will require changing buses four times. How long will it take? If I must be at work at nine A.M., it means leaving my house at six A.M.

The next morning, I wake and am out of the house by seven, already late. It starts to rain, and I don't have an umbrella. The wind blows full gale at the bus stop—I take it as a sign that nature doesn't want me to go to work. What will Jimmy Clancey, Dr. Katz, and the other guys think if I don't ever show up again? I should quit—it's just too complicated to get there—but sat least say goodbye. Do everything officially. So, I wait for the bus. I wait for what feels like an hour, but I lost my watch. It could be twenty minutes for all I know. Rain blows into me at a sharp angle, soaking me through.

A young blond woman with blue eyes rushes for shelter beneath the bus stop awning. She holds the hand of a small boy who looks to be about six years old. Blond like his mother, blond like my brother Chance, he catches me watching him and blushes, looking to his mom for comfort. She smiles at me, shakes out her umbrella, and brushes the rain off her boy's face and coat. Giving him a hug, she kisses his damp cheek and wraps him up in her arms as she takes a seat next to me. Safe now, he feels. Safe and cozy.

The mom smiles at me. "Are you waiting for the Detroit bus?"

"Yep."

"Sometimes it's late. It should be here any minute."

A familiar sting rises in my chest and I decide to leave, walking straight into the rain. Walking home, where Aretha Franklin's voice will brush the rain from my shoulders, singing "Oh Me Oh My (I'm a Fool For You Baby)".

I never got my last check, spoke with my supervisor, or boarded another bus to Brecksville. And I never saw Jimmy Clancey or Dr. Katz again.

Everything is falling apart. I never got it together to get a phone, and I can't call Hugh, don't want him to think I'm weak or know that I quit my job at the VA. The water isn't working, just a nasty rumbling sound coming from the pipes in my bathroom. Thankfully the kitchen sink water is running. The gas on the stove isn't working either. I'm afraid to call Hugh and admit defeat. I wash up in cold water and walk down West Twenty-Fifth to a diner to buy a cup of coffee and a fried egg sandwich. People stare at me like I just dropped down from Venus, so I take the sandwich home. It must be the boy's suit, but come on, it's just a suit, and boys have long hair too.

Quiet Fire plays on the hi-fi as the October rain pelts the sidewalk outside. Winter will be here soon enough. It's getting cold. Do I need gas to run the heat too? I stare at a piece of paper with Hugh's number, a whole series of numbers. The phone company, the gas company, the landlord, the police, the local hospital. The numbers seem to blur before my eyes while it dawns on me that I'm seventeen and don't know how to do any of this. People have been taking care of me for so many years now, feeding me, keeping a roof over my head, paying invisible bills to make sure everything runs smoothly. I'm too proud to call Hugh and ask for help. He might think I'm a complete idiot, and he can't call me because I never got a phone. All I want to do is stay here listening to music.

Gazing around at my silver palace, I can't decide whether it's spooky or beautiful. Whether I exist or am just a strange little dream in someone else's head. My reflection distorts in the aluminum foil. A stretched, fractured lump of a face staring back at me—my crippled heart, Hugo, in all his brokenhearted glory—while Richie Havens sings his heart out about freedom from the Woodstock soundtrack.

Freedom, he sings. *Sometimes I feel like a motherless child*. Maybe he feels like I do, feels that ache. Too much freedom isn't such a great thing after all.

I can't just sit here and rot, so I walk over to the Salvation Army. Lenny is in good spirits, the king of his own wondrous junkyard, whistling a tune. That wise grin, a sparkle in the eyes, as he picks through a new crate of goodies fresh off the truck. Come to think of it, he kind of looks like Redd Foxx in *Sanford and Son*, with his scruffy salt-and-pepper beard and that cap always cocked over his eye.

Lenny can tell I'm not feeling right today. I confess it would have taken me three hours to get to Brecksville by bus to my job at the VA, so I quit. In fact, I tell Lenny the short version of the Perry Mason truth and nothing but: about my parents, the foster homes, the whole shebang. I tell the stories like it's all a big joke, but he's not laughing.

He rubs his beard, considering. "That's it?"

"Yeah, but there's more if you want to hear—"

"You need a job. How about working here?"

I figured he'd kick me out of the store for lying, but instead he is slapping his hand on his thigh and offering me a job.

"Really?"

"Yep, really. Full-time as a clerk, helping me sort out all the treasures. I need the help."

"Thank you, thank you, thank you!"

Lenny is such a kind man. I feel like I want to dance, like it's all going to work out and I'm going to be okay out here. If it wasn't for Lenny and Hugh, I'd be sunk.

"Now I can only pay you minimum wage, a buck sixty an hour, but you'll get a twenty percent discount."

"Lenny, this is the best day of my life! I'm so excited!"

"Oh, don't you get too riled now. Welcome to the Salvation Army, where I'm about to make you *work* for that money!"

When the shipment comes in Mondays from the main center downtown, I'm a kid let loose in a candy store: clothes, kitchen stuff, books, records, tchotchkes, and jewelry—an overflowing pirate's booty. And I have the pick of the litter! It's strange, realizing some of these boxes might be filled with things that belonged to someone who just died. In the end, it's all just stuff passing from one hand to another, to be treasured or forgotten. Much like people, I guess.

Lenny keeps his eye on me as I pick through and sort things in piles. It's my job to hang the clothes and categorize the items. He calls out the prices; I write them down and tag each item with a small label.

"Don't you go stealing anything, or I'll fire you so fast your head will spin!"

He laughs, but I know he means it. Lenny treats me well. He buys lunch at least three times a week, and even though I don't get benefits here like I did at the hospital, Lenny tells me that if anything happens and I get sick, he'll take care of it. He just might be as alone as I am.

But I'm no good. As soon as the man turns his back, I steal anything I fancy, anything small enough to sneak into my clothes and jacket, except for the Little Flower—a statue of Saint Thèrése of Lisieux! My favorite saint, the one Grandma would talk about with her shower of roses. She is mine, even if I have to blow the rest of my savings to pay for her. She's as tall as I am, wearing her nun's habit and clutching a bouquet of roses and a crucifix. In her sad, kind eyes, I can't help but see Grandma looking back at me. I jump on her and cling like a monkey to a tree.

"She's mine! I've got to have her!"

Lenny says he can't just give her to me for free; if I want Saint Thèrése, I need to pay him back for all the stuff I've been stealing. Damn. I can't believe he's known all this time.

"Ten dollars should do it for the payback of stolen goods. Five for Saint Thèrése. And a promise that you'll never steal again. I mean it, Maddie. Deal?"

I've got to laugh. There he goes with his fifteen dollars again. He calls me on the thievery so matter-of-factly, like he has watched every boost, and says I can pay him off slowly, as always. Feeling like an ingrate, I vow never to steal from this good man again. And I mean it this time.

I arrive at the bottom of the steps wheeling Saint Thérèse in the red wagon, flabbergasted about my own idiocy. There's no way I'm going to get this lady up my stairs without causing a tragic break to her or to the both of us.

"Oh, Mary, look! There's a little creature out here transporting a nun in a wagon!"

I hear squeals from above. Two women hang over the railing of the porch above. One has a do-rag tied around her head; the other's head is decorated with pink curlers.

"Mona, clutch your pearls! It's Saint Thérèse and the boy Jesus! Well, hello there, handsome!"

Both wave their fingers, pinkies-first in comma shapes. Girlie and dramatic. Boom, I've figured out what's happening. I call up to them, wave, and bow.

"I'm your new neighbor!"

"Poor thing, you need help. We'll be right down!"

It takes them a minute, but here they come, all ladylike and giggly.

"I'm Mona, and this is Mary."

Mona has on short-shorts and a man's striped shirt pulled tight, tied underneath where her boobs should be. Mary is wearing a short oriental robe over jeans. They're both sporting cherry-red lipstick, which they didn't have on when they were screeching from the porch. They made themselves up for me! It's so flattering.

Mona looks me over, then tells Mary, "Kneel down and genuflect, darling, they've come to bring us a blessing!"

"I can't! My knees have had enough bruising for one week!"

They giggle, and Mary the blonde extends her hand.

"I'm Trixie, but we are *all* Marys. Pleased to meet you!"

The other queen curtsies and introduces herself. "And I am Mona Minnelli. We are the Holy Maudlins, the gifted ones residing above your head, darling."

I act shy and say my name softly, hoping it'll charm them. "People call me Capone."

Trixie gasps, while Mona raises her painted-on eyebrows.

"Capone! How priceless!"

They inspect my wardrobe with batting eyelashes: a pair of gray-striped boy's pants, old scruffy black boy's wingtips, and a Cub Scout shirt. My hair is tucked under an apple cap.

"Aha," says Mona. "A gentleman, are we?" Her eyes land on Saint Thérèse. "And did you rob her from a church or a graveyard, Capone?"

A flood of relief washes through me. Bona fide queer friends! Not one to be shy of theatrics in any way, shape, or form, I take off my cap and do a little bow—finally, more Artful Dodger than Oliver.

"I like to consider myself a gentleman, ladies. And no, I didn't steal her. I work over at the Salvation Army on West Twenty-Fifth Street."

I may as well have said "open sesame." They explode in a shower of excitement, eyelashes fluttering like butterfly wings.

"You work at Sally Army? Touch the stone, Mary!"

Mona wipes the air above her eyebrows with her middle finger, quite pleased.

"My, my, it's about time we had a man around the house! Come on, Trix, let's shift Miss Holy Thing inside and get to know our new neighbor."

As they lift and haul Saint Thérèse up the stairs, they sing that Helen Ready song, "I Am Woman!," and I love every minute of it, bum notes and all.

My first official visitors coo over Saint Thérèse as they walk her through the living room.

"Don't drop her, darling, or we'll end up in Hades!" and "We're already halfway to hell, honey, where have you been?" and "Thank God I'm not wearing my fuck-me pumps! Oops, forgive my wicked tongue, Saint Thèrése!"

They place her down gingerly, facing the couch in the front window, and then turn a circle as they take in the silver bachelor pad.

"I was impressed by Andy Warhol's Factory," I say, cap in hand.

"That's quite evident." Mona grimaces at her crumpled reflection.

"What a fabulous idea! It's like being in a fun house!" says Trixie, who goes directly for the record player. "Mona, look! She has 'Moon River'!"

Trixie is blond, bubbly, and petite. She's wearing fake eyelashes but no other makeup besides red lipstick on very full, pretty lips. Mona is the brainy one with the colorful language. Trixie tries her best to keep up. She finds another record she's far more excited about.

"Capone, what's your first name? You don't look like an Al, not to diminish your, um, reputation, darling," says Mona. Trixie swans around to "Sex Machine," by Sly and the Family Stone.

"My real name is Maddie. But you can call me Bird."

"So many names! Maddie's cute, but Bird sounds right."

Having my new friends call me Bird is a way of flipping my darkest nights into light. Every time the queens say my name, the memory of what happened in the snow, and in Hough, flies off and away from me.

Mona spots the photo of Jack tacked up on the wall.

"That's my uncle. He's an MP in Vietnam."

"Oooh, he is handsome! Does he like ladyboys?" Trixie is all aflutter.

"Shut your piehole, Trixie. Come upstairs and join us tonight, will you, Bird? How about dinner at eight?"

Mona holds her hand out for me to shake or touch or kiss, I don't know which. I bow and decide on a shake, and her hand is graceful. Warm and soft. Mona wears her dark hair pulled back in a headband, like Marlo Thomas. She has brown eyes and high cheekbones and is quite a bit older than Trixie. A dignified queen, she moves with a regal glide.

Off they flutter. A current of happiness rushes through my body. Queer friends. Queer, like me. I've tumbled into a nest of drag queens! I pinch myself hard. *Impossible . . . things are happening every day!*

17

THE HOLY MAUDLINS

The Maudlins have decorated their house like a show palace. Two windows are rimmed in blue Christmas lights, and a doorway arch between the dining and living rooms sparkles in red. A painting of Paris at night is outlined in yellow bulbs that have left sharp heat marks on the lavender-painted wall. Feathers everywhere: on lampshades, rimming pillows, hugging necks, and adorning shoulders. It's like they raided an aviary and plucked every poor bird dry in the service of feathering themselves and their nest. And quite a homey nest it is.

Trixie is setting the table to the soundtrack of *Funny Girl*. Very much the Mother Superior, Mona introduces me to three other queens in attendance: Lola (dark-haired, young, doe-eyed, and glittery in a rock 'n' roll style), Diana (very tall, thin, and glamorous, like her heroine, Miss Diana Ross), and Juanita (short, slightly chubby in cut-off jeans and a bad wig attempt at a Marlo Thomas flip).

"Ladies, meet Bird."

"Ooh, how handsome! How do you like our boudoir, Bird? Elegant enough for you?" says Lola, wrapping her long silver nails around a fancy glass full of something red and sparkling.

"Lola darling, you should see Bird's bachelor den downstairs. It's a veritable hall of fun house mirrors." says Mona, lifting a brow.

They all seem to be talking at once, moving around the room like a flock of preening swans to Barbra Streisand, who sings "I'm the Greatest Star" in the background. When they're not trilling out some clever little crumpet of words, they're singing along to *Babs! Babs!* like theater royalty on parade. Diana crosses her legs demurely, peeking out at me from beneath heavily lidded eyes. Her conch shell necklace is creamy against her velvety skin.

"You're obviously a boy, but most importantly, are you gay? Do you like boys? Or girls?"

The room falls silent.

"I like girls and hope to marry one someday. A brainy strawberry blonde, or a sexy brunette who writes books."

The gasps, the laughter, the dramatic gestures and expressions! Trixie grabs a Japanese fan and starts fluttering around me like a butterfly on diet pills.

"I'll be your blond geisha girl, Birdie. How about it?"

Mona slaps her away. "I told you, Bird's the perfect gentleman. Would you care for a cocktail, Birdie?"

They all start at once.

"Or a cockatiel?"

"We forgawk! Bird doesn't like cawk!"

And on it goes. Getting a word in with this flock takes some effort.

"What is Diana having?"

"Cranberry juice and vodka, darling," answers Diana. "Can I mix one up for you?"

Hours and feathers seem to fly past in a blur of entertainment and information. They keep handing me vodka cranberries while telling me the only time they can be themselves like this is at a gay bar called the Change, and here at home. Clearly, the world isn't ready for such divinity. I tell them they are holy beings, wave a wobbly sign of the cross over each, and they squeal in delight. Plastered Juanita starts singing that depressing Carpenters song "Goodbye to Love."

The song ends and she wails, *"How could he do that to me!"* causing Mona (who is already at her wit's end about her own love problems) to snap. She slams a glass down onto the table, silencing the room.

"Get off the cross, Mary. We can use the wood for kindling!"

I find myself singing a duet with Lola on "You Are Woman, I Am Man." I must have learned the words quickly, or maybe someone wrote them out. Lola is tugging on my tie, running her fingers through my hair on the slow and dreamy bit at the end. I gag on the word *"Let's . . ."* and moments later am hugging the toilet bowl, spewing up spaghetti Bolognese.

The ladies tell me it's high time I learn how to hold my liquor. To be part of this flock, I'd better learn to keep pace with the boozing. These girls drink circles around Kitty Ballou, a significant feat. There's always a moment where what begins as hilarity flips into hysterical emotional outbursts, deep crying fits, and catfights. When they start to carry on like this, Mona calls them the Sisters of the Three *M*'s: Maudlin, Morbid, and Moronic.

"All right, Maudlins, the histrionics stop here! You sound like a gaggle of pathetic drunken geese! Snap out of it! Now off to bed with you!"

The very worst of the Maudlin culprits attempts to grab a gin bottle off the table on her way out. Mona's voice stops her in her tracks.

"Put the bottle down slowly, Juanita."

"What bottle?!" Juanita is stone drunk, trying to slip the bottle under her skirt.

"Put it down. And don't look back, or I'll turn you into a pillar of salt!"

Pouting, Juanita follows orders and scuttles off.

The queens visit Sally Army, asking me for discounts or boosting stuff when Lenny isn't looking. I don't exactly aid them in their criminal activities. But I do turn a blind eye while keeping my promise not to steal from Lenny. I saw Lola whisk a used ball gown beneath her trench coat and waltz out the door, all purity and innocence. Who am I to judge when nearly a rack of decent boy's clothes is home in my closet, having hitched a ride there beneath my own houndstooth overcoat? That was then, when the Artful Dodger in me ruled. It's different now. And I did pay Lenny back for the clothes.

Everything seems to be breaking down in my place. I sleep at home most nights unless I pass out upstairs on the sofa, but my gas was turned off, and the plumbing is lousy. At least the toilet upstairs flushes without bucket assistance. I still listen to my records and keep clothes and things here, but the girls seem to like having me around. They cook dinner and always invite me. It's nothing fancy—

spaghetti or soup most nights, and pork chops when we all chip in on the weekends.

"No eating fish ever in this household, not even on a Friday!" they screech.

They call women "fish," and all that pertains to fish is smelly and disgusting—present company, famous singers (like Babs), and Hollywood royalty not included.

I'm learning to hold my liquor as the man of the flock—Omar Sharif and Joel Grey rolled into one. They've crowned me as their troupe's drag king. There's a big show coming up at the Change, a notorious downtown gay bar, and they want me to star in the show! Even though I'm two feet shorter than the queens, I still take their arms, treating them as the ladies they are. If I had to date any of them seriously, it would be Lola. She knocks me out—especially when she sings "I Don't Know How to Love Him" (the Yvonne Elliman version, NOT the Helen Reddy version). Lola flirts with me like a girl does with a guy. It's sexy.

Mona treats me like a son she's exceptionally proud of. She's motherly in the most considerate, protective way; maybe because she's older than the rest of the flock. One evening after our rehearsal at the Change, Mona asks me to come home with her so we can rehearse our duet together, "Money," from *Cabaret*. The others stay at the Change to dance and drink.

Mona pops popcorn, and we watch a Greta Garbo movie on television. It's my first experience of Garbo, who is spellbinding! I fall madly in love, helped along by the little details Mona's able to provide about the great Garbo. The movie is *Anna Christie*. Mona seems to know every word of Garbo's dialogue. I thought she'd lose her marbles when Anna is at the bar and says, "Give me a whiskey with ginger ale on the side, and don't be stingy, baby."

Mona mouths the words, then starts weeping, dabbing at her eyes with a hankie. "Too priceless," she says.

I ask about Mona's life, and she tells me her real name is Nathanial. She came from a wealthy family in Shaker Heights and went to Case

Western Reserve University, majoring in English literature. Mona wanted to be a scholar and a teacher, but when her family found out she was gay and dressed in women's clothes, they kicked her out and cut off her funds for school. Now she works at the May Company as a window dresser, but never in drag. She'd lose her job, word would spread, and she'd never be hired by anyone ever again.

Sometimes Mona's broken heart peeks through the Max Factor concealer. Like when she sings "Do You Want to Dance?," by Bette Midler. What life does to people like Mona, I feel it too. Like when men stare at me on the bus or walking down the street, trying to figure out if I'm a boy or a girl. The confusion in their eyes turning into meanness. It scares me. I would lie down on a railroad track for Mona. She's my fairy godmother, like in the Cinderella story. And I'm not embarrassed at all to be her baby Bird.

Mona asks if I've had sweethearts before. I tell her about Nina and Samantha Tamorini. I tell her the story about my foster sister Izzy. Izzy was never my girlfriend, but I sure did care about her, like a real sister. I tell her about my lonely girl, my secret love—a fantasy that feels very real to me. I don't tell Mona about the Vietnam vet and the gun. I refuse to think of those days, of him. But I'll wonder what happened to Texas and her girlfriend, Bernice, wonder what became of their lives until the day I lift off from this planet.

Mona calls me a Casanova when I go on about girls. She has a particular type: macho guys with dark hair, she says. Especially Poles and Italians, usually of the "blue-collar persuasion," preferably construction workers or telephone line repairmen. Her present boyfriend's name is Danny, and he's married with two kids. I never see Danny come around, though. Mona says he will be at the show.

Our show will consist of ensemble numbers and duets from *Cabaret* and *Funny Girl*. Lola will do songs by Marlene Dietrich, and Diana, songs by her namesake, Diana Ross. Juanita is Lesley Gore (which explains the new gold flip), and Trixie will do Loretta Lynn and Helen Reddy. For all the "divine and decadent" numbers, Mona the Queen Mum is the choreographer and performer of the Liza Minnelli and Judy Garland songs, transforming effortlessly from daughter to mother.

The Change is run by a dapper older fellow named Bob. Bob's got a face like a good-natured basset hound. The first words out of his mouth to me: "Where's your ID, kid?"

Mona jumps in. "She's eighteen, Bob. Someone robbed her in the alley behind your bar, so her ID is gone. Leave the kid alone. Where else can she go to feel accepted?"

Mona winks at him. He gives me the once-over, grumbles, and walks away.

"Bob has to pay off the cops *and* the Mafia to keep the place open," she says. "They take advantage of the situation and shake him down left and right. Friday nights, you'll see how many of them come in here sniffing around for blow jobs. They call us filth, but here they come again, pigs rooting in our truffle bed. It's diabolical."

To get into Bob's good graces, I spend the afternoons after rehearsals sweeping the dance floor and polishing the oak bar. He's a hard one to please.

"Don't think swingin' a broom will make me any happier about letting you in here, kid. And don't even dream about drinking in here until you give me a birth certificate, got it?"

Drinking (and drinking money) is never a problem for me at the Change. Eager to see me smashed and bold, the girls sneak me vodka cranberries because they love to dance with me. And when I'm on my way to being smashed, my dance moves get wicked.

The Change is in a shady part of town, on Prospect Avenue and East Fourteenth Street where the hookers hang out. There isn't a sign to mark the bar, just a peephole and a doorman named Billy on the other side of it. If he thinks you're not Change material, you don't get in because "this is a private club, members only."

There are two floors. As you walk in, there's a bar to your left and, just past the bar, a stage big enough for Mona's troupe to spread out a bit, but small enough to fall off if you're drunk and make the wrong move. A dance floor is in front of the stage, with big plastic tiles lit from below and a spinning mirrored disco ball above. The lights from the floor tiles pulse to the rhythm of the records, and the place has a great sound system.

When a fresh female face comes to the club, she'll usually sit upstairs at the bar and act timid, looking to see if there are real lesbians around. Downstairs is where the queer girls hang out, and the scene isn't half as cool or glamorous as the one upstairs. Clearly, Bob doesn't care too much for dykes, as he calls us. (I don't like the words for lesbians. *Bull dyke, bull dagger, lezzie, truck driver, muff diver,* well, I just cannot relate.) Sweaty brick walls and red light is about all we get. I don't hang out down there, would rather be upstairs with the showgirls. Besides, there aren't any cute girls to hit on in the basement. It's either boring white girls or reform-school stud types, and I'm into femmes only. No one is about to make a lady out of me.

A few cool studs hang out upstairs. I make friends with a girl named Future. Like me, she likes hanging with the gay boys and the showgirls. Future looks like a pretty boy with beautiful hazel eyes and a short cropped 'fro. She's real skinny, wears a gas station attendant's uniform, and is in the Job Corps learning how to be a mechanic. She has this habit of nodding her head like everything is cool and nothing could ever upset her. I figure it's because she smokes so much reefer.

Bob won't let anyone smoke pot in the bar, so sometimes we go outside to the alley and I hang out with Future while she smokes. When the boys in the alley see us coming, they usually zip up and move around the corner. Sometimes they yell at us, *"You dykes need to find your own place to suck pussy!"* which completely cracks us up. We look at each other like two straight boys—*as if we would ever touch each other!* Future asks if I want a toke. I prefer liquor and Lucky Strikes. Pot just makes me paranoid. I tell her about the time I sniffed glue and nearly punched in a TV set and how reefer makes me feel the same way.

Future introduces me to her friend Charlene (Charlie) Brown. Charlie is a stud, like us, and a fly dancer. Always laughing, always finding the ridiculousness in things. She'll grab me and whisper, "Dag, did you see that new queen's broken heel? No wonder, look at those size eleven feet trying to squeeze into a seven! Trying to keep dancing so her wannabe man won't notice! Puh-leeeeze!"

The three of us hang together at the bar, on the lookout for pretty femmes coming through. That is, when we're not dancing with the showgirls. Mona and the Maudlins call us the Boychicks.

Eddie Kendricks is crooning out his eleven minutes of disco, and we're all on the dance floor, my eyes watching Earl. He's over six feet tall and skinny, real shy when he's not on the floor. But when he's dancing, every muscle in his body moves in elegant rhythm. He's a glitter boy, hair cropped short and dressed in tight scoop-necked T-shirts with suspenders and tons of skinny silver bracelets up and down his slim wrists. His skintight jeans are rolled up to show off insanely high platforms and glittery socks. With legs so long and his butt sitting so high, his body seems to defy gravity. Earl assists Mona in the window dressing department at the May Company. He's her right-hand man for the show, setting the lights for the stage, making sure the curtain fabric hangs just so at our rehearsals. He brings Mona the perfect French café chair for her number "Mein Herr" from his kitchen set. Earl is devoted. I'm gonna start dressing like Earl, a style that matches my David Bowie obsession.

Bob is warming up to me, maybe because he's impressed with our rehearsals. The excitement is contagious. We all can sense our show will be something else. The night after our dress rehearsal, Mona takes me aside and asks me to shut my eyes and open my hand. She drops something hard into my palm and closes my fingers around it tight. When I open my fist, I'm in shock. It's an emerald!

"Please, Bird, I hope you don't think it's a real emerald! But it is gorgeous, isn't it? Like your eyes when they catch the stage lights."

Mona and I are in line at the Cleveland Music Hall, about to witness the greatest event of our lives; David Bowie's Ziggy Stardust show! We've been listening to his records nonstop, and Mona never stops singing "Queen Bitch." My personal favorite is "Oh! You Pretty

Things," and when he sings about a Homo Superior, I imagine Mona dressed in a sequined nun's habit, roller-skating through Marycrest to the horror of the Good Shepherds. This new record hits us like an earthquake. It's so gay! The crowd is singing snippets of Bowie songs, all dressed up with boas, feathers, and glitter everywhere.

I've dyed my hair bright orange like Ziggy's, wearing high platforms—once white, now covered in super-glued green glitter—with striped bell-bottoms and a glittery sheer top. *Push on!* Mona's in a silver halter pantsuit and a Liza Minnelli wig. Her eyelashes are silver too, and she's sporting a mole above the corner of her shiny red mouth.

"Darling, I have to tinkle, be right back."

Her Royal Highness Mona strolls down the line toward the restroom, with all eyes following.

"Hey. Um . . . remember me?"

I can't believe my eyes. Izzy Treadwell is standing there.

All I can say is "Yeah." She's nervous, keeps shifting around. I feel numb.

"Did you ever get the letters?"

My eyes don't leave the floor. What is she talking about?

"What letters?"

"My mom and me, um, we wrote you letters. We sent them to that Catholic school."

It hits me like a punch. The nuns at Marycrest had a policy to open all incoming and outgoing mail, in case a letter might be "upsetting" to a girl. Marie and Izzy had been writing to me? The nuns kept their letters from me. I just thought of the Treadwells as more people who were happy to forget I existed. If I had known, if only I had known . . .

"Nope, never saw any letters."

Izzy shifts her weight, still with that tomboyish way of hers. Tomboy guilt in her voice.

"Well . . . I'm sorry. About what happened. I'm . . . I'm really sorry. Okay?"

She reaches out to touch my arm. I yank my body away like her hand is a hot razor.

I want to ask her about Marie, I want to, but keep my head down, avoiding her as she nods in that surrendering kind of pose, and she says, "Oh, okay then," and because I refuse to even look at her, she finally walks away.

Mona returns. "Who's the cute little dyke you were talking to?"

"Nobody special. Just a girl I used to know."

18
SHOWTIME!

Comment ça va?

Do you feel good?

I bet you do!

I'm onstage wearing a bow tie, suspenders, and a bowler hat, with every word to the songs of *Cabaret* burned into my brain. I wish Kitty could see me singing the part of her old boyfriend. Mona made me up to *perfection* with what she calls a bee-stung lipstick line and fake eyelashes that are incredibly uncomfortable but look super-glamorous.

Even Bob is happy tonight, beaming from the bar as he leans over and exchanges comments and hugs with his friends. Why shouldn't he take some credit? If not for Bob, the show wouldn't exist. The place is packed, and the girls are stunning, breathtaking. It isn't only about the costumes or the makeup; it's about the glow. All the heartache they endure melts away onstage. They are born again. Nothing matters but the lights, the music, and the adoring crowd. The rest of the cruel world can go straight to hell!

The crowd explodes as the *Cabaret* girls march out one by one, including Juanita (playing Helga), who got smashed before the show and started crying, on the pity pot about how she is a lousy performer, nobody loves her, blah blah blah. Sure enough, when I'm introducing them in the opening number—*"Texas, Frenchie, Fritzie . . . und Helga . . ."* — guess who prances out like a cute little suckling in a sausage casing, then proceeds to stumble right off the edge of the stage?

Helga.

Mona is horrified, but she can't exactly stop mid-number. After all, she's Sally Bowles, and the show must go on. The crowd roars with laughter, thinking it's part of the act. A muscular guy dressed in sailor whites catches Juanita and rolls her back onto the stage. The ruckus occurs during the instrumental part of the song while all the queens dance around displaying their wares, so it couldn't be a more perfectly timed mistake. Juanita's face lights up like a firecracker. She's become the hit of the number! I take advantage of the moment and escort her back to her place in the lineup, like it was all planned. She sucks in the adulation, glowing like a bride on a march up a wedding aisle.

We all squeeze into a small dressing room next to Bob's office to change our clothes and use the mirror, but the room is too tiny for such an entourage of superstars, resulting in high-pitched screeches and "Move over, Mary!s." I give up entirely and use the bathroom. There is no such thing as competing for a mirror with a flock of queens in wigs and high heels.

The first act is a triumph! It's my very first time on a stage, and I feel so at home with my actress partners. Charlie congratulates me, and Future pats me on the back and says someone is looking for me at intermission, some girl who says she knows me from Blossom Hill. Could it be Slick? If only!

I spy Nitti's gap-toothed grin across the room, dimples and squinty eyes watching me from the side of the dance floor. She rushes over.

"L'il Bit! Girl, I can't believe it, look at you, all mackin' and pimpin' on the outs. What you doing here, and up onstage too?"

"Hey, Nitti. What's goin' on?"

I try to be cool, but Nitti was one of the girls who betrayed me. Does she think I've forgotten?

"I'm free and ready to party, Bit! This is my girl, Coco, and Leroy."

Nitti's friends seem a little strange to me. First off, Coco is old, maybe thirty or even forty; it's hard to tell. She's wearing a bad wig and too much makeup, a leopard miniskirt, and super-high heels, and she has a huge handbag almost the size of a suitcase. This does not look like anybody Nitti would mack on, more like a hooker who blew in from the corner after a rough night. And Leroy is downright nasty, darting eyes peering from under a wide-brimmed hat.

Nitti is head-to-head with Leroy conspiring about something. They give me a sideways look and a nod, then Coco asks me where the bathroom is. I point it out to her. She hobbles over on her five-inch heels, clearly stoned.

I'm about to walk away when Nitti grabs my arm.

"L'il Bit, do me a favor. I need you to hold this for a minute."

Nitti slips something heavy into my tux jacket pocket. I curl my fingers around the shape of it, and the realization burns my hand. It's a gun.

"Nitti, what the hell?"

"A .38 Special, girl! With a barrel fulla bullets. Just hold on to it for a while. Come on now, gangsta. I'll be back for it."

Nitti slaps her hand on my back as Leroy gives me a sleazy smile. I feel sick.

"L'il Capone, packin' heat!" Nitti laughs, and off the trio slides through the crowd.

Why didn't I just shove it back in her hand? The gun feels alive, a metal snake filled with venom. I hustle Future and Charlie toward the bathroom. Coco nearly knocks us down on her way out.

"Look at you three fine-ass little muthafuckahs!" she says, hobbling off with her wig twisted to the side.

I open my pocket and show Future and Charlie the gun.

"Whoa. Shit! What the fuck?" Charlie jumps back a few feet.

"It's not mine. It's that girl Nitti's. I knew her in Blossom Hill."

Future is spooked. "Why did she give it to you? Something ain't right," she says, shaking her head.

"She wants me to hold it for her."

Future and Charlie inspect my face, looking for an answer about what I'm gonna do.

"You better give that thing back, girl," says Charlie. "You don't need that kind of trouble. Hell, she may have shot somebody with that gun!"

"Hand it over."

Future holds out her hand. I give her the gun. She pulls a bandanna from her pocket and carefully wipes the gun off. Hands it back to me with the rag wrapped around it, and I know what to do.

"I'll need you two to watch, make sure she doesn't try to pull anything," I say.

If Mona knew what was happening, she'd burst a blood vessel. I stick my hand in my other pocket, touching the emerald. Mona has given me back my bad eye.

The Boychicks follow me out of the bathroom, and sure enough, there's Nitti, laughing at the bar with Leroy and Coco. I approach while Future moves over to Bob, whispering in his ear. Bob wipes the rim of a glass real slow, staring down Nitti and her buddies.

I slide up to Nitti, real cool.

"Nitti, you need to take this back."

"Come on, L'il Bit! Dag, girl, don't tell me you can't handle it."

"I don't want to handle it, Nitti. Take it back."

She grins at me, screwing her eyebrows together like I must be kidding.

Mona is motioning to me from the side of the stage to hurry. The girls are all lined up, and the show's second half is ready to begin.

"It's yours for now," says Nitti, and turns her back on me.

Bob walks over stone-faced. He knows something's up. He asks Leroy, "Can I get any of you another drink? Or have you had your fill?"

While Bob's throwing *get out* hints at Leroy, I muster up all the nerve in my body and slip the gun out of my pocket and onto Nitti's lap. I back away fast with my hands outstretched.

"Poof! Magic, Nitti!"

Nitti quickly scrambles the piece into her own pocket, eyeballs popping. "You never were shit, L'il Bit, thinkin' you a playa. Mutha-fuckah, you still ain't shit! And who are these sorry-ass bull daggers up here behind you?"

Future grins her sleepy smile at Nitty, and Charlie shoots her a middle finger while the three of us stroll.

Mona and I hit the stage and launch straight into the song "Money" from *Cabaret*. We are *perfection*, as she'd say, and the crowd is eating it up, howling in delight. Especially when we try to bump pelvises like Liza and Joel; in those heels, she's so tall that her privates practically slap me in the face, which the crowd thinks is hilarious. Good thing she's got her business tucked somewhere inside the pantyhose.

Midway through the song, I see a commotion in the back of the bar: two cops are escorting Nitti, Leroy, and Coco toward the door.

Out they go on their sleazy cans. Future and Charlie push through to the front of the stage, giving me *everything's cool!* smiles while Mona and I pump our groins to the sound of coins hitting a slot. We're triumphant! The crowd goes nuts for Joel and Liza.

After that night, Bob never growled at me again. I enjoyed all the vodka cranberries I desired, on the house. And Nitti and her friends never returned to the Change.

A real rock 'n' roll band is playing the Change tonight! The show-girls turn a bit catty when Bob asks if they're excited about seeing a glitter band. Mona's wearing her haughty, bored look.

"I guess your house performers are chopped liver now?" asks Mona.

Bob serves up a round of drinks on the house, assuring them that no skinny, drug-addict rockers will ever surpass the sheer beauty and extraordinary talents of his queens. They purr.

Mona is too proud to stand near the stage or show any interest in other performers, but Lola is thrilled to see a glitter band. She joins me at the front. We lean on the edge of the stage, acting cool, checking out the amplifiers, microphones, guitars, and drums. This is the first time I've seen rock 'n' roll instruments close enough to touch. It gives me a fizzy feeling in the pit of my stomach. I down my vodka cranberry.

"All the Young Dudes" plays on the sound system as the band climbs the side stairs and onto the stage, that climb, like a holy ceremony. There's a skinny guy with dark hair in a striped T-shirt—I think he'll sing lead—strapping on a red electric guitar. He's wearing shades and tight black jeans, looking like a Warhol superstar. Oh my God, the whole band looks fantastic. The drummer and the bass player have longish hair and mod clothes, and there's another guitar player with a haircut like David Cassidy's. A tall, leggy blonde is singing background vocals. She has a wild mane of curly hair, like the girl on the cover of the Mott the Hoople album—it shines out like a halo in the stage light, but you can tell she's no angel. Nope, this whole band is killer. Glitter on their eyelids, glittery platform shoes, glitter everywhere.

Blondie holds a tambourine and shakes it a little, looking confident and smart-assed. The musicians plug in, and the power of the guitar's first notes scream through the amplifiers. The crack of the snare drum, the bottom of the bass, rattling my stomach. I think I'm going to faint.

Striped T-shirt man steps up to the microphone and, with a soft, hoarse voice, says, "Hey, everybody, we're Cinderella Backstreet . . . (strum strum) . . . and it's a beautiful night. We're gonna do a song that you might think was written by Mott the Hoople, but it was actually . . . (strum, with reverence) . . . the great Mr. Lou Reed who penned it."

He plays a few notes on his guitar alone. Then the band kicks in, and my guts fall out.

Sweet Jane! Sweet Jane!

I'm mesmerized . . . I can't believe the rush, the vibrations, of the music moving through me. Lola is across the room now, in the same kind of trance while the band sends electric shocks through the crowd. The blonde can't sing—she sounds like a caterwauling animal—but who cares? She's perfect! This is real bona fide rock 'n' roll!

They go through a set of cover songs. Pretty raucous ones, and a song with a chorus that goes *I can't stand it any mo mo*. The crowd is eating this up, and you can tell that the lead guy, whose name is Peter, wants to keep everybody happy by playing up-tempo stuff. He introduces the band, then gets kind of quiet and says they're about to do a ballad he wrote with the same name as the band. He's trying to be funny, talking about Cinderella being a scullery maid. For some reason, it's not coming off so funny. Then he starts singing an incredibly sad song. It reminds me of Bob Dylan.

I wanna walk on down in the alley
Down where the light shines so very dimly
Out where the night is so complete
With Miss Cinderella Backstreet.

I reach in my pocket and squeeze the emerald, making a wish. The singer scans the crowd—his eyes land on me and stay there. That's when it hits: I want to be like him. I want to be a singer in a rock 'n' roll band.

19

FLYING IN FORMATION

Me and Mona, we drive. Below the Erector Set canopy of the Detroit-Superior Bridge, the sun slices through the girders above, flashing a rhythm to the hum of tires on the bridge's webbed surface. And the oldies radio station plays Betty Hutton singing "It Had to Be You", Mona's favorite song. It's one of those moments when what you hear, see, and feel all come together with no need to speak 'lest you break the wonder.

The car dips down around a curve as we turn onto Old River Road. Mona steers the old Chevy Impala with her right hand and holds a cigarette with the left, smoke curling around glossy scarlet nails that Miss Sally Bowles herself would be envious of. She's a picture, all right. One I hope to never lose sight of.

She taps ash into the tray and asks, "Did you find a phone at Sally Army?"

"Yep, a nice one. But not a princess."

"If anybody knows you're not the princess-phone type, Birdie, wouldn't it be me?"

Mona had asked if I wanted to do anything special on my birthday, and this is it, driving around the Flats today, listening to the radio, and a good supper later. I turn eighteen and legal today. A cause for celebration! She thought I was nuts for wanting to visit the Cuyahoga—a "swill pit," she calls it—but being a fairy godmother, my wish is her command. Mona has been helping me figure things out, like how to get a telephone account and how to force my landlord into fixing the plumbing—first with charm, then threats. She says, "You draw more bees with honey, but when sweetness won't work, the Department of Sanitation will!"

The Cuyahoga comes into view. It looks the same as it did long ago, when I came here as a little kid with Big Al and we watched fire dance on top of the dirty water. The riverbank is still filled with slag heaps and soot-covered warehouses of corrugated tin. Drainage pipes and rusted iron. The muddy, the brown, the bleak, and Republic Steel lording over the whole of it, a giant beast blasting smoke and sulfur. The wind coming in from Lake Erie blows ribbons of horizontal fumes off the smokestacks. There are no fires burning on the river today, no fires except for the one swirling inside me.

We park and get out of the car. Not a soul around as we walk over to the river's edge to take in the sad vista, me with a deep satisfied breath over my birthday wish come true: to spend it with Mona.

"Darling, why would you want to come here? It's all so dirty and gothic."

Mona sways in her caftan to the music leaking from the car. She takes my hand, and we do a two-step . . . *It had to be you* . . .

"I like ugly things that also have their own beauty. Like Maria Callas when she sings."

She arches an eyebrow at me and smirks. "Maria Callas is hardly ugly. She is a statuesque beauty. But I get it, that agonized face on her top octave."

She places her arm around my shoulders. I watch a cluster of air bubbles break the surface of the water—a pocket of gas maybe, something still alive down there holding on. A miracle of science.

"You think you might call your folks, let them know where you are? Now that you have a phone?"

Mona has never asked about my folks before.

"What folks? I'm an orphan."

I pick up a chunk of ore and pull my arm back, a pitcher on the mound. The ore flies, arcing out over the lake and breaking the water's calm surface into rings.

I don't tell Mona that the first call I made on my new phone was to Grandma Jo. I wanted to find Jack. How sad she sounded when she told me Kitty's still in the hospital. Jack has returned from Vietnam with an honorable discharge, but he's not so good . . . it's better I don't see him right now. He's got a job cleaning a church. He's all in one piece but doesn't talk much. "Something happened to that boy," she said. "Something happened."

She never asked what happened to me.

I don't tell Mona how my body shook when I got off the phone, shook so hard it had to rest for a few seconds and then start up again, and I couldn't stop it or do anything but stare into space for a long, long time. I don't tell Mona that I died a few times. That the things I'm afraid of have already happened. Things that make me feel invisible. Things I can guess people will not want me to tell them, about good and evil, and the word I fear most that makes me go on when the shaking stops. A word like a promise, like the golden fire inside, filling me with the sharp smell of oranges and foreign perfumes, exotic teas and books. Of glimmers of people who use words like *open sesames*.

"Ah, who needs 'em! We have our own family now, don't we? And when you leave this godforsaken place, you'll have us to return to." Mona arches her neck swanlike, gaze pointed toward some mysterious distance.

"Leave? Who says I'm leaving?"

Mona lights up another cigarette and nods her head, a fortune teller now, squinting and dancing her fingers around the curl of cigarette smoke, like she's pulling secrets from the air.

"I see your future, darling, and it isn't here in this dump of a town."

"You think I'd leave you behind? Never!"

"I certainly can't go with you. Forsake my queens? They'd be utterly lost without me. 'Woe to the idol shepherd that leaveth the flock.'"

"Are you quoting Bible passages at me, mademoiselle?"

"Zechariah, chapter and verse."

"Well, how about this. Genesis, chapter twenty-one, I think: 'And Abraham set seven ewe lambs of the flock by themselves.'"

"How cryptic, Birdie! By themselves to do what, exactly?"

"To witness. That's us, our family. We are the witnesses; we are the flock. I think it means to *be* ourselves, *by* ourselves, if that makes sense. To tell the stories. No matter what the world might think of us."

"Hmm . . . to be witness? Or to be lambs to the slaughter? Now that is the question!"

Mona speaks with a Shakespearean flourish and a curtsy toward the river. A gust of wind blows the caftan around her knees. She pulls the fabric close.

"Oh, wise sage, the wind! We must flee! I have to tinkle; meet me in the car."

Mona tosses me the keys and walks toward the river's edge for privacy. I climb into the driver's seat and rev the engine.

"And don't think I'm letting you drive just because it's your birthday! When we get home, call Future and Charlie about tonight, dinner at eight. Chicken cacciatore, your favorite!"

The Cuyahoga pulls my eyes to its surface where I watch them all: the lost ones and the ones who lost me too along the way. Dancing on the water, on this dirty river. I ease them back down into the deep, turn up the radio, and sing.

ACKNOWLEDGMENTS

I'd like to thank the following for their belief in this book and their continuing support throughout its journey into print: my ride-or-die Natalie Hill, Hugh W. Harris, Dorothy Allison, Nona Hendryx, Vicki Wickham, Peter Laughner, Lizzie Borden, Lydia Lunch, Janet Hamill, Mary Ann Livchak, Stephanie Cabot, Logan Garrison, Gerry Howard, Liz Graves, Susan Berman, Lynn Kuennen, Fenton Bailey, Randy Barbato, Gordon Lish, Jerry Stahl, Chris Heiser, Olivia Smith, Margaret Wimberger, Will Tavlin, Allison Miriam Smith, Molly Walls, Roger Trilling, Jiminie Ha, John Clifford, Hannah Tinti, and Rey Roldan. Thanks to the Virginia Center for the Creative Arts and the Albert and Elaine Borchard Foundation for the fellowships and residencies. My deepest gratitude to Michael Zilkha—for placing such care into the making of this book and for his uncompromising vision, beginning with Ze Records and continuing into Ze Books.